C000258980

The Wandering
Civil Servant of
Stradivarius

The Wandering Civil Servant of Stradivarius

Themes and Variations

DESMOND CECIL CMG

QUARTET BOOKS

First published in 2021 by Quartet Books Limited
A member of the Namara Group
27 Goodge Street, London, W1T 2LD

A catalogue record for this book is available from the British Library

ISBN 9780704374812

Set in Monotype Dante by Tetragon, London
Printed and bound in Great Britain by
TJ Books Limited, Padstow, Cornwall

To my wife Ruth and to our four children, Thomas, Nicholas, Andrew and Sarah – and to the inspiration of music.

Contents

I

OVERTURE

A T A RELATIVELY ADVANCED AGE, BEING NOW IN MY LATE seventies, I have endeavoured to set down the key events and emotions of my life as a professional and amateur musician, international diplomat, linguist and traveller, nuclear environmental restoration adviser, antiquarian travel specialist bookseller, arts charity supporter, amateur cricketer, and a happy family man. This book represents, I hope, an honest attempt to guide the reader through the various changes of my career, usually generated by my internal emotional drive as well as by more prosaic external circumstances – while the dominant elements have always remained my love of music and its interpretation.

My family tell me that my character is basically introverted, slightly shy, albeit arrogant at times, and influenced by the appreciation of family and close friends. However, there are indeed strong emotions, and even occasional extrovert flashes. This is particularly true of interpreting music, when the extrovert starts to take over from the introvert, and I clearly know exactly what emotions I wish to transmit to others.

The musical themes have dominated my life. My passion, since my early teens, and continuing throughout the diplomatic and other variations in my career, albeit all interesting and fulfilling, has been and continues to be interpreting music – and especially playing and performing music on my violin, viola and oboe throughout my years spent around the world. Eventually I was fortunate to play on my own lovely, hitherto little known but authentic, late Stradivari violin, created by the master at the age of eighty – and which has now been formally entitled the 1724 'Cecil' Stradivari.

After five years in Switzerland studying with the eminent Max Rostal and working as a professional musician, I decided for myself that I had taken the violin professionally as far as my relatively late start, and what Rostal described as my 'English introversion', permitted. However, when I moved to diplomacy, I never regretted my Swiss violin years. Had I never had this opportunity, I might have been 'bitter and twisted' for the rest of my life. As it was, I knew for myself that I had taken the violin as far as I reasonably could, which brought me immense musical joy for the future.

Much as I enjoy going to concerts, especially given by friends in the music organisations which I support, my overwhelming passion is playing chamber music with like-minded friends and colleagues, every time interpreting afresh the glorious ideas of great composers over the centuries. We have all been gifted with a wonderful chamber music repertoire, duo sonatas, trios, quartets, quintets, sextets, septet, octets, where – unlike in orchestral music – the players are their own inspirational masters, faults and all. When we perform in charity and local concerts, others can judge our professional standards – we try to project our musical ideas, thoughts and passions to each other and to the listeners.

We are privileged to be able to do this – and it reinforces the vital need for arts charity work to provide similar opportunities for aspiring young musicians. I know from my own experience how difficult life can be for young musicians – of whom only a very few will ever make it to the top or even near the top – so whatever help we can all give them, often as much moral as well as financial, makes its own valuable contribution to our wider culture and human society as a whole.

When I drafted the chapters on variations such as the Foreign & Commonwealth Office (FCO), international diplomacy and subsequent nuclear environmental consultancy, which took me through many fascinating areas – intellectually and politically challenging – it became even clearer to me how strong the central themes of playing and interpreting music have been and continue to be, running like a magical thread throughout my life.

Nevertheless, diplomacy in Germany, the United Nations, Switzerland, Austria, Russia, the Middle East, the Balkans and the Americas brought its own intellectual and emotional challenges, which I was greatly privileged to have an opportunity to experience directly.

When I moved from diplomacy to international political consultancy, these challenges remained very relevant, albeit of a separate but related character. Approaching the complex UK, French and Russian civil-service machines from an external commercial perspective, rather than from an internal FCO perspective, was a real eye-opener. Also, I especially appreciated the opportunity to build friendships and partnerships in the 'window' of post-Soviet pre-Putin Russia, discovering a very human 'window' into the rich Russian culture after the relative formality of my earlier Soviet-era diplomatic contacts.

These memoirs are an attempt to set down in writing what these musical themes and these other significant variations have meant to me, and, I hope, have meant to others with whom I have had the joy and privilege of sharing work and friendship. I felt some trepidation in trying to describe my emotions, as for many years my writing attempts were formally proscribed by dry diplomatic restrictions and the Official Secrets Act – indeed my chapter on the Foreign & Commonwealth Office is inevitably anodyne, having been submitted to the relevant authorities for their prior perusal.

To date my only public writings have been my 1724 Stradivari monograph, published in 2017, and in 2019 a *Guardian* obituary of a close friend, the writer Dan van der Vat. However, I hope that these memoirs can progress beyond my dry diplomatic past and convey some of the emotions and joys which it has been my pleasure and privilege to appreciate.

Finally, my most grateful thanks are due to my many friends around the world, and of course to my lovely family and to Ruth, my dear, tolerant and critically perceptive wife for over half a century. Without their support, patience and love, none of this would have been possible.

2

Oxford – Where It All Began

Theme: Exposition I

OXFORD'S SHELDONIAN THEATRE WAS THE SCENE OF A life-changing moment for me where, as a teenage schoolboy, I was bewitched by Yehudi Menuhin's violin playing of solo Bach and Bartók on 12 May 1959. It marked the beginning of the end of my embryonic career as a scientist, as music took an ever-stronger hold in me.

Although I spent most of my youth in Oxford, I was actually born on 19 October 1941 in Uffington, Lincolnshire, the home of my mother's parents, while my father Rupert Cecil, born in 1917, was serving in the RAF at Scampton of the Dam Busters fame. He was studying biochemistry at Balliol College Oxford just before the Second World War and, anticipating future international events, joined the University Air Squadron, and then the RAF as War broke out. He served initially in RAF Bomber Command, doing two tours mainly on Lancasters, which most of his comrades did not survive, rose rapidly to the rank of Wing Commander, collecting two DFCs, and then before D-Day moved to British Scientific Intelligence headed by Professor R. V. Jones. For years he spoke little about the War, both because of the loss of his RAF comrades, and because of the Official Secrets Act. Years later, when R. V. Jones published his book *Most Secret War* in 1978, the family could finally read about our father's daring RAF pilot exploits and his subsequent secret work, illustrated by a photo of him helping to dismantle a German experimental reactor pile in 1945.

In 1943 when he started working with R. V. Jones, we moved to a semi-detached house in Claygate Lane in Hinchley Wood, the first home that I can remember. My father cycled into central London every day, claiming that this was as quick as the overall train journey. My mother thought at the time that I developed a dislike of wasps because of the sound of V1s, which were buzzing overhead at the time. After the War, my father moved back to Oxford University, becoming a Reader in Biochemistry, researching insulin and haemoglobin with Dorothy Hodgkin and Hans Krebs, and later Vice-Principal of the post-graduate Linacre College.

My mother, Rosemary Luker, born in 1920, had a lonely upbringing with strict parents, being taught by a governess rather than being allowed to go to school, although she developed into a sensitive pianist. She played regular piano trios, no doubt inspiring my later love of chamber music, and often accompanied me when I played solos in school concerts.

Her stern father Roland was a retired Army officer and her mother Aileen of Anglo-Irish background (see later) – they both died when I was very young and, as a consequence, I can hardly remember them. They lived in an old country house in Uffington, just outside Stamford, and by chance quite near Burghley House, the home of the 'other branch' of the Elizabethan Cecils. The Burghleys (Marquess of Exeter) were descended from the eldest son of William Cecil, Queen Elizabeth I's eminent Lord High Treasurer, and my family's Lord Salisbury branch from the second son, Robert.

Despite my youth, I can just recall my grandfather Roland threatening to 'horsewhip' me as a two-year-old, for (inadvertently) letting some sheep out of a paddock and on to his lawn. I wasn't sure what a horsewhip was, but it didn't sound very nice. However, in the end he didn't horsewhip me, and was no doubt only expressing his annoyance in his own ex-military, country-squire language.

Many years later Rosemary, recovering from a nervous breakdown, worked hard to break out from her strict isolated upbringing and to try to rediscover herself. She eventually achieved this with an external London

University degree in psychology, though sadly for me this worthy initiative greatly reduced her interest in playing music with me. She was also an active Quaker for many years, attending the Friends' Meeting House in St Giles, Oxford, and she loved tending the flowers in her garden.

She and Rupert had married in 1940 when they were both young, just twenty-three and twenty, and given the wartime and later frustrations the marriage did not survive. Inevitably the marital problems of our parents impacted the lives of their children, especially for me when my musical epiphany caused a divergence from my father's scientist ambitions for me. In effect, because of these sad parental circumstances, from about the age of fifteen the emotional influences on my subsequent musical development inevitably came from within me, rather than from parental guidance or support.

Rupert remarried, to a graduate student of his, Anna Hodson, by whom he had two children Flora and Maud. They moved to Islip north of Oxford, but this marriage also ran into difficulties and ended in divorce. He spent his remaining years in the village of Bayworth near Cumnor, was a special constable, an active member of the Campaign for the Protection of Rural England, and a lover of the River Thames – where he maintained a self-made canoe and where his ashes were eventually strewn.

My mother died in a nursing home near Oxford in 1995 aged seventy-five, and my father in the Oxford John Radcliffe Hospital following a collapse in 2004 aged eighty-seven. I had the sad duty of playing Bach on my violin at both their funerals in the Oxford Crematorium.

Rupert coming from the celebrated Cecil/Salisbury family, broke away from his august background during the War and afterwards, becoming a scientist. The Salisburys had changed the family name from Cecil to Gascoyne-Cecil when the 2nd Marquess of Salisbury had married a wealthy Miss Frances Gascoyne in 1821 and added her name as part of the deal. My father, as an act of independence, changed his name and those of his dependants back to Cecil by deed poll in1955. He claimed that this was because he never knew whether he would be listed alphabetically under G or C. I was certainly relieved, because when some of my more acerbic school friends heard about Gascoyne, they nicknamed me 'Gassy'.

After the War we first lived in a modest semi-detached house in Wharton Road in the Oxford suburb of Headington. Our neighbours for a short time were a pleasant couple whose children were much younger than us, so we had little contact. He was the curate of a local Church of England parish, before moving away to become the Vicar of Eynsham on the other side of Oxford. His name was Stuart Blanch, and he did not tell us that he would one day be Bishop of Liverpool, and subsequently the Archbishop of York.

As a further gesture of parental independence from the family background, we children all attended the local state Headington County Primary School, rather than a private school as might have been expected from the Cecil heritage. It was an enterprising establishment, bringing together a wide mixture of local children, some children of workers from the Morris Cowley car factory and a few children of Oxford dons. I have happy memories of the school, which was indeed enterprising. I recall our serious but kind class teacher Miss Mellor taking our class to Paris and being impressed with the sight of Notre Dame at the age of ten – which would not have happened with every such primary school.

I am eternally grateful that we went to a state school with all the other local children, rather than being sent away to some elitist private establishment. This had a major and positive impact on my later development. Many years later when I was working with British Nuclear Fuels, I heard at third hand that some of the North Country nuclear scientists were uneasy about having to work with an ex-diplomat/violinist with an 'aristo' name – subsequently I had feedback that they were surprised to discover for themselves that, apart from the Southern accent, I was almost a normal human being.

Some years later, for some obscure reason, I found myself visiting a notoriously tough North Country prison, where my state primary school experience was no disadvantage. The inmates, no doubt guilty of their

various charges, were very friendly, despite my southern accent, said that
I obviously wasn't guilty of any standard criminal offence, and speculated
without animosity that I might be some kind of foreign imposter. They
offered me a share of their cigarettes, and although I was not a cigarette-
smoker, I was touched by their generosity and joined my temporary new
friends in smoking a cigarette with them.

Our patrician Cecil grandparents were shocked that we all spoke what
they described as common 'Oxfordshire' rather than 'Oxford' English.
Rupert's father Victor was also a retired Army officer – he lost his three
brothers in the First World War and was himself seriously wounded.
He was subsequently a director of the Peruvian (railway) Corporation,
High Sheriff of Essex, a gentleman farmer, and was very aware of his
aristocratic Conservative background. He explained to us that he would
invite the doctor or the vicar to tea, but not to dinner. (We children did
not really understand this, especially as our fairly anti-social parents rarely
invited anyone to dinner.) However, he also made it clear to us that we
should respectfully address his senior farm staff as 'Mr...'. In return they
would address us as 'Master...' or 'Miss...'. He told us that when he was
a young officer, the two subjects which one did not discuss in the officers'
mess were 'women' and 'money' – vulgar subjects which might provoke
unseemly arguments. When the Profumo scandal broke in 1963, his comment was 'that's what one might expect from a foreigner'.

Victor's father was Lord William Cecil, Bishop of Exeter, second son
of the 3rd Marquess, Prime Minister under Queen Victoria – who was my
grandfather's godmother. I still have on my mantelpiece a handsome silver-
plated bowl inscribed 'To Victor Alexander Cecil from his Godmother
Victoria R.I. July 5 1891'.

Victor (nicknamed 'Popski') talked at length to me, my brother and
sister about our illustrious family history, no doubt trying to compensate for our own father's distancing himself from it. Years later when I
voted for the first time – Labour, as young men do – Victor wrote me a
stern letter comparing me with 'appeasers such as Sir Edward Grey and

Neville Chamberlain' – quite flattering, although this was not what Victor intended.

His wife, Stella (nicknamed 'Mimski'), of middle- rather than upper-class background, was rather less austere. She was proud of the cows which she bred on the farm, and which won numerous prizes. Although not a great music lover – she described the music of J. S. Bach as 'sewing machine' music – she was always most kind to me about my musical ambitions. She and Victor both offered us children a warm family refuge at their spacious Essex country home, which was particularly welcome as the parental marriage disintegrated.

I had a younger brother, Tim born in 1944, and younger sister June born in 1946. After taking a chemistry degree at Oxford Tim set up his own bus company in Flitwick near Luton, which he ran for many years. Tim, being of a practical scientific disposition, got on rather better with our father than I, with the intervention of music, did. Tim married a charming artist/potter Ursula Rotton and they had two children, Rob and Tom, with whom we are still in close family contact. Then in 2003 they sold up the Flitwick business and moved to an old house in Dinan in Brittany, where they became very integrated into the local community – and Tim enjoyed the local oysters and wine.

After Oxford, June married a teacher and enthusiastic musician, Michael Robb, known as Tim. They had two children, Geoffrey and Joanna, but later divorced. June, also a good musician, rather like our mother tried to discover herself, experimenting with various therapies which took her apart from her two brothers.

Sadly, they both died relatively young, June in 2007 of pancreatic cancer and Tim in 2017 of melanoma cancer which had spread. As I had done with our parents Rupert and Rosemary, I had the sad duty of playing Bach on my violin at both their funerals – June's on a windswept hill in Devon, and Tim's at a Franco-British ceremony in Brittany.

We were often joined at our grandparents' Essex home by our Essex cousins, Mike and Jenny, as the marriage of my father's brother Anthony (politically in the right-wing mould of his father), known as 'Hippo', also broke up. From Hippo's second marriage, to Alison, I am still in regular touch with Caroline, who runs her own PR agency and is married to Mihir Bose the well-known journalist and cricket writer. We have much in common – politics and the arts to cricket, although by chance we found ourselves on opposing sides in the Martin Neary / Westminster Abbey affair – Caroline's company supporting the Abbey, and I supporting Martin. We see the other cousins Rosalind and Richard less often but meet at family funerals – again with Bach on the violin.

Family holidays were relatively few and far between, although we did go twice to the seaside on the Gower Peninsula and Anglesey. However, I remember with great pleasure the trips which we made in the lovely unspoilt upper regions of the Thames on my father's small cabin cruiser *Wychwood*.

Although we were often reminded of the Cecil family history by our grandparents and school-teachers, I had little contact with the Hatfield House 'Salisbury' Cecils at the time. We did occasionally meet Lord David Cecil, who was an Oxford colleague of my father's, and we attended the funeral of 'Bobbity' Salisbury the 5th Marquess and Tory kingmaker at Hatfield House in 1972.

I have been told that officially I am, as the eldest son of the eldest son, etc., eleventh in the (male only) line of succession to the marquessate, and some years earlier I might have been even closer with some of the machinations which fuelled the Ealing comedy film *Kind Hearts and Coronets*. However, oddly perhaps, maybe because of the state-school upbringing, although I was very aware of the illustrious Cecil / Salisbury background, I did not flaunt it. Indeed, I felt distinctly uneasy when, during history lessons, the teacher would inevitably make some reference to one of my distinguished ancestors, while I was bracing myself and hoping that he would not.

Years later through diplomacy I got to know Bobbity's grandson, my twice-removed cousin Robert, then Lord Cranborne and an active Conservative politician, and we got on very well together personally if not always politically. Later, when he had become the 7th Marquess of Salisbury, I invited him to join me for an Athenæum Talk (see later) which I was giving in 2012 on Queen Victoria's famous Prime Minister the 3rd Marquess, in which I noted that the Prime Minister had surprisingly liberal personal views behind the public Conservative exterior. For example, during a youthful world tour in 1851 he publicly expressed his sympathy with the black South Africans and the New Zealand Maoris. He was later nicknamed 'The Housemaids' Markiss', when he introduced legislation to stop housemaids being made to clean upper-floor windows from outside, after a young lady fell and was killed.

More recently, when our own children and grandchildren unsurprisingly expressed their growing interest in their aristocratic heritage, I wrote to Cousin Robert and asked if we could bring them to Hatfield House. He very kindly invited us to a family lunch, together with a private viewing of the House, Gardens and Maze, and with a closely fought family game of croquet – which, of course, he insisted on winning.

After Headington County Primary School, I was fortunate to pass the 11-plus and go on a state-aided place to Magdalen College School (MCS), which then, as a direct grant school and now as an independent school, enjoys a high academic reputation. In Form One, I quickly made friends and am still in contact with the Needham twins, Roland (with whom I still play correspondence chess) and Robert, Tony Brewer (later Bristol University Professor, sadly died in 2017), Will Wyatt (of subsequent BBC fame) – and then with the post-state school 'posh' Dragon School intake in Form Three, John Cooke (a rival for the Latin prize, and whose cousin Ruth I later married) and Tim Hunt (subsequent Nobel Prize Winner). Under the renowned Headmaster Bob Stanier, the academic standard at MCS was understandably high, with Latin (useful for a later understanding of German and Russian grammar) and Greek up till O-level, and then sciences and humanities till A-level.

From Headington I cycled down Headington Hill every morning, and every evening back up again – sometimes walking after a long day. With our 'rough' local friends, the Foster-Jones (Morris Cowley workers, despite the double-barrelled name) family, we played regularly in the 'wilderness' of the Rock Edge overgrown quarry, imagining it to be wilder than it was – and still is. We also climbed up Shotover Hill, a historic nature park, for games and exploration with 'secret' camps. My mother acquired a Shetland pony, which she kept in a field near Shotover. I much enjoyed riding bareback for many hours through the fields and woods of South Oxfordshire. I also became quite an expert with the catapult, until one day one of my friends challenged me to shoot at a jenny wren some yards away. I did so without thinking, killed it, and was so upset that I never fired at a living creature again.

However, the 'rough' Headington Quarry area was the only place where I faced actual physical violence, Lebanon, Cuba and NW Russia notwithstanding. For some reason, a fight broke out between two local teenage gangs. Although I was only a disinterested bystander, a local youth with a knife pinned me to the ground. I had to use all my youthful strength to throw him off – which I fortunately managed to do.

One passion which developed in my early teens was that of trainspotting with like-minded school friends, in the days when steam locomotives had character and originality. Oxford being on the Western Region, we were able to collect in our Ian Allan Notebooks many of the local engines, especially the Castle, Grange and King classes, which we found very exotic. We were able to augment our Western Region access with trips to Didcot and Reading stations to clock up the main-line engines. We got permission to visit Swindon railway sheds, which was a gold-mine for Western Region locomotives. When I visited my grandparents in Essex, I could add Eastern Region locomotives to the collection, to be followed on subsequent travels by Southern, London Midland and the other regions. A great highlight was the King's Cross railway shed, which for some reason we could not get permission to visit. So, we decided to 'bunk' the sheds, climbing over fences and moving surreptitiously round the assembled locomotives, pencils and notebooks at the ready, before escaping back over the fences.

Somewhat to our surprise we managed to get in and out of this reputedly secure protected area without being spotted or challenged – no doubt this would be much harder nowadays in the security-conscious environment of the twenty-first century.

After Headington we moved in 1956 to Cumnor on the other side of Oxford, where my father satisfied his anti-social needs by building an isolated Swedish cedar-wood bungalow in a large field. We children did not like the isolation, and we missed our local friends. After cycling up and down Headington Hill, we now had to cycle up and down Cumnor Hill.

Quite early on, as I cycled up Cumnor Hill, some local lads, no doubt provoked by my 'posh' MCS coloured blazer, rode up behind me and their leader tried to knock me off my cycle. Fortunately, I saw him coming and took evasive action. By chance I had had plenty of practice at cycle games and, after a bit of manoeuvring, managed to knock the leader of the lads off his cycle. Interestingly, far from causing enmity, the incident created a kind of 'laddish' bond. The next time that we met on Cumnor Hill, I was expecting to have to take evasive action again, but somewhat to my surprise and indeed to my pleasure, I was greeted as an honorary lad.

Needless to say however we had little social life in our isolated Cumnor bungalow, but by now our friends were scattered all over Oxford – but the ability to drive a motor scooter and later a car eased the logistics.

At Magdalen College School the musical inspiration which we received from the (first ever permanent) Music Master Chris Bishop (subsequently recording director with HMV) generated a high standard of concerts, and the establishment of a Bach Gesellschaft, almost revolutionary in the 1950s. He was also an excellent teacher of the English language and its structure – in my view vital even for native English speakers – and literature.

Other serious 'thinking' teachers from whom I learnt a lot included Frank Garside, E. W. Stoneman, 'Fred' Porter, Dennis Clarke, Leo Fenn and especially the Art Master 'Basil' Field, also a 'cellist. As so often in life, it was the quiet thinkers rather than the authoritarian extroverts who showed us – especially me – what the outside world was really about.

Inspired by 'Basil' we established a 'Casals Club' in the Art Room next to the Big School, when in the Sixth Form we congregated for 'cultured' discussions over self-brewed coffee.

MCS, being an old-established school, had traditional disciplinary standards, with prefects as well as masters being allowed, indeed encouraged, to beat recalcitrant schoolboys. Frankly I thought that this barbaric practice did as much long-term harm to the prefects as to their victims. I recall an incident in the 'Muni' queue (the municipal restaurant across the road, since we had no restaurant for day boys), when the prefects caught some of my friends misbehaving (probably no more than high spirits) and caned them all. Since I had also been misbehaving but for some reason not caught, out of loyalty to my caned friends I owned up to Headmaster Stanier. He thanked me for my honesty and said that he would have to beat me too, but I could tell from his reluctance and gentle touch that his heart was not in it. Some of us persuaded our parents to lobby against corporal punishment, with my father reacting against his traditional upbringing and to my delight playing a leading role. Eventually Stanier, a liberal thinker with a deep conscience, abolished it.

This experience awakened in me a strong opposition to corporal punishment, and a lifelong aversion to excessive authority – which grew during my later career. By chance we recently saw at Glyndebourne a performance of Händel's *Rinaldo*, which was set in a pre-war 'English public school' with corporal punishment inflicted on the pupils. The critics loved it – I hated it! I would subsequently strive for consensus, if possible, rather than instruction, however necessary this may be at times. At times in my subsequent FCO career this may have been portrayed by an orthodox few as a weakness, but I have always regarded it as a strength. In parallel, my Headington state-school experience and friendships inspired an innate liberalism and dislike of 'class' elitism – which if anything has grown stronger over the years.

Inspired by my father's wartime experiences I joined the RAF Section of the School's Combined Cadet Force (CCF). This involved visits to RAF

Stations, such as Scampton where my father had served. I can recall the excitement of flying in small planes, such as Tiger Moths, when the instructor would let me take over the controls for short periods when we were safely aloft. The first such flight was immensely exciting as we soared up into the sky, and indeed for a short time I even dreamt of joining the RAF.

I also played the oboe in the CCF Band, and although unmilitary in demeanour, found myself promoted overnight to the lofty rank of Band Sergeant (subsequently Warrant Officer), when the well-established previous Band Sergeant suddenly disappeared from the School – for a reason not uncommon in boys-only schools in those days.

Given my scientific background I designed a small model ejector seat, based on the Martin-Baker MK 1A Seat. My model, still proudly on my mantelpiece to this day, was six inches high, fitted with a hand-made parachute, and powered by home-ground black gunpowder in a piston/cylinder at the back. When ignited with a Jetex fuse it shot up some hundred feet, before (mostly) descending safely back to earth by parachute. At the CCF Centenary Celebration in 1960 I was tasked with demonstrating this to the visiting military VIPs – who clearly did not believe that it would work. I invited the senior visiting officer, General Sir Montagu Stopford, GCB, KBE, DSO, MC, to press the button, warning him that there would be a loud bang. Perhaps because the General had lunched well beforehand, he did not take the warning seriously, and practically fell over (giggles all round) when the bang occurred, and the ejector seat flew skywards. Happy days!

MCS had a high reputation for sport, especially rugby, hockey, cricket and athletics – especially with Roger Bannister's (a subsequent Athenæum colleague) famous Iffley Road ground just down the road. Although I was initially keen on sport participation, gradually music took over. I remember my father, who had enjoyed his sport at his public school, Stowe, trying to persuade me to give up 'this music stuff' for a term and get into the Rugby 2nd XV, and focus on my science studies. But it was too late, and the intervention of music at the expense of sport and science caused an emotional barrier to develop between my father and me – sad but probably inevitable.

At O- and A-levels, following in my father's footsteps, I concentrated on sciences, initially getting high marks – also for intelligence tests, Mensa membership, etc. However, although I could do all that was required, my interest in science was waning. I applied for The Queen's College Oxford, where they had well-known Chemistry teachers, and was awarded a Chemistry place a year early. I did not spend my last year in the MCS Upper Sixth, but instead of wisely upping sticks and seeing something of the outside world, I continued to work on my chemistry, without either enthusiasm or success. This was a big mistake.

However, despite my later music-related frustrations at MCS, I am the first to acknowledge that I, like most of my contemporaries, benefitted greatly from the School's academic excellence, strong cultural activities and increasingly liberal attitudes – especially from the 'thinking' masters.

Before we all went to University, a group of school friends, the Needham twins, Tony Brewer and I, bought a clapped-out Ford van, which we called 'Schroink', cut out the sides to insert windows, and set out across the Channel to explore Europe in 1961– mainly France, Germany, Austria and Switzerland – with at the time only basic schoolboy French and German.

While we were in a Tyrolean mountain valley in Austria, my friends decided that they wanted to climb a mountain and then descend into the next valley. At the same time, I wanted to go to Gstaad in Switzerland to visit the Menuhin Festival for the first time. Accordingly, we parted and agreed to meet at the Hotel Post (we thought that there must be one) in a village in the next valley in three days' time. I then drove solo across Europe, heard a wonderful Menuhin Gstaad concert (over the years the first of many), on this occasion with the Maestro playing Mozart. I also remember the concert being introduced by the daunting local priest, Pfarrer Hirsch, who made it seriously clear that there was to be no applause in his church – things have relaxed since then. I then drove back to the agreed rendezvous. Somewhat to my surprise, there they all were, indeed at the Hotel Post, happily sipping Austrian beer, and we were all reunited. What we would have done in those pre-mobile-phone days if they had not been there, who knows? But we never had the slightest worry.

This was my first venture abroad, apart from the Paris trip with the enterprising Miss Mellor at primary school. We had great fun, saw something of the outside world, and eventually got home safely – despite finding that the front wheel bearings were so loose that we had to lock the steering against the camber at any significant speed. A year later, with Tim Hunt, John Cooke and another friend Peter Pusey, we did much the same in a slightly more reliable Bedford van in a similar European tour, but this time also venturing to romantic Italy and the then-Communist Northern Yugoslavia. These trips were both hugely exciting explorations into hitherto unknown European territory and culture for all of us – and of course prepared the way for future experiences.

In 1961 I moved from Cumnor into Oxford city to study Chemistry at Queen's. For the first two years I lived in College, initially in shared rooms which I found irksome, although regular visits from my new girlfriend Ruth provided very pleasant distraction. In those days, women were not permitted in College in the evenings, but the College staff were always most helpful – offering discreet after-hours exit routes for the young lady. However, the studies were not a success, given my growing obsession with music, which the University musicians encouraged. I can recall asking my school friends the Needhams to do my science practicals for me, to avoid giving up any music time. Soon I had agreed with my reluctant parents that I would stay on to get a degree, and then go abroad for full-time professional music study. I decided to switch from Chemistry to Philosophy, Politics and Economics (PPE), since I thought that this would offer a broader outlook on life. When I rang my College Chemistry Tutor Morrin Acheson late at night to inform him, he was unamused. Ironically, when I volunteered to help the College forty years later, I became good friends with him and my Philosophy Tutor Brian McGuinness. Morrin said that he had understood the internal dilemma which I was going through, but I cannot recall him showing this at the time.

Eventually, after only working seriously for my final term, I scraped a Third-Class Bachelor of Arts Degree (BA), which shocked my parents and Ruth's family. Oddly enough, since the Oxford system allowed one to purchase a Master of Arts (MA) Degree a few years later for a modest sum, the long-term damage was minimal. Certainly, the Foreign & Commonwealth Office Selection Boards seemed less interested in this than in other overseas and linguistic experiences. With hindsight, my Oxford years were wasted, although I profited from playing a great deal of music at a high level. Whether an earlier move into full-time professional violin study would have made any difference to my longer-term and eventually unfulfilled ambition to become a top soloist – who knows? Life is what you make it.

*

I had virtually no contact with Oxford for forty years, until the then Provost of Queen's, Alan Budd, previously Founding Member of the Bank of England's Monetary Policy Committee, invited me to a College Gaudy Dinner and sat me next to him. We immediately 'clicked', having mutual interests in music, politics and cricket (we would both sit on the top balcony of the Pavilion at Lord's, watching the cricket intently and not talking to anyone until the next interval). He invited me to join the College's Appeal (subsequently Development) Committee, the formal College *alumni* body working on fund-raising and wider development. This work continued under the next Provost Paul Madden, a nuclear scientist with whom I would chat about nuclear reprocessing, and his Development Officer Andrew Timms – later College Bursar. As I write, the work continues under the new Provost Claire Craig, another scientist, and her new Development Officer Justin Jacobs. We *alumni* members of the Development Committee all get inspiration from trying to help our former College, and to support future young students.

I was able, through drawing on my foreign contacts, to revive the 'Florey European Studentships' – Howard Florey, a previous Provost of Queen's and Nobel Prize Winner, had initiated these for European post-graduate students, but they had lapsed for lack of funding. I was able to find German, French and Swiss funding, and negotiate the academic conditions with the foreign funders – and European post-graduate students returned to Queen's.

A couple of years later I received a letter from the University, saying that, for my voluntary work in reviving the Florey European Studentships, I had been nominated for a 'Distinguished Friend of Oxford University Award' – a long way from a distant Third Class degree. In 2012 I was duly presented with this Award in a formal ceremony by the Vice-Chancellor Andrew Hamilton – ending this chapter where it all began – at Oxford's Sheldonian Theatre.

3

FAMILY

Theme: Exposition II

IN MY FINAL YEAR AT SCHOOL, 1960, I MET MY SCHOOLFRIEND John Cooke's cousin, Ruth Sachs, who was visiting the Cooke family in Oxford. She lived in Putney, and her parents were German-Jewish refugees who had come here in 1938. They were in fact non-practising Jews, subsequently converted to Christianity in England, and rather more German than Jewish, but this was clearly not acceptable to the Nazis. Ruth, who was born in Wimbledon on 15 October 1943, came with us when we drove my school friends Tim Hunt and John Cooke to Cambridge in the Bedford van. She and I then drove back to Oxford, a night drive complicated by a puncture near Dunstable, and I dropped her at her sister Ursula Owen's flat in North Oxford in the small hours. Two days later I got a postcard from her, inviting me round for 'super' – spelling was never her strong point. Anyway, the supper was super, the attraction was mutual, and the rest is history.

My father was initially concerned that I had a 'German' girlfriend, with memories of the War still strong in his mind, but was relieved to find that she was not a blonde Aryan, but of German-Jewish origin – like many of his Oxford University scientist colleagues. Ruth's somewhat formal German father, Werner, had already found his first English son-in-law Roger Owen, a Middle East academic at St. Anthony's, rather too informal (unsurprisingly we got on well together), and Ruth's new boyfriend, tieless in sandals, confirmed his suspicions of English idiosyncrasy. Apparently, I had to 'mend my ways', which I'm not sure if I ever did – but in the end we all lived happily ever after, or at least found a way of getting along.

Ruth's mother Emma – known to all as Fips, after the popular humorist Wilhem Busch's cartoon character 'Fipps der Affe' (tomboy/monkey rather than ape) – was a good violinist, with a nice violin labelled 'Amati' (although probably of Czech nineteenth-century origin), which our son Andrew still plays. Fips spent many years in mental hospitals, and no doubt inevitably the marriage with Werner broke up. She eventually lived in Oxford, playing in a local orchestra, working as an Oxfam volunteer, and belonging to the congregation of St Andrew's Church, Linton Road, where Ruth and I later got married. Ruth's elder brother Peter, who with his then Dutch wife Ellen gave us kind hospitality, initially referred to his little sister's new boyfriend as a 'drip', but later qualified this as a 'truculent drip' – with which I could not disagree.

Ruth and I became inseparable and went on holiday together on the West Coast of Scotland, which was considered quite an adventure for the 1960s, even sending the families a cheeky postcard from Gretna Green, still reputed for unauthorised under-age marriages. Our grey mini-van, with a mattress inside, became our temporary mobile home – once on Shotover we were awakened by a policeman knocking on the window, but purely to see if we were both OK. After a couple of years, we decided to get married, even though we each had a year of our hospital/university training to complete. I was twenty-two and she was twenty, technically needing parental consent, which fortunately was forthcoming, albeit reluctantly. We were married on June 20, 1964 in St. Andrew's Church, Linton Road, Oxford, by her friend Norman Motley, Rector of St Michael's Cornhill and founder of the Othona Community in Bradwell-on-Sea which Ruth attended. With grand-parental/mortgage help we bought a one-bedroom flat in Holland Road, London, and during Oxford term-time she joined me in a bedroom which I had rented from a musician friend. Commuting was facilitated by my Vespa scooter, and by her ancient Ford Popular 'Crummy' which she shared with a lifelong nursing friend Gillian Heyes, later Peace.

When we first met, Ruth was still at Putney High School, about to go to St George's Hospital to embark on her lifelong ambition to be a nurse. She was and is one of nature's kind people, dedicating her life to helping others, whether patients, lonely neighbours, children in distress, family and the less-privileged anywhere. She worked as a nurse at the Inselspital when we moved to Berne for my violin study, and then at local hospitals in our Geneva and Vienna diplomatic postings, and while in Vienna she helped to set up a palliative care movement with Viennese friends with whom she is still in close contact.

Back in the UK she worked at local hospices, and with a friend Sheila Hurton, founder of Voices for Hospices, she set up a charity to support the Shepherd's Hospice in Sierra Leone, with its redoubtable founder and director Gabriel Madiye. She has twice visited the Hospice in Freetown and experienced for herself the immense African challenges, and now chairs the charity, the UK Friends of the Shepherd's Hospice. She has also worked in neuro-surgical ICU, as a health visitor, and served on a Community Health Council. She was a volunteer 'gamesmaker' for the 2012 London Olympics – where in the job-interview she related how her mother had not put up her arm to the 'Heil Hitler' at the 1936 Berlin Olympics. Although not a natural practising musician, she loves music and to her credit took up the 'cello in her late sixties, managing to play simple duets with her husband and others.

More than half a century later I can only say that marriage to Ruth was one of my better decisions in life. She has been immensely supportive in the various changes in my life and career. At the same time, she quite properly has also been my strongest critic when I have strayed – intellectual arrogance, masculine weaknesses, a glass of wine too many during a tedious dinner party, talking too much about myself rather than listening to others. After all these years we have, if anything, become even closer.

Our partnership allowed both of us to develop in our own ways. Although I eventually became the main breadwinner, Ruth, who is not cut out for staying at home, always found work wherever we lived. While bringing up the children this was often part-time, including working weekends when I became the *pater familias*. Sometimes it is easier to be a father when the wife is out working. Ruth's work and our children were often the key to our integration into local communities.

We have been fortunate to be able to raise a lovely family. We decided to have children when we were both young, so that we could enjoy them at first hand as they grew up. At the time we did not have financial security but went ahead anyway as we so much wanted to have children then. Ruth decided that we should have four children – maybe as a reaction to both our three-children families – and I did my duty. I was privileged to be present at the birth of all our four children; it was a spiritually uplifting experience to be able to see and hold one's children from the very beginning, which I can only recommend for all future parents.

As I said, we generally managed to combine jobs and looking after the children. When I was a violinist, I could usually combine this with daytime babysitting when Ruth was out working. As the children grew up, our neighbours and their older children, especially in Swiss Chavannes-des-Bois, would kindly keep an eye on them for us. Anyhow we nearly always coped – with the odd scare. Once in Switzerland, while we were both at some diplomatic function, the neighbour's grown-up children kept an eye on ours. We telephoned at the end of the function to check if everything was OK – '*pas exactement*' came the reply. Andrew had been running round the garden, cut his head open, and was rushed to hospital by the neighbours. Fortunately, there was no serious damage.

Thomas and Nicholas were born in 1966 and 1968 in the Frauenspital in Berne when I was an impecunious violinist there. The young Thomas could not say Nicholas properly, garbling it as 'Lee', for his baby brother. They were close friends, and some outsiders thought that 'Tom-n-Lee' was the name of a single child. Andrew in 1971 and Sarah in 1972 followed, both born in our Esher house, when we were back in the UK. They all went to the local Church of England Primary School in Esher, and then in our village of Chavannes-des-Bois outside Geneva, when I was posted to the UK Mission to the United Nations, they all went to the local Swiss school in Versoix with the other village children – totalling forty of which our four made up 10 per cent, thereby hastening integration into village life.

Whenever possible we kept them with us on overseas postings, sending them to local schools rather than the FCO practice of sending them back to UK boarding schools. The positive side of this was family integration as we all grew up together, and we proud parents could rejoice in their development and creativity, occasional naughtiness notwithstanding. Another positive side for them was fluency in French and German. The negative side was that they changed schools often – Sarah counted thirty-two changes of school for the four of them – which meant finding new friends and environments, with both positive and negative aspects.

After Geneva when we returned to the UK, Thomas and Nicholas were accepted by Tiffin state grammar school in Kingston – Nicholas remaining there throughout his secondary education – while Andrew and Sarah went back to the local Church of England primary school, and later Andrew briefly to Hampton School. Thomas then got an FCO-sponsored place at the United World Colleges (UWC) Atlantic Sixth Form College in South Wales. When we moved to Vienna, Andrew and Sarah went initially to a Viennese local school, later to the International School, and then also to the FCO-places at Atlantic Sixth Form College. Afterwards all four went to their various UK universities, Thomas to read Medicine at Southampton, Nicholas French and German at Exeter, Andrew Law at Bristol and Sarah Psychology at St Andrew's.

Thomas initially wanted to be a helicopter rescue pilot, but was then persuade by a careers master to go into medicine. After Southampton Medical School, where he first met his future wife Alison Wyborn – also a doctor who trained as a GP and now works in breast care – he did junior doctor rotation in the South of England. He was privileged to work briefly in the MEDSTAR Trauma Center in Washington DC, and, later on, in laparoscopic colorectal surgery with Joel Leroy in Strasbourg. He became a Consultant Colorectal Surgeon in Basingstoke in 2002 and is now the Clinical Director of the Peritoneal Malignancy Institute in Basingstoke, the largest such unit in the world. He lectures extensively nationally and internationally on laparoscopic colorectal surgery, with various publications, and is on the Medical Advisory Board of Bowel Cancer UK.

Nicholas after Exeter University went on a Health Projects Abroad project in Tanzania, where, by chance, he met his future wife Jo Barron – now a chartered surveyor working for the British Heart Foundation. On his return he went to journalist school in Cardiff, subsequently worked on the *Western Morning News* in Exeter and Plymouth, and the *Western Daily Press* in Ross-on-Wye and Bristol. He then became a regional lobby correspondent for *Central Press*, before moving to the *Sun* and working with Trevor Kavanagh. Afterwards he became Political Correspondent for the *Evening Standard*, where he has been for some years, and is now Deputy Political Editor working closely with the Political Editor Joe Murphy.

After university Andrew worked initially in a ski chalet in Val d'Isère, then for six months in Brussels as a *stagiaire* with European Commissioner Leon Brittan (whose wife, Diana, was one of my father's pupils). He then moved into Public Relations first with a Brussels *boutique* company Cabinet Stewart, and later with Hill and Knowlton. He decided to enhance his qualifications at *Insead* in Fontainebleau, picking up an MBA and, as his future wife, his landlord's daughter Christine Evans – a strategic marketer and gender-equality thoughtleader. He then moved via Paris eventually back to Brussels, working for Yahoo and later Amazon – for whom he appeared before a House of Commons Select Committee and was 'savaged' on television by the Chair Margaret Hodge (for which she subsequently privately apologised to me) for adroitly evading her questions on Amazon activities. Then he moved to Burson Marsteller – now Burson, Cohn & Wolfe – responsible for their client relations in Europe, Africa and the Middle East, and most recently being promoted to CEO in Brussels.

Sarah was always keen on psychology and sports – she was an Austrian junior hockey champion, playing as a back for the local Viennese Club

SV Arminen. After university she became a Chartered Sport psychologist and has worked for the English Institute of Sport (EIS) since 2005. She has worked extensively with Olympic, Paralympic, World and European medallists across five Olympic cycles, including athletics, canoeing, fencing, rugby, shooting, snow-sport and tennis. Sarah started with 'Help for Heroes' in 2013, was the lead sport psychologist for the UK team at four Invictus Games, is mentoring sport psychologists within the EIS, and sits on the UK Sport Mental Health Steering Group. She uses the expertise which she has developed to enable athletes to deliver under pressure, and to support coaches and performance staff to fulfil their full potential. Sarah has remained single, while being a universal aunt to numerous children of her many friends.

While they naturally went their own ways as they grew up and progressed with their diverse and interesting careers, we always remained close friends. We have been on many family holidays together, in the UK, exploring Germany, Italy, Yugoslavia, and of course family skiing holidays in France, Austria and Switzerland to this day. They have brought many of their own friends to our home, which has enhanced our lives.

As the years pass by, they have if anything become even closer to their parents. We share interests in sport – still skiing together after all this time – politics, medicine, music and travel. During the coronavirus pandemic they initiated, and all joined in a family Zoom twice a week to maintain family spirit while we were in self-isolation, for which we were very grateful. Ruth and I are extremely lucky to enjoy close happy relations with all of them – of whom we are inordinately proud.

Finally, they have, so far, produced six lovely grandchildren, within easy reach in Surrey, Hampshire and Brussels, who are growing up fast, developing into their own distinct personalities, and who bring great pleasure to their proud grandparents – whom they naturally out-ski these days, but with tactful kindness. Thomas and Alison's son, Toby, has just graduated in Economics from Bath University, and their daughter, Jemima, is reading Psychology at Birmingham. Nicholas and Jo's eldest,

Christopher, is reading Philosophy, Politics and Economics at Durham, and their youngest, Matthew, has just finished at Hampton School and will study International Relations and Politics at Bath. Andrew and Christine's Alexandre and Tara, the youngest of our grandchildren, are in their early teens. They are at the Brussels bilingual Lycée Français, both lively and artistic, and fittingly Belgian and British in their outlooks on life.

The toughest period in our family life was in May 2004. I was at Lord's watching England play New Zealand at cricket, when the public-address system – mobile phones being banned in the Pavilion – asked 'Mr Desmond Cecil to go to the Pavilion Office as soon as possible'. I did so (missing out on Kiwi Richardson's century) and was ordered to ring Nicholas immediately – to be told that Thomas was seriously ill at his own Basingstoke Hospital and that we should go straight there. Apparently, Thomas, then aged thirty-seven, thought that he had a bad attack of hay-fever, checked into his own hospital and then developed severe breathing difficulties. These worsened dramatically and he was taken on a ventilator and unconscious by emergency ambulance with police escort to the Royal Brompton Hospital in London. The family all gathered in the hospital to maintain a twenty-four-hour watch. His condition continued to worsen, and the hospital confirmed a deterioration in a defective heart valve which had been diagnosed earlier. We were told that if they operated to replace it, the chances of survival were 40/60, but near zero if they did not. His wife Alison, a GP herself, had to take the tough decision to go ahead with the operation. Fortunately, the heart surgeon, whom I later got to know, had made the correct diagnosis and performed the operation well. After a few 'touch-and-go' days, Thomas started to improve, and the hospital told us that we could end the twenty-four-hour vigil. Full recovery naturally took somewhat longer, and Thomas needed time to be told and understand what had happened – we spent hours together chatting about it at local hostelries. Happily, within a year he was back to a full and active life, although on permanent Warfarin, working and even skiing again. We were lucky. At the same time, my father died at the age of eighty-seven after a full life – sad, but a predictable course of events, unlike with one's children.

Homes

After we came back from Berne in 1970 for me to join the Foreign & Commonwealth Office, we sold our Holland Road flat, the rent from which had been useful in supporting our musical existence. Ruth's Aunt Emmie, a 'cellist with whom I played regular string quartets, and in the family oil business in her non-musical life, kindly lent us a small house in the peaceful environment of Welwyn Garden City, from where I commuted by train to work on a daily basis for the first time in my life.

We then bought a pleasant Edwardian house in the (relatively) down-market end of Esher in Imber Park Road, near the Metropolitan Police Sports Ground. It was detached, and although not particularly big at the time we were able to build out an extra room on the top (second) floor. A few years ago, we visited it again during a local garden event, and found that the new owners had extended it even more. It had a nice garden and we had friendly neighbours, including the Abineri actor family. As a WWII memento the brickwork above the front door had been (quite elegantly) scarred by VI flying-bomb fragments. The location was convenient for commuting to London and the FCO from nearby Esher Station, was not far from Heathrow and within easy driving distance of our parents who then lived mainly in the Oxford area. It was well placed for local schools, and close to the open spaces of Weston Green Common, where our former friendly black-and-white border collie Gypsy loved running with us and the children.

While in Bonn, Geneva and Vienna we let out the house, returning to it between postings. In Vienna we were spoilt with a relatively spacious living room which we could use for 'house concerts'. The UK taxpayers kindly paid for this, as they did for all overseas diplomatic premises, and we looked for something similar when back in the UK. We searched in London itself – too expensive for anything spacious, and out in the country – too far from the cultural life of London.

Eventually in 1992 we found a lovely old house, half of an original large 'villa' in Palace Road near Hampton Court, a couple of miles north of our Esher house. The house had been divided into two in the middle of the twentieth century. The old part, retaining many original features, had been built in 1845, shortly before the railway had first come to Hampton Court, and it had been significantly extended over the years. It has a spacious garden, big enough for a croquet if not mini-cricket game, the original title deed stating that we could build a 'beer-house' only at the bottom end of the garden, and a large living room where we can seat forty to fifty people for a 'house concert'. Its original Victorian cellar is big enough to house a three-quarter-size slate snooker table, which has brought much old-fashioned pleasure to family and visitors over the years. The cellar also serves as a cool, secluded space to store wines. The house is near Hampton Court Palace, Hampton Court Station for London commuting, and the River Thames, where our new friendly black-and-white border collie Clara (after Schumann) loves running and swimming after tennis balls, this time with us and the grandchildren.

We have now been living happily in Palace Road for twenty-eight years, much longer than anywhere else in our peripatetic married half-century plus, although more recently interspersed with regular visits to our 'idyllic' second home in the Swiss Alps – which will be described later, as will the other homes in which we lived during our musical and diplomatic years abroad.

4

MUSIC – THE FOCUS OF MY LIFE

Theme: Oboe Studies

A S A YOUNG CHILD I WAS NOT ESPECIALLY INTERESTED IN MUSIC.
My mother had studied the piano seriously, and my father liked
'lighter' classical music, so at least we children were accustomed to the
sound of music at home, and I taught myself to play the descant, treble
(both plastic) and tenor (wooden) Dolmetsch recorders with increasing
enthusiasm.

This all changed in 1952 when at the age of eleven I went to Magdalen
College School and was playing baroque works on the recorders regularly
in concerts. The Headmaster, Bob Stanier, announced that he had a spare,
basic, oboe to lend out, and it fell to me as the recorder player to take up
his offer. Apparently, my oboe proficiency developed very rapidly, and I
sought out, with financial help from my parents, a Boosey & Hawkes
'Imperial' Conservatoire-system oboe, which was considered at the time
to be an above average instrument.

Over the years I had various key improvements, such as low-B/C# and
Bb/Ab connections, done by a well-known oboe repairer called Charles
(Charlie) Morley who lived near King's Cross, and later worked part-time
for the woodwind specialists, Howarth of London. He was not always
on the telephone, and in those days before emails, one simply had to
travel to King's Cross in the hope that the promised work had been done
on time – which was not always the case, although the finished product
was always excellent. Modern oboe construction technique has moved

on, but my upgraded instrument became very serviceable, and I can still play it to this day.

I took lessons, not in fact from an oboe player, but from a semi-professional flute player, Eric Ashcroft, who worked at the Cowley car factory during the day and often played the flute in the Oxford Playhouse orchestra during the evenings. He was a charming but strict teacher, who always began the lessons with what he called 'memory exercises', when we would play together through scales and arpeggios in all the keys – without doubt very useful training for a young musician. I rapidly progressed through the oboe repertoire from the eighteenth century sonatas by Bach, Händel, Telemann, Loeillet and others, to the concertos by Mozart and Haydn and the Mozart oboe quartet. The nineteenth century was somewhat limited, other than the challenging Saint-Saëns sonata and the French *conservatoire* pieces, but the twentieth century was richer with, not only the well-known Strauss and Vaughan Williams concertos, but excellent works by Martinů, Nielsen, Poulenc, Hindemith and others.

There were also numerous British works including those inspired by the great oboist Léon Goossens, for which the oboe world owes him a great debt – Pitfield, Arnold, Benjamin, Berkeley, Bowen, Addinsell, Jacob, Boughton, Rubbra (which I had the privilege of playing with the composer – he was somewhat academic and austere when discussing his Oboe Sonata beforehand, but quickly became musically engrossed once we started to play it together), and many others. I much appreciated the opportunity to get to know these works by composers who might have been less known at the time – and to learn to appreciate their serious musicality, virtuosity and lyrical style.

Like many young oboists I benefitted from the transcriptions of Corelli, Pergolesi and others by the distinguished oboist Evelyn Rothwell (Lady Barbirolli). While at school, I corresponded with her about 'discovering' new oboe works, such as 'transcriptions' of concertos probably by Mozart, Haydn and others, and she always responded kindly to my well-intentioned, if at times naive, ideas. I later got to know her personally through the Royal Philharmonic Society Council. She was always very open and responsive to the various suggestions, easy to correspond with and, notwithstanding her professional eminence, a good listener – and of course a great champion of the oboe, its playing and its literature.

Although initially taught by a flute player, I somehow managed to master, not only the oboe technique but also the mysteries of oboe-reed manufacture, regularly dealing with and learning from Harry Baker a well-known reed-maker in Welling, South-East London (who later published a book on reed making). When I was in my final year at Oxford University, I was invited by the Headmaster of Abingdon School, James Cobban, to become the part-time oboe teacher at the school, which as an impecunious student I accepted with alacrity. When he also asked me to teach the clarinet, I did so, remembering Eric Ashcroft's example of teaching another wind instrument.

Later, while still at school, I also studied with Professor Joy Boughton in Barnes. She, the daughter of composer Rutland Boughton and herself a pupil of Léon Goossens, was one of the country's finest oboists, and the dedicatee of Britten's *Six Metamorphoses after Ovid* for Solo Oboe. These became an integral part of my own repertoire. She became a good friend, as well as a kind and serious teacher, and also gave me valuable advice on the subject of reed making and maintenance – vital to all oboists. Among my proud possessions is still my original copy of the Britten, with Joy's handwritten pencil diagrams of reed intricacies.

While still at school my oboe-playing developed rapidly, passing Grade 8 with high Distinction, and with sonata and concerto performances of much of the oboe repertoire, not only at school but around Oxford. As a schoolboy I auditioned with Ruth Railton for the National Youth Orchestra of Great Britain and was appointed first reserve oboist.

I recall playing Händel and Haydn solo oboe concertos with orchestra in Oxford Town Hall. The *Oxford Times* wrote: 'Cecil's relaxed and confident technique in a work [Haydn], bristling with obstacles for the unwary, soon put us at our ease and enabled us to give full appreciation to the beautiful limpid tone of his playing and to be reminded of the expressive range of the instrument.'

By coincidence, in 2017 I was invited by Oxford Home Start, a charity which supports families in need with young children, to play solo violin 'lollipops' in a Home Start charity concert. This was organised by the charity's Oxford Chair, Alison Madden, wife of The Queen's College Provost, together with the Mayor of Oxford and other VIPs, in Oxford Town Hall – sixty years on from playing oboe concertos there. This experience brought back happy memories of my Oxford musical youth – and indeed a couple of members of the 2017 audience came up to me afterwards and said that they vaguely remembered me from sixty years ago. Life's personal treasures have no time limit.

At school I was strongly supported by our then Music Master, Chris Bishop, who later became a distinguished recording producer for EMI. We are still in touch, and to this day he has not 'forgiven' me for switching from oboe to violin. As mentioned earlier, supported by Chris Bishop, a group of musicians, including harpsichordist Roger Golder and trumpeter David Martin, established a 'Bach Gesellschaft' for what we considered to be semi-authentic performances of Bach, Händel, Telemann, Loeillet and others – quite a rarity in the late 1950s. We would hire a harpsichord from Robert Goble, an admired local maker based in the Headington suburb of Oxford, which we young 'period experts' considered to be more authentic than the better-known Dolmetsch harpsichords. We played with single instruments per part, without period instruments of course in those days, and maybe a little too much *vibrato* for today's 'authentic' specialists, but still quite something for the 1950s…

I recall playing *Brandenburg Concertos* Nos. 2, 3, 4 and 5 (which I directed from the solo violin), several times, including in the eighteenth century Holywell Music Room. A fellow-pupil composer A. A. Brown, wrote an oboe concerto for me, which we performed with orchestra in Holywell.

The *Oxford Times* wrote:

Brandenburg Concerto No.5 directed by D. H. Cecil, the player of the violin part ... he gave a firm lead to the other players and produced consistently good tone and phrasing ... musical premiere of a concerto for oboe and orchestra composed by one of the senior boys of the school, A. A. Brown – a work of far more than schoolboy quality in which the soloist D. H. Cecil displayed his versatility ... solo part calls for considerable virtuosity but D. H. Cecil was quite equal to the occasion.

This switching between violin and oboe in the same concert could cause confusion. Some years later in Berne I played violin in the Vivaldi *Four-Violin Concerto* in the first half of a concert and then the oboe in the Bach *Violin and Oboe Concerto* after the interval. The *Berner Zeitung* critic made some negative comment about my bowing technique in the Bach – in which of course I was playing the oboe. No doubt the critic had left at half-time – as they often do – and then improvised!

I had just left school in 1961 when I travelled to Munich to compete in the International Oboe Competition. At the time I spoke very few words of German and had hardly travelled outside the UK. Nevertheless, I was made to feel at home in Munich. In the competition itself I performed the Strauss and Vaughan Williams concertos, the latter's English style somewhat mystifying the resident German accompanist, and of course the Britten *Six Metamorphoses after Ovid*. Among the judges was Léon Goossens, who duly reported back to his ex-pupil, my own teacher Joy Boughton. Needless to add, though I did not disgrace myself on a first 'international' appearance, the competition was won by the Swiss Heinz Holliger, who went on to become one of the world's great oboists.

Theme: Violin/Viola Studies

Despite my youthful progress as an oboist, all this was to change when Yehudi Menuhin performed solo Bach, the E major and D minor partitas, and the Bartók Solo Sonata (written for him) at the Sheldonian Theatre in Oxford on 12 May 1959. I had never heard music played like that before, was completely bewitched by it, and decided then and there to take up the violin as well as the oboe. Much as I loved and still love the clear and plaintive sound of the oboe, the singing tone of a fine violin well played goes straight to my heart.

Despite his technical problems later in his career, Yehudi was and remains for me one of the very greatest musicians of the twentieth century. I heard him play many times over the years, was privileged to meet him and later to get to know his family well. On a trip across Europe in a battered Ford van with school friends in 1961, as I have related, I visited for the first time the Gstaad Festival which he established with Louis Kentner his pianist brother-in-law, the French 'cellist Maurice Gendron, the British composer and pianist Benjamin Britten and the British tenor Peter Pears in 1957 – and many years later I was privileged to become the International Representative of the Festival, as I'll describe later.

After this life-changing experience with Menuhin at the Sheldonian, I started violin lessons with the school violin teacher Rachel Schiele. She had studied with May Harrison, of the celebrated musical Harrison sisters, and later in life with her own sister Pamela established an organic farming foundation. She was intensely musical, and a perceptive teacher. With the arrogance of youth, I assumed that, since I could already perform much of the oboe concert repertoire, switching to the violin would be straight-forward. Indeed, initial progress was rapid, and I passed Grade 8 within a year.

Little did I realise at the time that the next sixty years would be a much greater challenge. Soon I was able to play the solo violin in *Brandenburg Concertos* 4 and 5 with the school orchestra, and as 'Gypsy Desmondo' in school cabaret acts the Kreisler 'Old Viennese Dances' – pieces which I love to perform to this day. I also greatly appreciated the vast chamber music literature which the violin offered, in comparison with the somewhat limited possibilities for the oboe.

Inevitably, once the initial technical facility had been transferred from oboe to violin, the difficulties set in – the unnatural position of the violin, intonation, vibrato, sensitivities of bow control, left hand/right hand coordination, every aspect of technique – all the reasons why most great violinists started before the age of ten. Nevertheless, my overwhelming desire to create great music on the violin encouraged and indeed compelled me to work even harder to meet the challenges.

After crossing the bridge over the Cherwell from Magdalen College School to Oxford University in 1961, the dual musical commitment continued to grow. I played principal oboe in concert and opera performances with the Oxford University Orchestra under Professor Jack Westrup, whom I both admired and liked personally. While he could initially appear dry and academic, once one got to know him, one learnt to appreciate his musicality, mischievous wit, and his deep scholarship. I also played in the Oxford University Wind Quintet, my predecessor being the distinguished professional oboist Neil Black, and we gave concerts with twentieth century repertoire, including Paul Hindemith, Darius Milhaud, Jacques Ibert and Malcolm Arnold.

I was drafted into an Oxford concert to play oboe with a professional orchestra under Adrian Boult, a wonderful experience for any young musician. I clearly remember the serene musicianship, the patrician but kindly manner, and his impeccably expressive long baton, which always told us exactly what he wanted and where we were. However, behind the serene exterior one quickly sensed the strict musical discipline, which combined with expressiveness and deep knowledge made him the great conductor which he was.

However, I gradually switched to first violin in the University Orchestra, and in the various college orchestras with their enterprising performances of the baroque/classical symphony/concerto literature – sometimes conducted by colleagues such as László Heltay, with his now renowned *Schola Cantorum*, Duncan Bythell and David Tall, a Delius fan – and often without a conductor, with me directing from the first violin desk. (With a smallish group this can be most beneficial for ensemble, the players all listening to each other, rather than trying to follow the beat of a detached conductor.) To the detriment of my university studies I spent more and more time working on the violin, developing repertoire such as the major sonatas and concertos, and – still inspired by Yehudi – the Bach solo sonatas and partitas, which remain my musical ideals to this day.

I took some lessons with well-known violinists, such as Alan Loveday and Frederick Grinke, who were recommended to me as names, and who were politely helpful, if not enthusiastic. However, good fortune, in the shape of a recommendation from Elizabeth Matesky, a Jascha Heifetz pupil and the then girlfriend of fellow Oxford violinist John Roberts, put me in touch with Sascha Lasserson. Lasserson had studied in Russia with Leopold Auer's fabulous St Petersburg class before the First World War. He came to London in 1914, where he remained for the rest of his life. He was a quiet, slightly shy man, an extraordinary violinist who had performed the Glazunov concerto under Glazunov himself, but, perhaps suffering from concert nerves, had then dedicated the rest of his life to teaching from his modest apartment in North Kensington. His son Michael Lasserson published in 2005 *Sascha Lasserson – Portrait of a Teacher: Reminiscences of Sascha by his pupils*, which related the extraordinary contribution which his teaching made to many violinists, both professional and amateur. I was invited to contribute a chapter to the book, which I did with pride and gratitude.

I wrote:

...as one got to know this apparently quiet unassuming little man, one realised the immense depth of his violinistic, musical and human personality ... the lessons were highlighted by fascinating musical insights. Here was a man who had known and played with so many of the Russian greats – Auer, Heifetz, Elman and Glazunov among many others. In the middle of a lesson he would modestly let slip a casual remark about how Glazunov had conducted him in a performance of the violin concerto or of how Heifetz had tackled a particularly tricky corner. For those who were prepared to listen, these remarks were worth their weight in gold.

Sascha became both a friend and a mentor, as well as a formal teacher. He patiently guided me through the violin literature, which he knew intimately, tossing off concerto excerpts perfectly from memory, and, perhaps more importantly, through the inevitable technical handicaps which my late start had encumbered me with. If he could not enable me to overcome these handicaps, he could at least make me more aware of them and how to cope with them while playing.

Years later, when we were living in Geneva, Swiss professional music friends recommended as a teacher Edy Gyr, formerly a violinist with the Orchestre de la Suisse Romande – rather than go back to the analytical approach of Rostal. This was a wise recommendation, since he, like my pre-Rostal teacher in London Sascha Lasserson, helped to build up his pupils' technique and musical confidence. I recall working with him on the solo sonatas of Bach, Bartók and especially those of Eugène Ysaÿe. He was a quiet, unassuming man, who nevertheless saw straight through his pupils and their aspirations. When I played something badly, he simply looked at me and said, 'C'est pas digne de vous,' which was more effective than any outburst of criticism.

Years later, after my formal study with Max Rostal in Berne, I wondered whether I might have been wiser to have stayed with Lasserson in London. But – such is life. My belief and lifelong practice has always been to look forward rather than back, while at the same time learning from the lessons of history.

However, during my time at Oxford University, I had decided to move to Berne in Switzerland to study with Professor Max Rostal, one of the most renowned teachers in Europe. The deal with my parents was that I should get my Oxford degree first, which, although frustrating at the time, with hindsight was probably wise.

Rostal was born of Jewish parents in the then-Austrian Silesia in 1905. He was a former child prodigy who had studied in the 1920s with the renowned teacher and violinist Carl Flesch in Germany, whom he found strict and formal, but whose world-respected methods delivered serious results. In 1933, with the rise of Nazism and his Jewish background, Rostal had moved from the Berlin Hochschule to London, where he taught at the Guildhall School of Music. He moved from London to Berne in 1957, where he taught at the Conservatoire, also commuting regularly to Cologne where he taught at the Hochschule für Musik. Among his many famous pupils were the three upper strings of the Amadeus Quartet, who had been interned with Rostal as 'enemy aliens' on the Isle of Man at the beginning of the War. The Amadeus violist Peter Schidlof had in fact later been 'mothered' by Ruth's 'Aunt' (actually, her mother's cousin) Steffi Hess in the Lake District. In 1965 we went to hear Rostal playing at the Goethe Institute in London, and afterwards I spoke to him about possible study with him in Switzerland.

He invited me to the Cumberland Hotel, where he was staying in London, to play to him. After I had played, he looked intently at me. I can still recall his first question – 'Are you Jewish?' In response to my curious 'I don't think so', he went on, 'That's a pity, because you should be Jewish to play the violin properly.' After a pause he continued, 'Well, you look a bit Jewish, so I'll take you.'

Accordingly, in 1965, once I had graduated, we moved to Switzerland, initially for Rostal's annual summer course in Adelboden in the Bernese Oberland. Then in October 1965 we moved permanently to Berne. Despite his years in London, Rostal remained very formal and Germanic and was addressed by his students as 'Herr Professor', although towards the end of my studies he, quite unexpectedly, instructed me that I was now allowed to address him as 'Max' and to use the 'Du' form. Underneath the austere exterior he was a kindly man, and in time he became a much valued friend.

He had a reputation, no doubt well deserved, for being tight-fisted with money. However, once when I was performing at his master class in

Adelboden, he said that if I re-played a certain passage better, he would give me five centimes. Apparently, I did play it better, because he then handed over the five-centime coin, much to the amusement of the audience. I still treasure that coin, which is safely preserved in my violin case to this day.

Although I came prepared with the usual 'masterworks', violin lessons with Rostal began, as many fine teachers do with their pupils, by going back to basics – posture, bow-hold, left-hand position, and then slow bow strokes moving to Flesch-school scales and arpeggios, etc. We would meet at least once a week in his spacious house near the Aare River, just over the bridge from Berne Old Town. His charming (then) wife Caroline would offer us coffee, while waiting for the work to begin. After some weeks we moved on to the Etudes, Kreutzer, Rode, Dont and others – familiar to all young violinists. These provided the inevitable hurdles, some of which were overcome quickly, others much later. I remember Rode's second study in octaves, which, unlike some other double-stoppings, I could manage relatively easily. 'Thank God for that,' exclaimed Max.

Max held his violin well to the left, which suited me with my long arms. He had his chin rest on the left side of the tailpiece, which I was never happy with – years later I moved to a central chin rest and have been happy ever since. He used a soft shoulder pad and was relaxed about what kind of shoulder-rest his pupils used. Like many others, I experimented with the various models, Resonans, Menuhin, Wolf and other designs, which all claimed to be the perfect solution. However, I never felt at ease with any of these, and later reverted to playing with no shoulder-rest, simply putting the violin on my collar bone and holding it horizontally with the left hand – as I can recall the renowned Hungarian violinist and teacher Tibor Varga demonstrating very clearly at a Dartington Hall summer master class.

Changing position needed some thumb flexibility, which Max was a master of, and the slight ridge at the back of the chin rest prevented the violin from slipping away when changing down. The left-hand fingers were supported by the left-hand thumb, thereby enhancing inherent vibrato, and taking away the pressure between shoulder and chin. Most young violinists from the conservatoires are encouraged to use shoulder rests, and one can see the negative results in shoulder tension and visible chin sores (which fortunately I do not suffer from, despite intensive playing). Once I had overcome the initial dynamics of playing without a shoulder-rest, I never looked back. I always felt that the violin sounded more natural and free without a mechanical clamp at the back – as Jascha Heifetz, Yehudi Menuhin (once he had dispensed with his own designed shoulder-rest) and many other greats, including Anne-Sophie Mutter today, have demonstrated. The only problem is that they all play much better than I do!

Another problem which most violinists have is that the fourth little finger is almost invariably shorter than the other three. Max demonstrated how one could 'set' the left hand according to the little finger, and then develop the flexibility to stretch backwards with the longer ones. This was of special advantage to me, as my little finger on my left hand has been relatively much shorter than the longer ones since birth. At one stage I had even considered reversing the arms, bowing with the left and fingering with the right, as one sometimes sees in orchestras – which would of course have meant major violin re-adjustments. Fortunately, with the guidance of Max I was able to avoid such a drastic measure, but to this day I still slightly adjust the downward movement of my little finger to ensure the secure stopping of the string to deliver a firm tone.

However, many years later, when I had returned to playing cricket after leaving professional music, my little finger was broken. After a particularly 'social' late night, I had the next day dropped two catches at first slip, where I normally had 'safe hands'. I was banished to the deep, when to my horror I saw a high ball coming straight towards me – and duly dropped this one as well. The next morning Ruth took me into our garden for some catching practice. She has a right arm like a rattlesnake, and suddenly I felt a snap and twang as I dropped another catch. My unsympathetic 'nurse' wife told me to stop moaning and to bathe it in hot salt water, but eventually conceded that the little finger was broken. Fortunately, it mended, and was afterwards stronger than ever. However, a couple of days later I was due to perform Mendelssohn's first piano trio for the Kingston & District Chamber Music Society. Rather than cancel, I quickly re-fingered it for the first three fingers (which the key of D minor and the inherent open strings facilitate), and the performance went ahead. The audience seemed happy, and the only slightly curious comment that I heard afterwards was that I had used quite a bit of *glissando* – not surprising in the three-fingered circumstances.

Max also favoured the 'Russian' bow-hold, rotating the forearm and holding the bow behind the first joint of the first finger – although releasing this slightly as he approached the nut. He argued that this provided stronger tone through natural unforced pressure. He claimed that the 'German' bow-hold, using the second joint in the first finger and lower elbow with bent wrist, caused the player to force the tone – although conceding that for example Josef Szigeti (who used this bow-hold) was a very fine musician and violinist. I tried the 'Russian' style for some years, but found that the pronation of the forearm caused unnecessary tension, and eventually moved to the 'Franco-Belgian' bow-hold, with the bow in, rather than behind, the first joint, allowing greater flexibility at the nut, and with horizontal wrist and forearm. We are all built differently.

After a few months on Etudes, he allowed me to return to 'real' music and I recall that the first two pieces were the Schubert *First Sonatina* and the Brahms *Second Sonata*, both rather more challenging than they might appear. We then progressed to the wider repertoire, including the standard sonatas and concertos, and especially my great love – the Bach solo sonatas and partitas. Max continually advised me to play more extrovertly – 'more Jewish'. He said that he knew that I felt the music inwardly, but that would not be apparent to someone in the back stalls. He then demonstrated what he meant, to which I commented that I found it verging on the vulgar – to which he responded that this was always a problem for the 'introverted English'.

Max had developed a technique, which I use to this day, for changing position on the string by 'crawling' up and down, supported by the thumb, which avoided slides – except of course when they were intended *glissandi*, as they often were with someone who had learnt the violin in the early part of the twentieth century. Similarly, he was a strong believer in enhancing the tone with a near-permanent integral *vibrato*. Like many of his pupils, I followed this advice, although later on I did significantly reduce my use of *vibrato* in baroque works – although never going to the lengths of some 'period' players today who prefer 'bulges' to *vibrato*. To them I would advise studying Leopold Mozart's *Versuch einer gründlichen Violinschule* of 1756 (*Treatise on the Fundamental Principles of Violin Playing* – published by OUP, 1948), in which he writes at length about the appropriate use of *tremolo/vibrato*.

Max's approach to interpretation, naturally in the Germanic footsteps of his master Carl Flesch, was very analytical. While I found many of his ideas very satisfying, they could at times be intellectual rather than inspirational. For example, he favoured melodic lines changing positions on a single string, whereas I felt that the polyphony of for example Bach was better served by using separate strings. However, when I challenged him and suggested a different fingering or bowing, he would smile and ask, 'Who plays the violin better, you or I?' He added that, when I was no longer studying with him, he would be more than happy for me to try new ideas. Indeed I did this, and rather than amend his markings for the Bach solo sonatas, for example, after I had moved on I bought new *Urtext* editions and reworked the fingerings and bowings as I felt best suited the music and my own preferences.

Partly because he felt that the viola might be more suited to my 'English introverted' nature, and partly because I was tall with long arms, he advised me to spend a whole year working just on the viola. I wisely accepted his advice and developed a very fulfilling relationship with the viola, while still retaining my overwhelming love for the violin. We worked on the Schubert *'Arpeggione'* Sonata and the Bartók Viola Concerto, two wonderful and demanding works. The transcriptions of the Bach solo 'cello suites, up an octave but in the same original keys (except the 6th suite which is written for a five-stringed instrument), are deeply satisfying, and technically less daunting than the violin solo sonatas when one is looking to relax – to this day I still play them regularly. I also greatly enjoyed playing viola in chamber music, as have musicians from Mozart to Menuhin, the viola part being deeply immersed in the very heart of the music, while letting the first violin sweat over the difficult passages.

Incidentally, once when we were discussing technical matters in general, he referred to the issues which Yehudi Menuhin had later on in his career – mainly with the bow, where he had problems approaching the nut, but also affecting the left hand and intonation. While Max greatly admired Menuhin's musical genius and worked with him on musical projects, his own approach to the technical issues was quite Germanic, as befitted a pupil of Carl Flesch. He said that the problem with Yehudi was that, since he could play everything at a very early age, he had never really studied how he played the violin, nor had a 'proper teacher' – describing Yehudi's mentor George Enescu as a 'gypsy' (although a musical genius). When Yehudi developed his technical problems, according to Max he should have concentrated on 'scales and arpeggios' (Ysaÿe said much the same to the young Yehudi as far back as 1927), but instead 'he fell into the hands of the New York charlatans' (Max's exact words).

My view is that it was rather more complex than 'scales and arpeggios'. Even relatively late in his career Yehudi could struggle with an apparently technically straight-forward work, like for example a Mozart Concerto at the beginning of a concert, and then after the interval play say the technically more difficult Brahms Concerto quite magnificently. Once in Gstaad I heard him mess up the Beethoven Quartet op.18, no. 4, and yet after the interval play the challenging first violin part in the Schubert two-cello Quintet op.163 sublimely. Genius cannot always be explained simply.

Max was very happy to use me as an oboist (naturally unpaid) in his professional orchestra, Camerata Bern, at his annual festival/master class in Adelboden, where I had the privilege of playing alongside Terence MacDonagh, principal oboe of the BBC Symphony and Royal Philharmonic Orchestras. Terence, one of the finest oboists of his day, was great company to play with. He was always amused that, while he was paid for the Adelboden concerts, I as one of Max's violin students, and although playing the same oboe score as Terence, was not. An interesting comment from Max was that, while he was concerned about my rhythmic imprecisions on the violin, they were not noticeable when I played the oboe in his professional orchestra – no doubt because of the oboe being untroubled by the physical dynamics and complications of string-instrument bowing.

As the years with Max progressed, it became increasingly clear to me that, whatever my technical and musical weaknesses or 'English introversion', the basic problem was that I had switched from oboe to violin far too late. I should have started, if not at the age of five, then certainly not in my later teens if I wanted to become a top soloist. I also recognised that many of my fellow pupils, although greatly talented and having started at a much younger age than me, were also finding the pinnacles of the professional violin world, where only a very few make it to the very top, increasingly daunting.

Many years after Berne, when I had long left the professional music scene, we went to a Prom concert given by the Orchestre de Chambre de Lausanne. We were sitting near the stage and suddenly I saw a familiar looking face at the back of the second violins. It was Isabel Demenga (sister of the renowned Demenga 'cellist brothers) forty years on – at the interval we had a brief trip down memory lane. I always thought that Isabel, who had once given a stunning performance of the Bach A minor solo violin sonata, was one of Rostal's best pupils, and at a level above me. I could only console myself at the Prom that, had I been a bit better, I could have progressed to the back desk of the Lausanne second violins!

As the months went by, I gradually decided that although I had benefitted enormously from my five years in Berne – the extraordinary musical

45

and technical lessons that I had learnt from Max, playing and teaching as a professional – I was not going to achieve my initial ambition of becoming a top soloist. Rather than continue with orchestral playing and teaching, or try music administration, I recognised that the time had come to move on.

Happily, the personal friendship continued after I had stopped studying with him, and we would meet from time to time. When I was at the British Embassy in Bonn a few years later, Max was still teaching nearby at the Cologne Hochschule. He would sometimes ask me to join him in Cologne to play string quartets with him and friends but made it quite clear that I would play second violin!

After Rostal's death in 1991 a group of his former pupils then in the UK gathered all together in a chamber orchestra – I played the viola – to give a public London concert in his memory.

I never regretted those five years with Rostal. Had I not had the chance to try, and eventually to decide for myself, I might have been 'bitter and twisted' for the rest of my life. As it was, I had tried my best, had learnt a huge amount, about music, languages and life as well as about playing the violin/viola, and had decided of my own free will to move on. We were of course very sad to leave Berne and Switzerland, having spent our early married life there and brought our first two children into the world, and made many lifelong friends – not to mention the advantages of having learnt the various Swiss languages and being integrated into another culture. Fortunately, I was strongly supported by Ruth and by Max, and was able to take this decision myself with some, but not permanent, heartache.

We could now move on to the next stage of our life together. What it was to be was at this stage still unclear…

5

SWITZERLAND

Theme: Music and Life in Berne

IN THE SUMMER OF 1965, AFTER I HAD GRADUATED FROM OXFORD, we visited Switzerland briefly, to attend Max Rostal's masterclass in Adelboden. In October, two days after Ruth had taken her State Registered Nurse Finals, we held a goodbye party with our friends in our London flat, and the next morning set off in our grey mini-van for our new future in Switzerland. We arrived in Berne, initially for six months, to set up house there. Through the good offices of Hugh Blaschko, an Oxford University acquaintance of both our families, we were offered a flat on the fifth floor (no lift) of a building in Viktoriarain, just across the Viktoria Bridge over the Aare River from the Old Town. Berne, the capital of Switzerland, is in the thirteenth century Canton Berne which has a visibly male – the Bernese insist on this – bear in its flag.

The Viktoriarain flat belonged to a Bernese secondary school teacher, Vreni Lüthi, who was going on a year's French course in Provence, and who kindly agreed that we could rent her flat. Very shortly after our arrival, another Bernese secondary school teacher, Gerhard Schafroth, who lived two floors down, knocked on our door and introduced himself. He very kindly took us under his wing and half a century later we remain close family friends, skiing together for many years, and still regularly visiting him and his family in Spiez on the Lake of Thun. The Swiss, a bit like the English, are somewhat reserved at first, but once a friendship is established it is for life.

After Viktoriarain, we moved to a new attic flat in the Western suburb of Bümpliz, where to help pay the rent we took on the job of *Hauswart* (concierge) – not a position which many British diplomats would have had in their earlier careers. This involved sweeping the stairs every day, clearing the snow, managing the washing cellar, and sometimes adjudicating between the Italian *Gastarbeiter* ('guest' workers) and their Swiss-German neighbours (with linguistic advantages for me). There was a particularly aggressive Zürich middle-aged lady taxi-driver one floor beneath us. As well as jeering that I sent my wife out to work as a nurse, and stayed at home all day playing the violin, she also had it in for the Italians. Once they found that their laundry had been thrown out of the washing cellar at midnight. When I challenged the taxi-lady whether she intended to start her own washing at midnight, she simply replied that her official time had started even though she did not want to use the washing cellar then, and that the *Schinke* (a derogatory dialect word for *Gastarbeiter*) had to get out.

We also had a charming young Basel lady in the flat immediately opposite us, who seemed to have many friendly visitors. It was only when we saw through our front-door 'spyhole' the perspiring faces of the male visitors regularly emerging after about half an hour, that we realised the 'professional' nature of their visits.

Finally, because of the strains of being a *Hauswart*, we moved out of Berne to the farming village of Illiswil near the Wohlensee, twenty minutes' drive from Berne where we experienced the charms and local politics of Swiss village life. Our flat, above a carpenter's workshop, came with a balcony and a vegetable garden which we could use.

Although Ruth, through her parents, spoke fluent accent-less if grammatically suspect German, initially I had only basic schoolboy German and French. While at Oxford University I had privately studied the Müller texts of *Lieder*, such as Schubert's *Winterreise* and *Schöne Müllerin*, giving me a somewhat esoteric German vocabulary, which rapidly became more practical with daily life in Berne. However, we quickly discovered that, although in German-speaking Switzerland all the locals wrote High

German, they all spoke almost exclusively their Swiss-German dialect, an Alemannic variant from many centuries ago, with significant linguistic differences – and virtually incomprehensible to a Northern German. To complicate matters further, we learnt that each canton, town, and sometimes district spoke a different form of the dialect. In the town of Berne, the dialect (*Bärndütsch*) had not only a different and guttural accent and at times vocabulary, but also grammar – still using the eighteenth-century formal *Ihr* und *Euch*, no future or imperfect tenses, and different genders for some nouns. Rostal, like many German speakers, refused to learn Swiss German, which he referred to as a *Halskrankheit* – throat illness.

Fortunately, our Swiss friends helped us to master this linguistic challenge. Gerhard introduced me to two fellow secondary teachers, Hans Steiner and Ernst Graenicher, and we met regularly for a boys only *Herrenabend* in local hostelries. In those days Swiss women did not have the federal vote, and married women could not open their own bank accounts. To support her impecunious musician husband, Ruth worked as a nurse at the Inselspital, also facilitated by Hugh Blaschko who knew Prof Reubi there, and paid her salary into my bank account. Political incorrectness notwithstanding, the *Herrenabend* conviviality quickly immersed me in *Bärndütsch*. At the same time, Ruth, working in the Inselspital with Swiss colleagues, soon learnt to move from her High German to the local dialect. To this day Swiss friends still tell us that, when we open our mouths, we pass, if not as native-born Bernese, then at least as natives from an unspecified nearby canton.

I was also given by my new Bernese friends a local lesson in the very Swiss art of making cheese fondue. This was then a typically Swiss men-only practice, with for once women being excluded from the kitchen. The cheese, usually Emmental, Gruyère or Vacherin according to canton, was stirred with a wooden spoon in an anti-clockwise figure-of-eight motion in Swiss Fendant white wine. Halfway through the meal a toast, *Le Coup du Milieu*, was drunk with Kirsch liqueur out of special small glasses. If a man lost his portion of bread from his fondue fork, his penalty was to buy another bottle of wine – if a woman did, she had to kiss a man to whom she was not married. Maybe the practice has changed since then, but perhaps not in traditional Berne…

The other Brit invited to join the *Herrenabend* was a local teacher and curate at the English Church in Berne, Peter Hawker, who with his Swiss wife Vreni became lifelong friends. He became Vicar of the English Church, later Archdeacon of Switzerland, and some years ago retired to Berne, where he still lives – sadly Vreni died in 2019. To earn some extra money Ruth and I taught music on Monday afternoons at the American International School in Berne. Ruth also did some part-time English teaching at the Langford Institute and, as I shall relate, I was mysteriously engaged by the Russian Embassy in Berne to teach English and German. An English lady in Berne, Valerie Morris, very kindly babysat for us while we were teaching, and I regularly played chess with her husband David, who by chance was Yehudi Menuhin's Swiss actuarial adviser. They were two more lovely friends from Berne days, also no longer with us. David kindly introduced us to Yehudi Menuhin, after the Maestro had given us a magisterial performance of the Elgar Violin Concerto. We also joined the Berner Kammerchor, Ruth being the keen singer rather than me, which was conducted by the eminent Fritz Indermühle, who kindly introduced us to members of his family and other Bernese musical friends.

In parallel with the Rostal study, musical friendships quickly developed, resulting in regular sonatas and chamber music with Swiss musicians. This developed into invitations to play professionally in local orchestral concerts – which flourished not only in the towns, but also in some of the more cultured smaller villages. Rostal invited me to play my oboe, which I still kept up, in his professional chamber orchestra for Adelboden, where, as mentioned, I had the pleasure of sharing a desk with the distinguished Royal Philharmonic Orchestra principal oboist Terence McDonagh.

Through my school music master, Chris Bishop, I was introduced to a conductor in Neuchâtel, Jean-Pierre Luther who ran the Printemps Musical de Neuchâtel Festival. He kindly invited me to lead his professional orchestra, and we recorded works by the Swiss composer René Gerber (I still have the LP). Unfortunately, this friendship came to an end after a disastrous performance of Vivaldi's *Concerto in B minor* for four violins. I had performed this several times in Berne with fellow soloists from Berne, including the Demenga sisters (see below). I had directed the chamber orchestra from the first violin desk, without any apparent mishaps. However, when we brought it to Neuchâtel, Jean-Pierre naturally wished to conduct it himself, which confused my Bernese colleagues. Whatever the reason, the first movement broke down and we had to start again and happily the second time it seemed to go well. However, Jean-Pierre's normally charming wife was furious about the slur on her husband's reputation with the local (Swiss-French) audience, which she blamed firmly on the Swiss-German soloists, some of whom she said had been showing off with solo Bach during the rehearsal – and of course on me, for bringing them over from Berne. What seemed perhaps a minor musical mishap was acerbated by Swiss politics, with me the 'guilty' foreigner in the middle.

Despite this incident, I have continued to lead from the first violin desk various chamber orchestra concerts over the years – and usually, if the players all listen to each other, the ensemble can often be better than with a conductor.

Some of my fellow Rostal pupils, such as Isabel and Catrin Demenga (sisters of renowned 'cellists Thomas and Patrick), Jean Piguet and Thomas Füri (who made a guest appearance in the 1997 *Titanic* film), subsequently achieved distinction in their Swiss careers. However, this tended to be at the top orchestral level, rather than that of international soloists, say from the Juilliard School in New York. Another fellow pupil was Larry Homolka, son of actor Oscar Homolka, and then owner of the 1722 'de Chaponay' Stradivari violin, which I saw again and played in 2003, when looking for my own Stradivari violin.

Some of us also took chamber-music lessons from a fine violist, Dénes Marton, from the well-known Parrenin Quartet. Born in Hungary he settled in Berne to continue his career of chamber music performance and teaching. He was a sensitive musician from whom we learnt a great deal about the art and skills of chamber music. Alas, he was killed in a car accident in France in 1970.

We also met at Rostal's Adelboden master class the American violinist Harry and 'cellist wife Sally Nordstrom, with whom we played chamber music by Beethoven and others. They later moved back to their home in Minnesota. Sally died some years ago, but half a century on we are still in touch with Harry each Christmas.

A Swiss fellow-violinist friend, Walter Ammon, kindly invited me, not only to join him playing in professional orchestral concerts – most Swiss villages, let alone towns and cities, regularly host classical concerts in their churches and halls – but also to take over some of his violin teaching in Biel/Bienne and at the state teacher seminar in the nearby town of Herzogenbuchsee. This latter job was hard work, with nine pupils, one after another, mainly teacher trainees who had to learn an instrument as part of their training. I can recall one pupil who, when her finger started to descend, I knew was going to mis-hit the same note as the previous week with the same exact intonation discrepancy. I had to brace myself each time. However, the work was well paid, which was important in the economics of the music world.

Furthermore, many years later I got a letter from the Swiss Government (a benevolent police state which keeps track of its foreign residents), saying that as a former Swiss state employee I was now entitled to a Swiss state pension of CHF 29 per month – not a fortune, but even after UK income tax had been deducted, still enough to buy a decent bottle of wine.

Early on in our Swiss sojourn, on Rostal's recommendation, I met the Bernese violin dealer Henry Werro, who had both a worldwide distinguished clientele and – like several violin dealers – a questionable reputation for a past allegedly shady deal, which he always strongly denied. He had been brought up in London within the sound of Bow Bells, and spoke English with a trace of cockney, which I sensed also extended to his Swiss German. He, his son Jean, an excellent violin maker, and their assistant Fräulein Weyermann, became good colleagues, and I learnt a great deal about violins and bows from them. Indeed, our son Thomas's first word was 'bow'!

One aspect of a Swiss 'practice' did emerge later, when I started to teach the violin at Herzogenbuchsee, and introduced some of my pupils to Werro. Once, when I was in his shop, he handed me an envelope full of Swiss francs, which he explained was the normal discreet 10 per cent commission for teachers on purchases by their pupils. Presumably Rostal got the same! Over the years I purchased several instruments and bows from Werro.

I also got to know the Geneva Maître Luthier and bow expert Pierre Vidoudez, from whom I purchased some fine bows, and with whom I enjoyed many a detailed discussion about violins and bows. In 1968 he gave me a copy of his monograph *Quelques considerations sur l'archet et les archetiers français*, to which he kindly added a handwritten dedication, 'En attendant les ouvrages sur la lutherie' – which eventually transpired forty-nine years later when I published my own monograph on my 1724 Stradivari violin.

The intended six months stay in Berne became five years. During these years there we became very integrated into the Bernese way of life, both linguistically and with many firm friendships. Our two eldest boys, Thomas and Nicholas, were born in the Berne Frauenspital, and legally could have become Swiss citizens – although this would have meant doing national service – which many Swiss men relished as an excuse to escape from their families and rejoin the lads for a few weeks every year. With its compulsory national service, neutral Switzerland has the largest peace-time army in Europe but has been most careful to stay out of European wars for many years. Every Swiss man under the age of forty-five keeps his army rifle at home, but the Swiss joke is that if a Swiss wanted to rob a bank, he would never use his army rifle – that would be against the law.

The Swiss have a soft spot, at times somewhat hidden, for the British, whom they think have similar personalities – as I said above, reserved at first, but then friends for life. Every year we, like all foreigners, had to report to the Fremdenpolizei, but as British, albeit impecunious, we were once invited to jump the long queues of the *Gastarbeiter* from Italy and Eastern Europe.

We learnt that Switzerland is an authentic democracy, with effective power very much in the hands of the cantonal and communal regional authorities, who are in turn subject to regular decisions made by local *referenda* on many domestic issues. The Federal Council in Berne consists of seven members, with its President rotating each year – indeed if you asked the average Swiss citizen who is the current President, they might have to think for a moment. Berne handles wider national issues such as defence and foreign policy, leaving daily matters to the regional authorities. With four official languages, German, French, Italian and Romansh (a Latin-based language spoken in the Eastern canton of Graubünden), one might think that this would impose tensions on the country – as elsewhere in Europe. However, apart from the French-speaking part of the German-speaking Canton of Berne breaking away to form a new Canton, Jura, forty years ago, life is peaceful – and very efficient, with of course the trains running on time. One of our British visitors was worried about missing a tight five-minute train connection and sought assurance from the local stationmaster – who replied that he did not understand the question.

When in 1970, after five years with Rostal, I had finally decided for myself that I was never going to do Yehudi or Jascha out of a job, and that rather than strive for an uncertain teaching/orchestral career, I would leave professional music and look for something else back in the UK. Little did we know then, that only six years later we should be returning to Switzerland – this time to French-speaking Geneva.

Variation: Life and Music in Geneva

In summer 1976, we arrived in Geneva, now with four children, to take up a position with the UK United Nations (UN) Mission as Press Officer and be responsible for some of the UK agencies, such as WIPO (intellectual property), WMO (meteorology), Narcotics, and others. This was our first contact with British 'officialdom' in Switzerland, having only visited the British Embassy during our music sojourn in Berne to renew passports or to register the births of our children.

Given the size of our family we did not take up the delightful small lakeside house of my predecessor, a keen sailor. After a month in the Motel-de-Founex, with a practical rather than romantic swimming pool, we found a spacious recently built house in the (then) small village of Chavannes-des-Bois, in a cul-de-sac named Pré-Olivier. On one side of the garden, in which our children taught the locals to play mini cricket, there was a large field and forest in which roamed wild boars, and on the other side was the cantonal border between Vaud and Geneva.

We decided to send our children to the local Swiss state school, just over the cantonal border in nearby Versoix. As our four represented 10 per cent of the village school population of forty, they quickly became integrated. On their second week at school, the coach-driver, M. Nicolas, thought that our son – by coincidence Nicholas – had been misbehaving and ejected him from the coach just before arriving back in the village. The other children showed touching loyalty to their new foreign fellow-pupil, walking back *en masse* to find him. M. Nicolas was severely reprimanded by Ruth in her then-rudimentary French and did not repeat his 'error'. The four children, initially speaking no French, were well looked after, seated next to English speakers and given extra French vocab lessons by the school. Shortly after Christmas, they all suddenly switched to completely fluent French, speaking it to each other although using increasingly accented English with us. When we returned to England four years later, not surprisingly their English remained accented for a time, and they were nicknamed 'Froggy'. But their fluent French stayed with them.

Oddly enough Pré-Olivier contained three Swiss-German families, which speeded our integration. Some months after our arrival, we had to receive a formal communal delegation consisting of the village mayor and a couple of colleagues, whom we knew well. They explained that the village, being in the Canton of Vaud (founded in 1803, the only Swiss canton to have a written motto *Liberté et Patrie* in its flag), had to pay the Canton of Geneva for the education of their children over the border in Versoix. This also meant that Vaud was paying Geneva for our (foreign) children. Could we make an appropriate contribution? Fortunately, the FCO, being spared the much higher fees from the usual diplomatic practice of sending children back to UK boarding school, was happy to contribute.

We stayed for the whole four years of the UN posting happily in Chavannes-des-Bois. My drive to work took ten minutes through the woods with only one set of traffic lights. Ruth subsequently worked as a nurse at La Clairière in Mies, a similar journey away. The French frontier, for cheaper shopping with our CD diplomatic status, was two minutes away, and the nearest ski slope at La Faucille was only half an hour away – we could even decide on a Saturday mid-afternoon that we felt like a little family ski. Our children, at their Swiss school, had regular *vacances de ski* when the whole class was ensconced in a remote cabin high in the mountains, surrounded by deep snow – hence they all learnt off-piste as easily as piste skiing. When we finally drove away from Chavannes–des-Bois to return to England in 1980, following a village goodbye picnic by the River Versoix on the Swiss/French border, there was not a dry eye in the car.

Music carried on from where it had left off six years earlier in Berne. Chamber music and concerts continued with friends from Berne days, and I quickly found a new regular Geneva string quartet. With Ludwig Baeumer, an excellent 'cellist from WIPO (killed in the Swissair crash of 1998), and violinist Werner Kubischta and violist Günther Lütjens from CERN (European Organisation for Nuclear Research), we met weekly and played much of the string quartet literature. I recall a *Schubertiade* when we played Schubert's complete chamber music repertoire over a long but deeply satisfying all-day-and-evening session. When we finally left Geneva the string quartet gave us as a goodbye present a lovely set of twenty-one prints of the La Côte wine villages on the northern slopes of Lake Geneva – still on our wall today.

Other musicians with whom I played chamber music include violinist Alan Tartakoff, violist Lyn Parker (subsequently UK Ambassador in The Hague), and pianist Bill Lugg, with whom we gave house concerts, including the whole of Vivaldi's *Four Seasons* at a colleague's wedding party.

Variation: Les Diablerets

To own a mountain property for our family skiers had always been a dream for Ruth. In 1999 we received some German Government restitution money for Ruth's German-Jewish family having to flee from Nazi Germany in 1938. Our son Andrew suggested that Ruth should now stop dreaming about a mountain property, and finally get one. We eventually decided that, rather than looking for rented accommodation for family ski-holidays each year, we should buy our own place somewhere in the Alps.

After extensive searching in the Alpine areas of France and Switzerland, we finally decided on the village of Les Diablerets, just below the Col du Pillon leading to Gstaad. It is on the Eastern border of the Canton of Vaud – by chance our Chavannes-des-Bois house was on the Western border. In our Berne and Geneva days we had often driven through Les Diablerets, but never actually skied there. In fact, although not particularly well known as a ski-resort, it enjoys, as well as its own two ski areas, access to all-year glacier skiing at 3,000 metres and direct liaison with the extensive Villars area.

In 2000 we were fortunate to buy at a reasonable price by Swiss standards, and certainly by the standards of the more fashionable resorts like Verbier or Gstaad, a South-facing chalet, with stunning views over the mountains, sun from morning to evening, and the pleasant noise from two small rippling streams at the bottom of our garden. Accordingly, we subsequently officially named the chalet 'Les Ruisselets' (the streamlets).

Since the chalet was part of a 'PPE' (shared leasehold area of land), there were some initial and probably inevitable problems with our immediate neighbours over car access and parking. However, a few years later, a change in Swiss law enabled us to buy the freehold of the land and build an additional parking space – subsidised by the neighbours as part of the deal. The problems evaporated, some of the neighbours moved, and now we all live in perfect harmony, well integrated into the village, even addressed by our first names and *tutoyed* by some of the locals.

Fortunately, all our children and grandchildren love the chalet, obviously for the skiing in the winter, but also for the beautiful Swiss summer mountain scenery, wild-flowers and the idyllic, peaceful mountain walks down what in winter are busy ski-slopes. Since we had both fallen in love with Switzerland, its people, cultures and landscapes, it gives us especial pleasure that our children have over the years also grown to appreciate what Switzerland means to us.

Theme: Music Again

The reader will recall how, in 1961, just after leaving school, four of us youngsters bought a clapped-out Ford van and toured Europe. While they were all up an Austrian mountain, I drove across Switzerland to visit the Gstaad Menuhin Festival, which was founded in 1956 by my musical 'hero'. This was the first of many visits to the Festival over the years, to hear the maestro and his friends.

In 2001, when we had just settled in Les Diablerets, I telephoned the Festival President, Leonz Blunschi, and (in *Bärndütsch*) explained that I was a British, former Swiss violinist, and offered to work for the Festival. He sounded mystified by a Brit speaking fluent *Bärndütsch*, but like a good Swiss, he asked how much this might cost. When I explained that I was only too happy to help the Festival without charging, he arranged for me to meet him, his future Artistic Director Christoph Müller ('cellist with the Basel Kammerorchester) and his Funding Director Hans-Ueli Tschanz. After an exploratory chat with the somewhat bemused Swiss team, we agreed on a mutual-cooperation plan to include PR, fund-raising, artist contacts, and raising the UK profile of the Festival. Leonz Blunschi, mayor and hotelier, who with his wife Gisela became a close friend and made it clear that we should immediately be on first name/*Du* terms with him and indeed with the whole Festival team.

What followed over the succeeding years turned out to be one of the happiest musical experiences of my life. Ruth and I were immediately accepted into the Gstaad 'family', and in return for my efforts to support the Festival, were given complimentary staff passes which gave us access to all concerts. The venue's proximity, close to Les Diablerets, only half an hour away from Gstaad, was a big practical advantage. I was able to get regular free-of-charge publicity about the Festival into the UK musical and wider press and to persuade successive Swiss Ambassadors in London to host receptions to publicise the Festival, often with young musicians from the Yehudi Menuhin School in Surrey. Encouraging UK visitors to come to the Festival was always going to be difficult, given the CHF/£ exchange rate, but with Ruth's help we made some progress. I was also able, through personal contacts, to introduce the Festival to Swiss funding sources, with both direct cash results and future promises.

Christoph Müller, who brought the Festival back to the founding 'vision of Menuhin' after a negative post-Menuhin epoch, and I would discuss potential ideas and artists for the Festival, although I was careful not to stray into his professional domain. The Director of the Yehudi Menuhin Museum in Saanen and also local journalist, Dr Rolf Steiger (who by chance had worked at the Berne Inselspital at the same time as Ruth forty years earlier), and his wife Ursula also became good friends. He, together with Hans-Ueli Tschanz, had worked with Menuhin on the Festival management many years ago (described in their 2006 joint-ly-authored book *Gstaad und die Menuhins*), although they acknowledged that I, with my 1961 schoolboy visit, had been there even before they had. Rolf Steiger wrote an article – 'Der Brite Desmond Cecil CMG als "International Representative" des Festivals' – about my long-standing links with the Festival, with a photo of me in front of Saanen Church, for the local *Anzeiger von Saanen* newspaper in 2011.

To permit the use of the name Menuhin, the Festival must include a member of the Family on its Board. For a time, this was pianist son Jeremy, who would become another close friend. Some years ago, he was briefly replaced by his elder brother Gerard, who was immediately removed when he made a public anti-Semitic remark – particularly unfortunate for a son of a *Yehudi* – and Jeremy returned. (When Yehudi's Russian–Jewish parents Moshe and Marutha, then pregnant with Yehudi, arrived in New York in 1916 they were offered accommodation in a boarding house which proudly claimed 'No Jews, no Blacks'. The outraged Menuhins turned the offer down and resolved that the name of their first-born would make their Jewishness obvious – *Yehudi* from the Hebrew for Jewish.)

Yehudi's daughter Zamira and son-in-law Jonathan Benthall, whom we knew from the UK, and Yehudi's grandchildren Dominic and Nadia have been among the recent family visitors to the Festival. In 2016 the Athenæum Club (Yehudi was a member) planned an event with the Menuhin family to honour the centenary of his birth, which they asked me to organise. Together, with Jonathan Benthall (also a member) and Zamira Benthall-Menuhin, Malcolm Singer the Music Director of the Menuhin School which he has regularly conducted in Gstaad, Athenæum Menuhin memorabilia, and young Menuhin School violinist Andrew Samarasekara playing solo Bach and Bartók, we paid our respects to one of the great musicians and humanists of the twentieth century.

As in Yehudi's day much of the Festival's music, especially with the chamber and smaller ensembles, takes place in the historic fifteenth-century Saanen Mauritiuskirche, and also in the lovely small old churches nearby in Lauenen, Zweisimmen, Gsteig, Château-d'Œx, Rougement and Vers-l'Eglise. Leonz Blunschi kindly arranged for me to play Bach on my violin with the local organist in the Saanen church. I was privileged to hear my Stradivari humbly ringing out where Yehudi's once had. The big orchestral concerts later in the Festival are in the larger Festivalzelt, seating 2,000 people, as they were in Yehudi's latter years. This, although not especially romantic, has the practical advantage of bringing in the major sponsors.

Even though Menuhin died in 1999, his vision of great artists and young musicians, chamber and orchestral music, improvisation and jazz, the classics and new compositions – while respecting the past, always forward-looking – lives on, carefully nurtured by Christoph Müller, Leonz Blunschi and his successor Aldo Kropf, and the whole Gstaad team. Ruth and I are greatly privileged that our friendship and partnership with the Festival continues happily to this day. The theme of the 2021 Festival will be 'London', and I have been asked to help prepare the programme – which I do with great pleasure as a thank you for the friendship over the years.

*

For many years the Swiss Ambassador in London has organised the 'Swiss Ambassador's Award' for young, outstanding Swiss-based musicians to be given a prize-winning tour of the UK, London (Wigmore Hall), Manchester, Cardiff, Edinburgh, Belfast – star recipients have included Sol Gabetta, Louis Schwizgebel and Francesco Piemontesi. Very recently the current Swiss Ambassador, Alexandre Fasel, and his Head of Culture, David Kilian Beck, asked for my support in transforming this into an award for UK-based young musicians in recognition of our international cultural partnership. I was only too happy to help, in the light of what Switzerland has given me culturally, and have spent productive days with David Kilian Beck introducing him to my personal contacts in the music colleges around the UK. As a result, the first 'Swiss Ambassador's Award' to a young UK-trained musician was made in June 2020 to an emerging young British violinist, Roberto Ruisi, currently studying at the Royal College of Music in London. This will be followed by a UK-wide sponsored tour, although, because of the Coronavirus pandemic, probably in the Spring of 2021.

6

FOREIGN & COMMONWEALTH OFFICE (FCO)

Prelude

As is normal practice, this chapter has been submitted to the relevant authorities for their prior perusal. While some information has been withheld for official reasons, and with which I am content having signed the Official Secrets Act, the resulting text is both factual and accurate. I should add that my reminiscences are of a Foreign & Commonwealth Office between a quarter- and half-century ago – and the world has moved on.

Variations

When in 1969 I had decided to leave my Swiss professional musical life, I wrote from our Bernese home to numerous UK companies, banks, newspapers offering my services – overseas experience, fluency in several languages, Oxford degree way back. The polite answers were nearly all the same '...violin, interesting, but...' However, I went back to Oxford, where the University career advisers listened carefully and suggested the Foreign & Commonwealth Office (FCO), and I was duly invited for an interview. I was then put forward for the standard and lengthy selection process, further interviews, written exams, Civil Service Selection Board (CSSB) with other candidates, language aptitude test, and then the Final Selection Board (FSB). Interestingly the interviewers were intrigued rather than put off by my passion for the violin. Years later, when I myself sat on Final Selection Boards, we looked out for signs of originality, rather than rely only on academic excellence.

The result was that I was offered a position as a 'fast-stream' Second Secretary with what seemed for 1970 a princely salary of £2,317 p.a. – and unlike in the music world, it came in every month! I could now commute into London, from the house which Ruth's Aunt Emmie had lent us in a cherry-tree lined avenue in Welwyn Garden City, in diplomatically polished shoes.

London – (Moscow?)

I was sent on the usual FCO introductory and training courses, developing diplomatic, intra-personal and literary skills – and walking in suit and tie past the statue of my illustrious great-great-grandfather, the 3rd Marquess of Salisbury, Foreign Secretary and Prime Minister, at the foot of the main staircase – a far cry from the informality of professional music, but life is full of surprises.

Immediately afterwards, presumably because of my language aptitude test result, I was sent on an intensive Russian course with the formidable Countess Shuvalova at the excellent FCO Language School (later abolished as a cost-saving measure – maybe a belief that all foreigners spoke English?), as preparation for a Moscow posting.

With the Russian language progressing, the next step in preparation for my planned Moscow posting was a move to the Eastern Europe and Soviet Department (EESD). I was taken under the wing of Julian Bullard, the Head of the Department, and in my view and that of others, the best Permanent Under-Secretary that the FCO never had. Bullard, who became a loyal friend and mentor, was greatly supportive, as was his Under-Secretary Tom Brimelow, and he taught me a great deal about Whitehall and diplomacy which would be of much value during my later career. I noted with some amusement that the Deputy Head of the Department regularly re-wrote and lengthened my drafts (as no doubt Deputy Heads of Department are paid to do), and then Julian re-shortened them and restored them to something close to the original version.

As the time for my Moscow posting approached I exchanged letters with the then-Ambassador Duncan Wilson about diplomatic matters and, equally importantly, about music – his daughter was Elizabeth Wilson the 'cellist and the wife of pianist Radu Lupu – and with which musicians I might play my violin in Moscow.

However, this all came to naught because of *Operation Foot*, about which I was briefed in the EESD. *Operation Foot* was inspired by the then Conservative Government's laudable desire to restrict rampant Soviet espionage in the UK, especially after it had been exposed by the Soviet KGB defector Oleg Lyalin. In September 1971, the FCO Permanent Under-Secretary (PUS) Denis Greenhill summoned the Soviet *Chargé d'Affaires* Ivan Ippolitov and informed him that 105 Soviet diplomats would be expelled from London. If the Soviets over-reacted, he was informed that the UK Government would take further measures, going as far as breaking off relations with the Soviet Union.

Faced with this ultimatum the Soviets expelled only five British diplomats from Moscow at the time, mainly military and commercial officials whom they thought were of value to the UK. Predictably a lengthy period of frozen relations then ensued, and many future British diplomats, especially Russian speakers in whom the UK government had invested money and training and were perhaps seen as bargaining chips, had their future careers seriously affected. Shortly before *Foot* the incoming British Ambassador to Moscow, John Killick – who had been a paratrooper at Arnhem, a straight-talking and supportive colleague – at a diplomatic reception in London introduced me to Soviet *Chargé d'Affaires*, Ivan Ippolitov, as about to become 'one of my best Russian speakers in Moscow'. From the curious look on Ippolitov's face and with my prior knowledge of *Foot*, I reluctantly concluded that Moscow prospects might rapidly recede – which turned out to be the case.

Fortunately, I was never blacklisted, like some of the Soviet specialists in the FCO Research Department, but my visa application, with those of some other known Russian speakers, was put on indefinite hold by the Soviets. We all waited for months, most sympathetically supported by John Killick and his Head of Chancery, Ken Scott. Eventually the relevant FCO Minister decided that some of our names should be withdrawn from the list in a (misguided?) attempt to ease the tension.

Variation: (Paris?) – Bonn

So ... Moscow was put on hold, and the FCO offered me Paris as a consolation, and I was enrolled at the foreign diplomats' elite course at the Ecole Nationale d'Administration (ENA). However, because of a delicate staff complication in Bonn I was at the last minute asked to go there instead in 1973. Since I already had fluent German, I was to take over the position of the (junior) First Secretary covering German internal politics.

The preparatory advice which the FCO Western European Department gave me included reading *Der Spiegel* and *A Small Town in Germany*. The latter turned out to be particularly apposite when I first entered the long unromantic building on the Konrad-Adenauer-Allée, which reminded many of us of the Hoover Factory on the A4 road West of London. I recall John Le Carré's description of the dozens of people, many locally employed Germans, working away in the basement on I know not what. Le Carré had, of course, worked in Bonn in the 1960s (and had also studied in Berne – another link), before deciding that formal diplomacy and his writings were incompatible. The Embassy still retained his old house on the other side of the Rhine in Königswinter, which had been occupied by the Legal Adviser and then by another First Secretary.

Almost at once we were kindly invited to a welcome dinner at the home of the Defence Attaché and his wife, both charming people. However, the invitation was worded 'informal', and we were about to turn up casually dressed (as any ex-violinist would), when a thoughtful colleague pointed out that a Defence Attaché's 'informal' meant, if not 'black tie', then certainly 'dark suit and tie'.

The immediate professional shock was the rigidity of the Embassy structure, as described by Le Carré, and highlighted by the top-heavy formal morning meeting. This was presided over by the Minister (Deputy Ambassador) Reg Hibbert, supervised by the Ambassador 'Nicko' (or 'Nico') Henderson, both no doubt admirable diplomats individually. The dozen-plus Counsellors were regularly grilled and sometimes humiliated by their superiors. We twenty-plus Secretaries were to some extent spared from this – Reg made it clear that 'junior Secretaries are there to know the facts, but only to speak when required'.

Like the other 'juniors' I tried to follow this advice, although I was 'ambushed' some months later by a colleague who subsequently rose to high office himself. The Ambassador was telling us what guidance he had given to London before a meeting between Chancellor Brandt and Prime Minister Heath the next day, when my colleague interjected, 'Sir,' (as we were required to address the Ambassador in public), 'Desmond may have something to add.' In fact, I had been chatting with Brandt and others at an SPD party political (rather than government) event the night before, and he had described what he planned to say to Heath. However, this did not agree with what Nicko had already reported to London, and he was less than pleased with my involuntary contribution. Another Ambassador might have sent a follow-up telegram to London saying that his staff had been on the job and had gathered additional information, but that was not the Bonn style of the day! As a naive newcomer I no doubt thought that the duty of the Bonn Embassy was to report accurately on German politics, before becoming involved in Westminster politics...

A contributory factor to the rigidity of the upper Embassy management was that there were too many senior officials, and only a relative few
of these spoke remotely fluent German – others relying on the German
Foreign Ministry's daily English language bulletin. This combined with
the inevitable career infighting and an eye on Whitehall politics, under
the divisive leadership of Reg and Nicko, created an unhappy working
environment.

Privately, when he was not being autocratic, Reg could be charming. He had an excellent understanding of German politics, and he
gave me some most helpful advice on drafting content, judgement and
Whitehall style – which nobody else did. When Edward Heath visited
for high-level talks, Reg invited me, as the relevant, albeit junior, official to give the Prime Minister a briefing on German internal politics.
Heath appeared to be focused elsewhere while sipping his whisky, but
I noted the next morning at the official talks that he had remembered
every single detail.

Reg also asked me, as the 'in-house musician', to conduct the Embassy
choir, which was his pride and joy. Once, when we were rehearsing for a
Christmas concert, he instructed me to have one verse of 'Silent Night'
fast, the next slow, and the final one fast again – to make an impact. I
respectfully replied that my 'artistic' conscience had a problem with this.
An uncertain silence around the choir ensued, until Reg's wife Ann, a
lovely Welsh lady, interjected, 'Reg, why can't you admit that you might
be wrong for once in your life?' After a stunned pause, Reg suddenly burst
out laughing, as did the rest of the choir with some relief – and 'Silent
Night' proceeded at the proper tempo. Reg was also a participant at our
'Hauskonzerte' for our culture-loving Embassy colleagues and local musical friends, when he would recite poetry with due feeling, and afterwards
write us a fulsome letter of thanks.

While my actual diplomatic work was fascinating, as a naive newcomer
from the world of professional music, I was taken aback by the internal
back-biting and inter-departmental infighting in the 'senior' levels of the

Bonn Embassy. Many of my 'junior' colleagues were equally shocked – which created a long-standing bond between us.

On one occasion the Embassy Legal Adviser Frank Berman, later FCO Chief Legal Adviser, and with his wife Chris a good family friend to this day, and I drove down to Karlsruhe to observe the proceedings of the German Federal Constitutional Court on German Reunification. When we parked the car, Frank suddenly remembered that he had locked his keys inside it. For the next quarter of an hour we surreptitiously fished for the keys through a slightly open car window, hoping that a local would not spot us and report the British Embassy Legal Adviser and the Political Secretary to the police for attempted car theft. When we finally arrived at the Court, we listened with fascination to the proceedings, until I suddenly got a tap on the shoulder. Having done most of the driving from Bonn to Karlsruhe on a hot day, I must have drifted off. I opened my eyes to see the distinguished be-robed judges smiling but reminding us clearly that one was not allowed to doze during their deliberations. Fortunately, they were amused rather than offended that the British Embassy had inadvertently interrupted the proceedings of the German Federal Constitutional Court.

Frank reminisces about his Bonn experiences in an interview published in 2018.* He is, if anything even more critical than I was about the senior Embassy infighting and lack of German knowledge at the very top.

> Inevitably, when you have an Embassy of that size, it was a place of cliques … big egos…The trouble with Reg was that he sorted people into sheep and goats… Reg and Nico were completely different per-sonalities… I never had the feeling that Nico understood Germany… He certainly wasn't a German-speaker. I don't think that he even noticed among his staff those who could do the language and those who couldn't.

* https://www.chu.cam.ac.uk/media/uploads/files/Berman.pdf

However, on a positive note Frank does single out the 'terrific *esprit de corps* amongst the group of First Secretaries … who thought of ourselves as the engine room. It was a really outstandingly able collection of people who were there at the time: Nicholas Bayne, Nigel Broomfield: Desmond Cecil was there too.'

After we had left Bonn, the FCO Personnel Department showed me a confidential personal report on me from the Minister Reg Hibbert. Amid some qualified positive comments was the phrase, 'Desmond and Ruth would be more suited to a kibbutz than an embassy' – with which, as far as the then Bonn Embassy is concerned, I agree to this day.

I resolved that if my next Embassy suffered from similar internal tensions, I should have to resign from the FCO. Fortunately, this was not the case. My view was and remains that such infighting and excessive rank-consciousness is counter-productive, and I have always done my best to challenge it.

My musical experiences in Bonn, the birthplace of Ludwig van Beethoven, and elsewhere in Germany are described later.

(Paris?) – London again

After Bonn, I was again offered a Paris posting, but when I discovered that Nicko was to be the next Ambassador there, I declined the kind offer – no doubt before he could decline me.

I was then given a short-term posting covering South-Eastern Europe and especially Greco-Turkish issues after the Turkish invasion of Cyprus. This was a new geographical area to me, which I found interesting. From time to time I had the pleasure of lunching with Hugh Carleton Greene, previously Director-General of the BBC, to discuss Southern Europe political developments with him – at the time he was Chair of the European–Atlantic Action Committee on Greece, hence his widely respected in-depth Southern Europe political insights.

We met in the Martinez Spanish restaurant in Swallow Street, and he would always begin by ordering a couple of chilled glasses of Manzanilla – since then I have drunk no other sherry. Lunch with fresh fish would be accompanied by a bottle of excellent dry Spanish white wine. Halfway through the meal, Hugh would invariably ask, 'Do you think that we could manage another bottle, dear boy?' – with which I invariably acquiesced.

The Martinez was also a legendary haunt of journalists and publishers, who would often come over to our table to chat to us. I knew a few of them, but inevitably Hugh knew them all. I was never sure whether there was ever any diplomatic benefit from these lunches, but I certainly found the overall intellectual, literary and cultural range of our conversations – Hugh knew that I had been a professional musician, and we both had youthful German experiences – absolutely bewitching.

Variation: Geneva – United Nations

In 1976 I was sent with the family to the UK Mission to the UN in Geneva, a happy return to Switzerland. I was appointed as UK Press Officer to the UN and was responsible for diplomatic aspects of UK dealings with several UN Agencies. The UK Permanent Representative and Ambassador when I arrived was James Bottomley, who had previously been Ambassador in South Africa. He was courteous and helpful, giving advice where appropriate, but not interfering unduly, especially given the specialised and often technical nature of the work with the different UN Agencies – happily a very welcome and different atmosphere to that of the Embassy in Bonn. By chance his son Peter was a Tory MP, with whom I had some nuclear environmental dealings many years later.

The Press side of my job was normally about maintaining good relations with the UK and foreign Press Corps in the UN, a friendly and professional group. I made it a firm rule always to be as open with them as I was allowed, and never to tell them a direct falsehood. They reciprocated appropriately and most of them became trusted colleagues.

The only near incident of a leak that I can recall was once, when a visiting UK Minister, who had clearly enjoyed too much local hospitality, unwisely insisted on holding a Press Conference – at which he inevitably said too much. At the request of his worried officials, I telephoned around the journalists and, as a personal favour, asked for their discretion. They all respected this, albeit with a few jokes, apart from one well-known 'loose cannon'. The *doyen* of the UK Press Corps called me with a quiet warning, and I was able get hold of the said 'loose cannon' and repeat my request, adding that if he let me down, his information flow would dry up. He got the message.

Shortly after my arrival, the UK Government convened the 1976 Rhodesia Conference in Geneva, chaired by the open and affable Ivor Richard, UK Permanent Representative and Ambassador to the United Nations in New York. He brought his own personal Press Officer, but, despite my limited media experience, I was appointed Conference Press Officer. The first task was to be at the airport to greet the incoming VIPs – Ian Smith, P. K. van der Byl, Joshua Nkomo, Robert Mugabe, Rev. Canaan Banana (about whom the press made predictable banana-republic jokes) – and other dignitaries, attend their various press conferences, and monitor international and Swiss media reaction to the conference developments. The resident UK Press Corps was boosted by over five hundred international correspondents, accredited by my wife Ruth as a Conference 'temp', including UK media 'stars' such as David Spanier, Peter Snow and John Dickie – good company, as well as very professional. Many of them, including from ITN, BBC Panorama and Radio News subsequently wrote me warm personal thank-you letters.

I had to warn the journalists that Ian Smith's bodyguards were both nervous and armed, and that they should not be provoked. Once, when Ian Smith was emerging from the UN Building, the guards noticed a long 'tube' poking out of a fifth-floor window and started to go for their guns.

Fortunately, I realised that it was Peter Snow and his ITN team with a telephoto lens and was able to restrain the guards. Peter and I joke to this day about his life being saved, but question whether it might have been better journalism to have allowed a dramatic if violent conclusion...

At the end of the Rhodesia Conference in December 1976, Ivor Richard wrote to me from New York:

Dear Desmond,

It was fitting that at my last press conference in Geneva the Press should have expressed their gratitude to you in such forceful terms. I share with them the highest regard for all you personally did to ensure the smooth running of the Conference press arrangements. This was a very important achievement and one for which I send you my sincere thanks. With best wishes for 1977 to you and your family.

Yours sincerely, Ivor Richard

On another occasion Jeremy Thorpe, on bail for the notorious 'Rinka / Scott' case, had been allowed to come to Geneva with his wife Marion Stein to attend a meeting of the United Nations Association. I was instructed by the FCO News Department not to deny the visit if asked, which I of course I was. The Press Corps were at the airport in force when the Thorpes arrived, and took a photo of me carrying Jeremy's bag, with Marion cut out of the picture. They joked afterwards that if I did not give them plentiful information in future they would publish the photo of 'the happy couple eloping'. (If I look somewhat apprehensive in the photo, it is because I knew exactly what was going on.) That evening at the Residence of the new UK Ambassador, James Murray, the telephone rang constantly with press questions about the visit, to which I gave the standard replies. After a while Jeremy got bored and insisted on answering the telephone himself as 'Mr Cecil's Assistant', with alternating Scottish, Irish, Welsh accents – he was a brilliant mimic. The next day when the journalists commented that they were not aware that I had a Scottish,

Irish or Welsh assistant, I had to tell them that they had missed a scoop when talking directly to Jeremy.

On another occasion FCO News Department asked me to assist the veteran BBC Panorama journalist Tom Mangold, who had come to Geneva to investigate 'irregularities' within the United Nations. As instructed, I made the appropriate UN introductions for Tom and then let him get on with his 'revelations' – for which I subsequently received an official thank-you letter from the BBC. He was congenial company, when not being a serious investigator, and after Geneva we found that we were near neighbours in South-West London and stayed in touch on a personal basis.

When the UK Embassy in Berne decided to pension off their locally employed Press Officer, I was asked to double up between UN Geneva and the Swiss capital Berne. This brought me into contact with the Swiss-German media, with whom I could converse in their local dialect, gaining a national as well as an international/UN perspective on current events. I was also asked to marshal the Swiss press when HM The Queen and HRH Prince Philip paid an official visit to Switzerland, including the International Committee of the Red Cross (ICRC) in Geneva, culminating with a royal tour of the medieval Château de Chillon of Byron's *The Prisoner of Chillon* fame on the shores of Lake Geneva.

When the Thatcher Government took over in 1979, the new British Foreign Secretary Peter Carrington visited the UN Geneva for Balkan and other discussions. He impressed everyone with his calm competence, understanding and courtesy – after his somewhat abrasive predecessor David Owen. I recall him greeting his guards and drivers by name and enquiring about their families – which not every busy politician would find time for.

We at the UK Mission also had to coordinate 'secret' discussions in 1980 between British and Argentine Ministers (subsequently disclosed in the Official History), attempting to defuse the growing Falkland tensions. To maintain 'secrecy' the Mission booked the UK Minister into a Geneva lakeside hotel under another name, and tactfully had to remind him to sign the hotel register as 'John Smith' or whatever. The talks were amicable and even included discussion of the politically sensitive 'leaseback', but sadly they were not to succeed – as we saw in 1982.

Of the UN Agencies for which I was diplomatically responsible, the World Intellectual Property Organisation (WIPO) and the World Meteorological Organisation (WMO) were particularly enjoyable. I acted as diplomatic adviser to the Comptroller-General of the Patent Office for the WIPO and to the Director-General of the Meteorological Office for the WMO, working with their visiting teams. In particular, the WIPO demanded some sensitive political diplomacy, given the East-West, North-South political demands on intellectual property. On occasions, when the Patents Office team was absent, I had to sign formal treaties on behalf of the UK Government. Once a WIPO negotiation was delayed for days by a Soviet/West German clash about whether the FRG should be referred to as the 'Federal Republic, Germany' or the 'Federal Republic of Germany'. As a Russian speaker I was able to come up with the solution that treaties should be signed 'in the name of ... the FRG', since in Russian there is no difference between the genitive of a nominative and the genitive of a genitive.

A small matter perhaps, but it saved international taxpayers' money... When I left Geneva the Meteorological and Patent Office Heads, as had Ivor Richard, wrote generous letters of appreciation.

London again

After Geneva I had a short posting looking after new entrants. This was certainly a worthwhile assignment, both in the more formal mentoring, but also in wide-ranging informal discussion with the entrants about UK policy objectives. Some of them remain good friends of ours to this day. I then returned to Soviet affairs, both making use of my Russian and negotiating with other governments, especially Western European. One particularly happy and fruitful relationship was with France, despite the sometimes visible political tensions between the UK and French Governments.

While a potential Moscow posting remained on the horizon, I also worked in the FCO Planning Staff. This was a 'think-tank' under the leadership of Pauline Neville-Jones, a subsequent Tory Minister, with some bright FCO stars of the future, such as David Manning and Sherard Cowper-Coles, with whom I enjoyed working. As well as 'planning' papers for both practical and theoretical situations, we also travelled as a team around Europe, for example to Germany, to exchange 'planning' ideas with our counterparts in other foreign ministries.

Peter Hennessey eruditely described our activities, naming us all as the FCO 'think-tank' in a *Times* article of 31 October 1983 entitled 'Bright young things of the FO'. He went on to say:

In Mrs Thatcher's Whitehall some things are at a discount, diplomats and think tanks among them. It is mildly surprising, therefore, to find in the Foreign and Commonwealth Office a flourishing team of bright young officials licensed to think the unthinkable. What is more, Sir Geoffrey Howe, the Foreign Secretary, seems to relish their output. The Prime Minister uses their material for her speeches.

...*et voilà!*

I and an FCO colleague, Ivor Roberts, were involved in an 'FO high-ups' press-leak incident, which caused a minor stir at the time. Ivor and I have developed a tradition, now going back nearly half a century, to meet regularly in Turkish restaurants – in the old days to catch up with FCO gossip and nowadays to discuss cultural and political developments. The Turkish restaurants of London may have changed, but the tradition continues.

On this particular occasion we met at the excellent, but long since disappeared, Golden Horn in Wardour Street with Anthony Holden, a long-standing mutual friend, distinguished journalist (freelancing at the time, and previously Assistant Editor of *The Times*, until he fell out with the Murdoch regime) and poker grandee – see later. After the second bottle of very palatable Buzbag red wine, the conversation turned to somewhat delicate foreign-policy issues, on which Ivor spoke freely. At the time he was working in the FCO News Department, so I naively assumed that his comments were already in the public domain. The next morning Anthony splashed the conversation in his *Daily Express* column, quoting his sources as 'two FO high-ups'. At the senior FCO morning meeting that day, the Permanent Under-Secretary was less than amused, and ironically instructed Ivor as the News Department representative to track down and reprimand the two miscreant 'FO high-ups' – which, unsurprisingly, he failed to do.

Variation: Vienna – (Moscow)

In 1985 I was given what was to be our final overseas posting for the FCO. Although there was some talk of Rome, which would have been personally attractive – I have a lifelong cultural passion for things Italian, Stradivari violins included – the FCO decided on the Embassy in Vienna as Political Counsellor, for which I already had fluent German. The Ambassador Michael Alexander was a good friend from our time together in the UK Mission to the UN in Geneva where he had been Head of Chancery, and through our chess-playing link to his father Hugh Alexander (whose games I had studied seriously). He was succeeded by Robin O'Neill, who later became a respected Chairman of the Anglo-Austrian Society. Ruth and I remain in personal contact with him and his wife Helen to this day.

The British Embassy was then based in an imposing turn-of-the-century building in the Reisnerstrasse in the historic 3rd District of Vienna – Metternich was reputed to have said that the Balkans begin in the Rennweg (in the 3rd District). Certainly Vienna, lying at the far end of modern Austria (for example to the East of Communist Prague), cut off by the Iron Curtain from its former Austro-Hungarian imperial eastern provinces, was noticeably more Eastern than Western European – as a glance at all the Slav names in the Vienna telephone directory would confirm. When we arrived, I naively thought that, with fluent German and my German/Swiss diplomatic experiences, this would be another Western European posting – needless to say, I was somewhat mistaken as I got to know 'Balkan' Vienna.

Our Reisnerstrasse Embassy building, where we had been since 1948, close to the German, Soviet and Chinese Embassies, was old-fashioned, but certainly stylish and reminiscent of past glories. In due course inspectors came from London and decided that we had to move with the times – reflecting modern-day Austria in the late twentieth century. In any case the lease was about to expire, and we now had to accommodate UN and Disarmament Delegations as well as the bilateral Embassy staff. Although we were only paying a peppercorn rent for the Reisnerstrasse, we all moved out into a purpose-built and practical construction in the garden of the Ambassador's Metternichgasse Residence around the corner in the Jaurèsgasse (notwithstanding considerable local Viennese opposition). No doubt this was probably inevitable, although the saving to the UK taxpayer may have been minimal, but the transfer was accompanied by a slight feeling of historic regret. But we all must move on…

With the encroaching relaxations in the Communist Bloc countries immediately next door to Austria, my Russian language was particularly relevant in Vienna. In addition, given its geographical location and open borders, Vienna became a focal point for countering the challenges of international terrorism. We in the Embassy worked closely with our major allies and with the collaborative senior Austrian colleagues in the Interior Ministry.

This cooperation at official level was reinforced at ministerial level by an official visit to Vienna from the UK Home Secretary Douglas Hurd. Formal meetings with Austrian Interior Minister Karl Blecha, were enlivened by an Austrian hostage-rescue demonstration, and, Vienna being

Vienna, ending with a performance of *La Bohème* at the Vienna State Opera. The UK reciprocated by inviting Blecha, together with his officials, to London, for meetings with Hurd at the Home Office, and with the Ministry of Defence and other departments. Counterterrorism featured strongly in both visits – needless to say, the UK visit did not include an opera performance.

A relatively junior, but very able Embassy colleague and good German-speaker was Leigh Turner. Over the years we stayed in touch when our paths crossed diplomatically. In 2016 he returned to Vienna as Ambassador, now covering both the Austrian bilateral and multilateral United Nations duties – unlike thirty years previously when the various missions were separate – FCO cost-cutting. We met up again in London and Vienna, and while discussing my published Stradivarius monograph (see later), he said that some years previously when on unpaid leave from the FCO he had written travel articles for the *FT* and other journals. Since then his writing of novels and short stories under the name of Robert Pimm had developed into a more serious activity. We naturally compared notes about our literary aspirations.

Early on in my posting, Michael Alexander, busy with an official visit by HRH Prince Charles and Princess Diana, asked me to look after the Embassy while he was occupied with the Royals. Subsequently he and his successor Robin O'Neill both asked me to act as formal (communicated officially to the FCO and the Austrian Government) UK *Chargé d'Affaires* in their absences. This also facilitated diplomatic contacts with Western, Eastern and Austrian diplomats, officials and politicians during the fascinating period when the Cold War was drawing to its end.

Normal contacts and friendships with Eastern European diplomats developed quickly in the late 1980s. Most of them had, at least in spirit, distanced themselves from Soviet Communism. The Hungarian border became more open, the main shopping street Mariahilfestrasse becoming nicknamed the 'Magyarhilfestrasse', although there was still some shooting at the harder Czech border. Once, however, the East German Deputy

Ambassador, a pleasant colleague, almost surprised me by stressing during an affable lunch that he was still a Marxist, which very few of his Bloc colleagues would have said then.

Another diplomatic contact caused some initial alarm but ended amusingly. I was invited to lunch, to discuss political developments in general terms, by the Deputy Ambassador of a Middle Eastern country (which for obvious reasons I shall refer to as X – unlike former Minister Ted Rowlands who revealed in Parliament at the time of the 1982 Falklands War that the British Government was reading Argentine diplomatic traffic). As I knew little about X, I prepared myself by reading the standard FCO 'guidance telegram', which provides non-confidential background information on the relevant country for public use with other diplomats and with the press. Lunch was pleasant and non-controversial.

However, a few days later I received an alarming message from London that I had been unduly indiscreet and given away UK confidential information about X. I was told that the relevant UK agency had read a detailed account by my X lunch contact, which had provoked this alarm. Naturally, as this UK report was given a 'Top Secret' classification, people in London were concerned about my 'indiscretion'. Fortunately the British Ambassador in X then intervened to confirm that the report only contained the public information from the FCO 'guidance telegram' – which I had quite properly drawn on at the lunch, and which, somewhat to our surprise, the Deputy Ambassador of X had reported accurately. So – smiles and apologies all round, but interesting to see how people had over-reacted to the 'Top Secret' circumstance, without bothering to read the actual detail of the report.

As the Embassy's Russian speaker I liaised informally with the Soviet Ambassador and his colleagues in their Embassy, just across the street from the British Embassy, and facilitated 'confidential' meetings between the British and Soviet Foreign Ministers, Geoffrey Howe and Eduard Shevardnadze – and generally had perfectly amicable relationships with Soviet colleagues.

I also visited the Soviet Union in May 1988 for official discussions with the Soviet Foreign Ministry on Austrian EEC membership, and implications for Austrian neutrality. With our Moscow Head of Chancery, Rod Lyne – later Moscow Ambassador and an excellent colleague, especially on my later post-FCO Russian nuclear environmental projects for British Nuclear Fuels, I called on the Soviet Foreign Ministry, 2nd and 3rd European Departments for official diplomatic negotiations. These were both to discuss the Austrian-EEC question and, ironically, to protest about Soviet visa restrictions for UK diplomats awaiting posting. We officially briefed the Austrian Moscow Embassy on our Austrian/ EEC discussions.

I also called officially with the Embassy Press Officer on Soviet press agencies, *New Times* (Associate Editor L. Bezymensky and Departmental Editor Dmitriy Pogorzielskiy) and *Literaturnaya Gazeta* (Dr Arkady Vaxberg), to liaise over Western and emerging Soviet media activities, and I attended the Anglo-Soviet Writers Roundtable with Soviet and British journalists, some of the latter whom were already well known to me. The Soviet journalists had clearly been instructed in the spirit of *perestroika* to talk openly with Western officials, but some of them felt visibly confused and had to ask for our advice on what to discuss.

At these Soviet Foreign Ministry talks in 1988 I first met Grigory Karasin in the 2nd European Department. He was later Russian Ambassador in London, when I had the privilege of chairing a talk which he gave at the Athenæum – he reminisced to the audience about our earlier Soviet-era encounter. We also cooperated on UK/Russia nuclear environmental clean-up and cultural projects. When he left London as Ambassador in April 2005, he wrote me an official letter, personally expressing his 'sincere gratitude for your cooperation... for such a long time.'

We left Vienna in 1989 as the Iron Curtain was being raised.

My musical experiences in Vienna and elsewhere in Austria, the home of Mozart, Beethoven, Schubert and many others, are described later.

And Back to London – Middle East, Balkans and Americas

On return to London, I initially worked on counter-terrorist cooperation with European colleagues. Led by FCO Under-Secretary Duncan Slater and his Head of Security Coordination Andrew Green (later of 'Migration Watch' fame), we established an official inter-departmental 'Roadshow' to tour round our new Eastern European allies. We visited Poland, Czechoslovakia, Hungary and Bulgaria for official discussions. We were delighted to visit Warsaw, Prague, Budapest and Sofia, if not necessarily for the first time, nevertheless in circumstances where we could be completely relaxed and do some sight-seeing as if we were simply tourists.

We were warmly greeted by our new counter-terrorist colleagues, often composed of former Soviet Bloc security officials, but now apparently happy not to be under immediate Soviet influence. They were naturally only too keen to demonstrate to their new Western European friends their re-discovered loyalty to the international community. Later we also visited Moscow for rather more restrained official discussions but were even invited as honoured guests into the notorious Lubyanka KGB Headquarters.

Interesting Days After the Constraints of the Cold War

As the first Gulf War loomed in 1990, I was given a promotion into the Middle Eastern arena, despite having no local experience – perhaps the FCO thought that the 'Camel Corps'(a less than respectful nickname at the time for FCO Arabists) should be balanced by outside experience. During the first Gulf War our cooperation with the Americans was extremely close, each contributing their specific resources to the mutual effort. Unlike in the second Gulf War, there was no political dissension – Saddam had invaded a friendly state, Kuwait, and the UK had full UN backing, including from our Middle Eastern allies. Also, unlike in the second Gulf War, there were no controversial issues such as 'dodgy dossiers', renditions or internal political games.

My brief Middle Eastern incarnation took me to 'friendly' countries, Israel obviously, but also Jordan, Egypt, Syria, Morocco and Algeria. In the latter two my French turned out to be useful, as the Maghreb locals had problems with the classical MECAS (FCO Middle East Centre for Arab Studies in Lebanon) accents of my Arabist colleagues but were happy to converse in French.

I also visited Lebanon at the height of the hostage crisis for confidential local discussions about the British hostages. I recall being met at the Airport by a British Lance-Corporal, who told me that if there was any shooting I should lie flat on the floor of his armoured Land Rover – 'Is that f*****g clear?' he shouted, only afterwards adding a respectful, 'Sir!' My US colleagues were impressed that a British NCO should (quite correctly) have made it so explicitly clear to a 'senior officer' that he was in charge of my safety, which they were not sure an American counterpart would dare to do.

Despite the war damage, with hardly a building without bullet marks, I loved Beirut, and years later after my FCO days visited the whole country including the magnificent Bekaa Valley, which was clearly not possible during the first visit. All went well with the discussions until departure time when my British military guards took me to the Airport and saw that I was safely on the plane.

Unfortunately, after they had departed, the plane developed a technical problem and could not take off. I and the other passengers were decanted back into the Airport, which was still basically in Hezbollah territory. In those pre-mobile-phone days, I wondered how to tell my 'guards' that I was still on their territory, until I remembered that opposite the British Ambassador's Residence in Northern Beirut was a Middle East Airlines office. I asked the Airport MEA representative if they had a tie-line to their other office, which they did, and asked for their colleagues to cross the road and pass an urgent message for the British Ambassador, David Tatham, with whom I had been staying. This clearly worked, since half an hour later my 'guards' rushed back into the Airport, visibly sweating until they saw that I was safe. Had I been kidnapped in this unprotected interlude, it would have been serious for me, but would not have been good for their careers!

Years later I met ex-hostage Terry Waite at a German Embassy cultural event. We reminisced about our mutual Lebanese past, when of course he was still being held in solitary confinement. By then he seemed remarkably relaxed and open about his horrific experiences. We were joined by one of the London Philharmonic Orchestra team, Development Director Nick Jackman, a young man of slight build, and the three of us were chatting about music, when our LPO friend suddenly fainted and collapsed. As he fell, Terry (six foot seven) and I (six foot three) gently grabbed the young man and prevented him from reaching the floor. Fortunately, it was only a fainting fit because of the heat, and he quickly recovered – but Nick still amuses his LPO colleagues with the anecdote about him being 'saved' by the two charming, but large, gentlemen.

After this Middle Eastern incursion, I had a brief assignment to look at and advise on the worsening Balkan situation. This involved discussions with the relevant UK departments, and in the region with the local authorities and with the UK representatives. On one visit to talk to the British military commander, at the time based near Split, I was flown in an RAF Hercules. On the way back we diverted via Sarajevo to deliver supplies and pick up some locals. Since an Italian plane had been shot down a couple of days previously, we took special precautions, such as scattering *'window'* (tinfoil as a countermeasure to radar, dating back to the Second World War) as we approached Sarajevo. I was chatting with the pilot in the cockpit, when he suddenly told me to hang on to the back of his seat – nothing about 'fasten seat belts, fold up tables, seats in an upright position.' He then made what seemed a vertical dive to avoid any Bosnian Serb missiles. As I looked over his shoulder at the rapidly approaching ground, I reflected that if he did not pull out, at least the end would be quick. Fortunately, he did pull out, and I was allowed out of the aircraft at Sarajevo, with appropriate protective gear since the Airport was still under fire.

I also visited Skopje – where the Macedonian Foreign Minister joked that he could not understand why a British Minister (David Mellor) had resigned over an affair with an actress since 'that's what ministers and actresses do!' In Tirana I was invited by the Albanian President Berisha, a cardiologist, for a civilised meeting, and was taken on a private visit to the World Heritage site at Berat. I also revisited our old Geneva UN haunts for discussions with the Cyrus Vance / David Owen mediation process, with David Owen seemingly more relaxed and cordial than he had been as Foreign Secretary. At the end of this Balkan assignment I advised that the conflict was likely to escalate, including further South, and that the UK and allies would in the end have to intervene – in this case we might as well intervene sooner rather than later, but governments take their time...

I than had a couple of external career secondments, with the Sundridge Park 'Senior Executive Programme' and with the Board of P & O European Ferries (which I shall describe later), and I participated as an 'expert witness' in the Cabinet Office Top Management Programme. These were interesting and satisfying secondments, in that they gave me both an outside perspective and insights into then-current modern management ideas. However, some of these ideas were already challenged by P & O, who had experimented with them and then moved back to more 'tried and tested' practices. Similarly, when I had an interview with Arnold Weinstock, Managing Director of GEC, when later looking for post-FCO positions, he was even more vociferous in explaining how he preferred industry-proven rather than 'academic' theories.

I was then promoted to Under-Secretary level and given what turned out to be my final posting, responsible for the Americas. This obviously involved encouraging our links with the USA. There were regular visits to Washington DC for discussions with the various government departments, as well as to New York and the UN, also to Canada – Ottawa for official meetings, with excursions to Montreal and Halifax, and inevitably Miami Airport as a gateway to Central America.

This experience confirmed my conviction of the vital importance of the UK/US relationship – for both partners. If the Americans could at times be over-bearing, one could talk very frankly with them – no 'continental' niceties – and they would respond with equal frankness, no offence taken either way, to achieve a mutually productive way forward, from which we all benefitted. At a higher political level there could be frustrations for us officials, if only because most ministers had their own direct links with their opposite numbers and did not always brief their officials until afterwards. I recall that during the first Gulf War, we had regular pre-dawn Whitehall inter-departmental meetings in the FCO to coordinate the UK messages to the US – only to discover afterwards that No.10 had already been in contact with the White House the night before – but had omitted to inform the rest of us in Whitehall!

My 'domain' included the Caribbean, when – surprise, surprise – regional official gatherings were arranged to coincide with Test Matches. On one occasion I reluctantly had to leave the Test Match at the Kensington Oval for a lunch with a senior Barbadian official at a smart restaurant outside. He was particularly grumpy and complained that he had also left the Test Match – we quickly ended the lunch and rushed back together to the Oval. The work also included mutually beneficial work with the regional authorities – I can recall an illuminating dinner with the impressive and charming Dame Eugenia Charles, Prime Minister of Dominica, and officials at her flat in Roseau.

Other areas of responsibility included the whole of Latin America, Central and Southern. This was fascinating, both because of the vastness and variety of the area, and also because UK ministers visited rarely, thereby leaving the officials to do much of the work.

As I had no Spanish, I was sent on a three-week residential course at the Centro Andino de Estudios Latinoamericanos in Quito, Ecuador, i.e. to learn the rather purer *Latino* rather than the European Spanish version. I had fluent Italian, which was an advantage at first but not for long – when I got stuck, I tried to convert my Italian to Spanish, to the great amusement of the teachers. Once one got used to the altitude of 2,850m, with the active volcano Pichincha towering above at 4,794m, Quito was beautiful with its dozens of historic churches. The family with whom I lived was very hospitable, the father, a retired colonel, driving me around to see the sites, including the Equator ('Mitad del Mundo' standing with a foot in each hemisphere), and the children grilling me (with only limited success) on the detailed progress of the English football clubs. I was also introduced to the family friends, and since I had brought my violin with me, was invited to play in a *Latino* music jam-session with all the local musicians. The Spanish course was hard work, with additional homework to pass the FCO Higher Level Language Examination, but paid off in enabling serious discussions with the local officials and politicians without resorting to interpreters.

The obvious areas of UK Government interest included Argentina and Chile (Falklands and commerce), Brazil (commerce) and Columbia (oil and terrorism), as well as the varied British interests in the other countries, such as Venezuela, Mexico and Belize with their magnificent Maya ruins. In Belize I was taken over the dense jungles in an RAF helicopter for a unique 'vertical' view of the Caracol pyramid.

As part of my official 'Americas' preparation I had visited the Falklands by RAF TriStar, refuelling at Recife in Brazil rather than St Helena – with memories of Napoleon – because the runway there was being repaired. The other TriStar passengers were mainly Army/RAF and their families – I as a 'senior official' was privileged to be allotted three canvas seats, so that I could sleep horizontally. In the Falklands I had formal meetings with the Commanding Officer and with the Governor, David Tatham, a colleague with whom I had stayed when I visited Beirut earlier. As there were a couple of days before the return flight, the Army kindly showed me round the local sights and I had the privilege of seeing the beautiful, if cold and windy, scenery, Goose Green, and of course the penguins. Port Stanley reminded me of a small Scottish town of say fifty years previously. In the officers' mess, if they wanted a fresh seafood meal, they had to catch it themselves, as the Port Stanley shops only sold tinned versions – despite being surrounded by some of the most fertile fishing waters in the world.

In Buenos Aires, the local officials made a point of sticking a map of the Malvinas on their office walls before my visits, but personally they were always perfectly friendly. There were, of course, despite the Falklands, long-standing links with the UK – Harrods, Hurlingham Club, cricket, rugby, etc. There was a local joke that the citizens of Buenos Aires were Italians who spoke Spanish, thought that they lived in Paris, but wanted to be British. Likewise, the Chileans could not have been more hospitable, flying us down to the wonderfully impressive Torres del Paine National Park and then to dramatic Punta Arenas, close to the southern border with Argentina.

I also visited Cuba for political discussions. For the only time in my life I was physically mugged, by three men, when walking through the historic Old Town with a British Embassy colleague as guide and escort. We chased the muggers, who had grabbed my briefcase and who then escaped in a car. We reported the theft to the local police, and apparently the incident went high up the Cuban administration, reportedly even to Castro. Fortunately, I had left my passport and travel documents in the hotel safe, so the muggers only got away with credit cards (which were easily cancelled) and some dollars. The police presented three terrified-looking 'suspects' to us in the hope of closing off the incident and were clearly disappointed when we could not confirm the identification. I suspect that the incident was inspired by private rather than official motives but shall never know – fortunately there was no harm done.

On my final visit to the sub-continent I took Ruth (at my own expense). After official talks in Lima, we went privately to Cuzco and the astounding Incan Machu Picchu, before going 'off the air' (no mobile phones) to Lake Titicaca and across the Andes by coaches with the backpackers and the locals with their farm produce. We had a wonderful trip. We then turned up in Bolivia a week later, when I once again had to put on a suit and tie for an official dinner with the British Ambassador and his US colleague in La Paz – at 3,640m the highest capital in the world.

Because the UK had relatively few representatives strung out across this vast sub-continent, we regularly consulted other departments about how we might best coordinate our limited resources – we were all working to common objectives and paid by the same taxpayer.

At a time when the FCO was importing 'modern management' theories (while industry, after practical experience, was moving onwards from them – see the Weinstock reference above), I was criticised – ironically by one of those later singled out by the 'dodgy dossier' Chilcot Report – for being an 'old-fashioned' senior official. If 'old-fashioned' means respecting old-fashioned professional values of accuracy, discretion, teamwork and loyalty, I plead guilty.

In 1995, given internal FCO and wider Whitehall reorganisations, our UK family situation, and the thought that I was more likely to find an outside career in my early fifties rather than later, I decided that the time had come to move on.

I was grateful to be given goodbye parties by several Government departments – apparently this does not happen every day – perhaps reflecting my belief in teamwork rather than inter-departmental rivalries. When I called the switchboard to say that I was moving on and to give them my home number, I was touched by their response – I was 'one of the ones who was always polite and thanked them every time'. A little tear welled up.

However, after twenty-five very satisfying years and many friendships which I had greatly appreciated, the future beckoned. A few months after leaving the FCO I received a 'Strictly Personal' letter saying that 'the Secretary of State for Foreign and Commonwealth Affairs proposes to submit your name to The Queen for appointment as a Companion of the Most Distinguished Order of St Michael and St George (CMG)' – known

2. Father, Rupert, sketched by
an RAF colleague, 1942

1. With Mother, Rosemary, 1941

3. With grandparents, Victor (Popski) and Stella (Mimski), at their Essex home,
Downham. Left to Right: DC, Stella, brother Tim, father Rupert, cousin
Michael, aunt Mary, mother Rosemary, sister June, uncle Anthony, Victor. 1946

4. With brother Tim and sister June on Fox Hill, Oxford, *c.*1947

5. Young DC, March 1947

6. On board *Wychwood*. L to R: Tim, June, DC, with Rupert inside. *c.*1953

7. 'Gypsy Desmondo', whiskered, playing Kreisler's *Liebesfreud* with Roger Golder, Magdalen College School, 1960

8. Our old Ford van 'Schroink' broken down on the Gotthard Pass, Switzerland. Awaiting assistance – with Roland Needham and Tony Brewer listening to DC's violin. 1961

9. Wedding Reception, Oxford, 20 June 1964

10. Max Rostal, Berne, 1969

11. Youthful DC with Yehudi
Menuhin and David Morris, with
Ruth peeping in, Berne, 1966

12. With Jeremy Thorpe ('Happy couple
eloping' – the press cut Mrs Marion Thorpe
from the photo as a 'joke'), Geneva, 1978

13. With Chairman Ivor Richard, Geneva Rhodesia Conference, 1976

14. With Opposition leaders Joshua Nkomo and Robert Mugabe, Geneva Rhodesia Conference, 1976

15. With Rhodesia Prime Minister Ian Smith, Geneva Rhodesia Conference, 1976

16. With Thomas, Berne, 1968

17. Andrew and Sarah, Auvergne, 1978

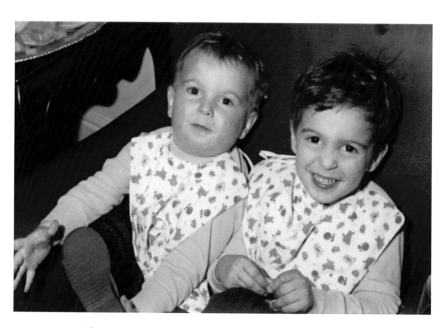

18. Thomas (R) and Nicholas (L) – 'Tom-n-Lee'. Berne, 1970

19. Opening the batting
with David Barmes for
Geneva Cricket Club, 1978

20. Royal visit by HM Queen Elizabeth
and HRH Prince Philip to International
Committee of the Red Cross, Geneva.
L to R: HRH, ICRC Delegate-General
Melchior Borsinger, DC keeping a
wary eye on the journalists. 1980

21. Signing World Intellectual Property Organisation (WIPO)
Agreement for the UK. WIPO Director-General Arpad Bogsch
(L), WIPO Director (also 'cellist) Ludwig Baeumer (R)

22. Greeted by Austrian
President Kurt Waldheim – with
Ambassador Robin O'Neill (L) and
Counsellor Tony Morgan (R)

23. First-day cut of Iron
Curtain barbed wire,
'Hegyeshalom May 1989'

24. Family music. L to R: Andrew, Sarah, Rozzie Barda,
Ruth, DC. Vienna, 1987. Photo by Clive Barda

in-house as 'Call Me God' – and early in the New Year, 1996, HM did the rest at Buckingham Palace. Naturally I felt proud to receive the award, but also fortunate – many of my colleagues delivered outstanding service over the years but received no public recognition.

*

More recently, in the light of the arguments over 'ethical' foreign policy and Iraq Two – which came after my time – I have been asked about moral issues in the public domain. One hears about officials put under pressure to implement decisions which they consider to be morally wrong and resigning, as for example some did over Iraq Two. All I can say is that, in all my years in the FCO, I was only once asked to do something that I considered morally questionable. I stated my belief clearly to my superiors, and said formally that if they persisted, I should have to resign from the FCO. In the event, I did not have to…

*

Another tribute, although oblique, to the UK FCO, was in the *Rheinischer Merkur* newspaper of 21 July 1987, which I unearthed recently. The Culture Editor, Wolf Schön, described a trip down the Rhine which he had made with some German friends, discovering among them a British diplomat from Vienna (yours truly). He went on to say that, when the tricky East-West disarmament negotiations broke down, 'Mister Cecil could add musical inspiration with his wonderfully singing Guarneri' (in fact Guadagnini). He added that, while a professional violinist could become a British diplomat, Foreign Minister Hans-Dietrich Genscher's Auswärtiges Amt, while representing the land of poets, thinkers and musicians, was so inflexible as only to allow lawyers to qualify for it. The Culture Editor praised 'English understatement', and by implication the flexibility and tolerance of the UK Foreign & Commonwealth Office.

*

…And of course my violin was a source of immense personal satisfaction and joy throughout my diplomatic career, to counter the inevitable day-to-day frustrations.

A few months after I had retired in 1995, I was invited with 'cellist Humphrey Maud (Ambassador in Buenos Aires) and pianist John Macgregor (Ambassador in Vienna) – both excellent musicians with whom I had played chamber music – to perform in an international charity concert in the historic FCO Locarno Suite. We played Haydn and Beethoven trios to a VIP diplomatic audience, who donated generous funds for various international charities – a happy final combination of diplomacy and music.

7

GERMANY

Variation: Bonn

M Y FIRST SIGNIFICANT ENCOUNTER WITH GERMANY, ALTHOUGH the country from which Ruth's German-Jewish refugee parents came in 1938, was in the 1960s when I was studying the violin with Professor Max Rostal in Berne. He was also Professor at the Hochschule in Cologne, and once a year his Swiss pupils followed him northwards for a master class in nearby Bonn University. We were housed in a university student hostel on the outskirts of the city, and when not busy with our violins could visit the majesty of Cologne's High Gothic cathedral towering over the Rhine or explore the intimacy of Beethoven's Bonn birthplace.

Bonn on the Rhine was and still is a university town, now twinned with Oxford since 1947. After the Second World War Chancellor Konrad Adenauer had somewhat controversially chosen Bonn as the new 'provisional capital' of post-War Germany, both because he himself came from the Rhineland (born in Cologne, where he had been Mayor from 1917 to 1933), and because he thought that a 'modest' university town would avoid the history of Prussianism (and by implication Berlin), which he blamed for the Nazi period, and potential rivalry with big cities like Frankfurt, Munich or Hamburg.

Both as an embryo violinist and later as a diplomat, I was bowled over by the grandeur of the Rhine. In our diplomatic days Ruth and I would stroll along its banks and note that the Germans on their Sunday walks would always be smartly dressed – often with suits. We would take the ferry over to Königswinter and enjoy a glass of elegant Rhine wine – and later a glass of the even more sensuous Moselle wine.

The parents of an Oxford 'cellist friend, Dietrich Bethge, also lived in the Westerwald south of Bonn. Dietrich's pastor father, Eberhard Bethge, had been a friend and colleague of the theologian Dietrich Bonhoeffer, who had been involved in the 1944 Stauffenberg plot to assassinate Hitler and was subsequently hanged by the Nazis. Dietrich's mother was Bonhoeffer's niece, Renate Schleicher, and also related to the von Dohnányi family. Eberhard was himself arrested by the Nazis, suspected of involvement in the plot and awaiting trial, before being released by the advancing Soviet army. Immediately after the war they moved to London, where he became Pastor at Bonhoeffer's former Lutheran church in Sydenham.

They were lovely people, with whom we often stayed while travelling across Europe, and from them we heard fascinating accounts of life under the Nazis, and afterwards. I still remember a comment by him about his neighbours in the Westerwald, who, although good citizens, looked back with nostalgia on the days of Hitler, who had improved the economy, brought the motorways and reformed the hunting laws...

Little did I realise then that a very few years later in 1973 we should be back in Bonn in a totally different diplomatic capacity for the Foreign & Commonwealth Office. The posting started badly when our Ford family car, a so-called 'Monday' car when everything seemed to go wrong, broke down late at night in Flemish-speaking Belgium. We were initially unable to communicate with the locals, who refused to speak French. However, we managed a working dialogue through Swiss-German and Flemish, both of Alemannic origin, and the locals kindly found a hotel for us and a garage to repair the car the next day.

When we eventually arrived in Bonn, as no suitable house was immediately available, we with our four young children were first housed in a 'junior' non-diplomatic flat in the suburb of Friesdorf. This was fine, but Embassy protocol, which allocated accommodation according to rank, insisted that we were required to move to 'senior' diplomatic premises, suitable for a junior First Secretary, when something became available. This happened when the Embassy found a house in the diplomatic suburb of Bad Godesberg – in fact, it was the former Guatemalan Embassy, although quite modest in size. Diplomatic Bad Godesberg was a far cry from the informality of music at Bonn University. Indeed, the formality of this particularly autocratic and notoriously top-heavy British Embassy required some acclimatisation after a life in the world of music.

In contrast with the stultifying bureaucracy of the British Embassy, the German political side of the work was deeply satisfying. The German Foreign Office / Auswärtiges Amt was, and perhaps still is, full of ex-lawyers; when they asked me what I had studied, I replied cheekily violin, not mentioning Oxford and PPE – but once they had got over the 'shock' they were very welcoming. West Germany was at that time a most open political society, and personal access to German politicians was relatively straight-forward for German speakers. The British, given the continuing presence of the Rhine Army and RAF bases, were still a significant local factor.

We were helped in that the CDU Headquarters (Konrad-Adenauer-Haus) was the Embassy's immediate neighbour, and at that time even shared our canteen when theirs was being re-furbished. I was able to develop close personal links with many senior CDU officials and politicians, especially with Wolfgang Bergsdorf, Helmut Kohl's *Chef de Cabinet*. When we were posted away from Bonn, he kindly hosted a formal goodbye party to which he invited a cross-party group of the politicians, press and officials with whom I had worked diplomatically. He and I became close family friends, and I regularly stayed at his Bad Godesberg home when I visited Bonn on FCO business after my Embassy posting, and later on cultural matters, when he became Head of the Culture / Media Department in the Interior Ministry and then President of Erfurt University.

Personal contacts in the CDU included many of the senior politicians, and from time to time even Helmut Kohl himself. Kohl, particularly late in the evening at a CDU party political event in a relaxed beer establishment, could be very approachable, informal and easy to talk with. Born in Ludwigshafen in the Rhineland-Palatinate, of which he later became Minister–President, bordering France, one of his lifelong political ambitions was Franco-German rapprochement. His CDU General Secretary Kurt Biedenkopf was somewhat more formal, probably given his role of coordinating the internal developments within the party. He did not get on particularly well with Kohl, and later their disagreements became public. In 1990 after reunification he became the first Minister–President of the new Free State of Saxony, based in Dresden. Then I got to know him a little better, through my own work with the Mendelssohn-Haus in nearby Leipzig, when he was a useful supporter of the cultural links. Another good friend in the CDU at the time was Peter Radunski, who later became a Senator in Berlin, when he and his wife Doris were very helpful with a 'Germany Panel 2000 Project' concert in Berlin for young British musicians which I organised (see below).

Likewise we had good contacts in: the SPD at their nearby Baracke Headquarters, including occasionally Brandt himself – again when more relaxed out of the office in some hostelry with his SPD party political rather than government colleagues (as mentioned earlier), although with the inevitable Chancellor constraints; the CSU, including Franz-Josef Strauss who was always easy to talk with; and the FDP, such as Werner Maihofer, Minister without Portfolio, an approachable liberal intellectual with whom, as well as politics, I would also discuss music and violins – he was a viola player, with whom I once played chamber music.

Regular participation in national and Länder party political conferences helped, allowing direct personal discussions late into the night – usually over 'social' drinking with corresponding damage to our youthful livers. I can recall a CSU conference in Munich where, with my Swiss-accented German I was almost welcomed as a non-Prussian – CDU/CSU Parliamentary Chairman Karl Carsten's pure North German accent grated somewhat on the Bavarians.

I can also recall, during a CDU conference in Hamburg, a group of young Western diplomats and journalists (no names, but some have since risen to distinguished positions) followed the advice of our German political hosts to check out the local 'culture' and visit an establishment in the notorious Reeperbahn. Needless to add this was very German, with local police visible along the street to ensure '*Ordnung*'. Naturally we did nothing to besmirch the professional reputations of the countries and newspapers which we represented, and limited our participation to socio-economic conversations with some of the performers when they were unwinding at the bar after their acts – one of which highlighted Black & Decker 'technology'. We were amused to notice that suddenly a spotlight descended on a table at the front of the establishment. The person, who was thus exposed and who looked to us just like a famous Bavarian politician, immediately tried to hide his face. But, if indeed he was who we thought he was, we doubted whether his subsequent political reputation would have suffered unduly.

We visited West Berlin for political discussions. At the time we were not permitted to visit East Berlin without a British military escort. However, we viewed the Berlin Wall, Checkpoint Charlie, and took the U-Bahn on an 'obligatory' journey without stopping through the heavily guarded Friedrichstrasse station in East Berlin. Even today when we travel on the U-Bahn through the now bustling Friedrichstrasse station, it brings back painful memories.

My professional contacts with the UK and Western press corps, especially with *The Times* Bonn Correspondent Dan van der Vat, helped with my understanding of Germany. Dan and his wife Chris, a teacher who was studying German, formed a close and long-standing family friendship with Ruth and me. We met regularly to compare German political notes, and both being professionals never enquired about the other's sources – although we both knew that they would be pretty similar. The main difference in our work was that Dan's copy usually appeared in *The Times* the next day, while my no-doubt similar copy reached the FCO about a week later, after being 'redrafted' by my seniors, such as Deputy Ambassador Reg Hibbert or even the Ambassador, and stamped 'Confidential'.

After Bonn, we continued to meet Dan and Chris (sadly, she died of cancer in 2013) on a very regular basis, including holidays together in Liverpool (where her father had been Anglican Dean of the Cathedral), France, Italy, Switzerland and Poland. Occasionally politics intervened, for example when Argentina invaded the Falklands on 2 April 1982. Dan and Chris, no fans of Tory Mrs Thatcher, saw this as her come-uppance. Without any inside information at all, I bet £10 that the Union Jack would be flying over Port Stanley again within three months – as indeed it was. Dan, always an honourable man, insisted on paying his debt with a signed copy of his latest book, *The Ship that Changed the World: The Escape of the 'Goeben' to the Dardanelles in 1914*. After *The Times* and a falling-out with Murdoch the newspaper's new owner, Dan moved to the *Guardian* where he became Chief Foreign Leader Writer and also responsible for foreign obituaries, before leaving journalism and becoming a successful naval history author. They became near neighbours in the UK, living on Eel Pie Island in Twickenham.

After the death of Chris, we continued to meet every few weeks, and Dan organised an annual music-loving group visit to the Proms. It was only two days after one of our Prom-planning meetings in a convivial Twickenham Italian restaurant that he suddenly died in May 2019. I had the sad duty of writing his obituary for the *Guardian*. To my surprise the *Guardian* later paid me the unrequested sum of £248.54. In consultation with his two daughters, Karen and Sara, we gave this to Diabetes UK as a donation in Dan's name.

Privately and musically we travelled all over Germany, from Bavaria to the Baltic, from the Rhineland-Palatinate to Saxony, greatly appreciating the varied landscapes and culture – as I relate later.

In 2019 we were invited to join a group of Ruth's (distant) family for the opening of the new James-Simon-Galerie on the Berlin Museumsinsel. James Simon (1851–1932), the son of Ruth's great-great-grandfather on her paternal grandmother's side, was a German-Jewish art collector and philanthropist, whose wealth came from the family cotton business. Over the years he collected a great many works of art from around the world, including the famous and controversial (Egypt has demanded its repatriation) 'Nefertiti' bust. He contributed greatly to Berlin's museum collections, and after the inevitable obscurity during the Nazi years, the city of Berlin and Prussian Cultural Foundations commissioned the British architect David Chipperfield to construct a splendid new Gallery on the Museumsinsel to honour the legacy of James Simon. This was formally opened by Chancellor Angela Merkel in July 2019 – she was reputed to be in questionable health at the time but was in fact very lively and talked to many people. Ruth and I, as invited family guests, got to know some of Ruth's more distant relatives, American, British and German – and of course some of the family intricacies.

With a wife of German-Jewish parentage I was naturally sensitive to anti-Semitism, but personally noticed hardly any, at least overtly, in Germany at the time. One evening, in fact 20 April 1974, at a Weinhaus with some young CDU politicians, a well-oiled man at a nearby table proposed a toast to what would have been the Führer's eighty-fifth birthday. Our hosts appeared genuinely shocked and apologised profusely to us for this reference to 'that criminal'. The comments which we overheard at Viennese dinner tables some fifteen years later were rather more worrying and will be described later.

Theme: Music

While in Bonn, I had played chamber music regularly with an enthusiastic string quartet from the Auswärtiges Amt with Manfred Osten, diplomat, Goethe authority and musician. Although German diplomats were very often lawyers by education, they had some good musicians. My old teacher Max Rostal, when he often visited Cologne, invited me to join his string quartet – naturally he insisted on playing first violin. Together with the British Council representative Raymond Adlam, a sensitive pianist and subsequently a colleague in Vienna, we organised regular Hauskonzerte with music and poetry, in which our Embassy colleagues and German friends enthusiastically participated.

After the Berlin Wall came down in 1989, I can recall the extraordinary experience for a 'Cold War' diplomat to be able to walk freely through Checkpoint Charlie for the first time. I still treasure my early 'hand-picked' sample of the Wall (as well as a 'first-day cut' of Austro-Hungarian Iron Curtain barbed wire – described later). When we first met our Leipzig Mendelssohn-Haus friends in 1997, the fall of the Berlin Wall was only eight years before and the East-West divergences and the socio-economic impact of the DDR were still very apparent. Some of our friends were nostalgic about the past when 'everything worked', at least for them, and they as '*Ossis*' (former East Germans) resented the '*Wessis*' (former West Germans) moving in and taking their 'jobs, apartments and girlfriends'. Others were delighted by the new-found freedom to talk, to travel, and, as they explained, to sit in a restaurant with us without worrying who was listening at the next table.

We were also able (with the help of Ruth's cousin John Cooke and one of my Baedeker guides, '*Berlin, 20 Auflage, 1927*' – see later) to track down some of my wife's family's former homes, both in West Berlin's Dahlem-Grunewald and in East Berlin's Jägerstrasse, where by coincidence Felix Mendelssohn's banker father Abraham had also lived.

In 1997 I was a member of a Royal Philharmonic Society (RPS) delegation visiting the music city of Leipzig to celebrate the inauguration of a statue in front of the Gewandhaus concert hall to commemorate Mendelssohn – some of his compositions had been commissioned by the RPS, which also supported the restoration of Mendelssohn's house. This was part of the Leipzig movement, to a large extent led by Maestro Kurt Masur, for many years the Leipzig Gewandhaus Orchestra Chief Conductor (*Kapellmeister*), to restore the musical reputation of Mendelssohn after it had been obliterated by the Nazis.

In our RPS group was John Denison, who had been a key UK arts administrator, running the British Council, Arts Council and South Bank music for many years. Before the War he had been a horn-player, including under Beecham with the LPO. He re-told how he had visited Germany then and indeed had met Winifred Wagner in Bayreuth. At a team dinner in the historic Auerbachs Keller, of Dr Faustus fame, we chatted and clicked immediately. After Leipzig we met regularly to discuss music matters over lunch at the Athenæum or his Garrick Club, until he died in 2006 at the venerable age of ninety-five.

As the only German-speaker in the RPS delegation, I made the official speech on behalf of the British link, together with that of Masur, who afterwards became a much-valued friend. Our Leipzig friends commented cynically that London had sent a delegation, but Berlin had not. Beneath his austere Maestro impression on the concert platform, Masur was privately a sensitive '*Mitteldeutscher Kapellmeister*', as he described himself. Ruth and I would sit round his kitchen table in the Leipzig suburb of Leutzsch, together with his wife Tomoko, singer and viola player, where he was an easy and at times humble conversationalist – slipping into using first names and '*Du*'.

Masur played a key role in the peaceful collapse of Communism in East Germany on 9 October 1989. When the huge crowds were gathered in front of the Gewandhaus in Leipzig's Karl-Marx-Platz (now Augustusplatz), menaced by the armed police, Masur told the police that there was now no going back, and that they should go home peacefully – which they did, and there was no bloodshed. Masur was one of the few universally respected East Germans who had the stature to say this. Nine days later Honecker resigned. Masur was later invited to become the first President of a non-Communist East Gemany, which he declined, reputedly saying, 'Am I so bad a conductor that I have to become a politician?'

In later life Masur may have acquired a reputation for focusing on the nineteenth-century classics. However, when he was a young conductor at the Komische Oper in Berlin in the 1960s, he promoted works by controversial young composers, which did not always please the strict cultural concepts of the East German Communist SED party (Socialist Unity

Party) – which Masur never joined. When he became Music Director of the New York Philharmonic in 1991, he regularly commissioned new works for the orchestra to perform. He was a master of the twentieth- as well as nineteenth-century masterpieces, from Stravinsky to Shostakovich, which he continued when he moved to become Principal Conductor of the London Philharmonic Orchestra in 2000. I recall a most moving performance of Britten's *War Requiem* in the Royal Festival Hall in 2005, subsequently recorded.

This was even more moving, being conducted by a German, who had been conscripted into the German paratroopers as a teenager late in 1944, before being captured by the American and British forces in May 1945. He was no Nazi, as demonstrated by his work to restore the music of Mendelssohn and his lifetime title as 'Honorary Conductor' of the Israel Philharmonic Orchestra. In 2012 he was awarded the 'Leo Baeck Award' for his humanitarian work in promoting tolerance and social justice.

In 2009 the then-German Ambassador in London, Georg Boomgaarden, asked me to arrange a London Philharmonic Orchestra (of which I was a Trustee) concert in the Royal Festival Hall with Kurt Masur (just retired as LPO Chief Conductor) to celebrate the twentieth anniversary of the fall of the Berlin Wall ('*Mauerfall*'). Masur was happy to do this, and very fittingly conducted a splendid performance of Mendelssohn's '*Elijah*'. At the reception afterwards I was asked to introduce Masur to the assembled German and UK political and cultural 'great and good' VIPs, and he spoke very movingly about Mendelssohn and '*Mauerfall*'.

In 2015 the new German Ambassador, Peter Ammon, asked if I could arrange something similar in September of that year to celebrate twenty-five years since German reunification. This time the LPO was in the middle of a Russian series and had no suitable German music planned. However, I was able to agree with the Managing Director of the Philharmonia Orchestra, David Whelton (with whom I regularly play violin and piano sonatas), to dedicate a Philharmonia Royal Festival Hall concert to this event. The concert was conducted by the distinguished

German Christoph von Dohnányi (who had anti-Nazi family links with my 'cellist friend Dietrich Bethge's mother – see above). Beethoven's Ninth Symphony was followed by the young German pianist Martin Helmchen playing the Schumann Piano Concerto – so it could not have been more German and appropriate for the event, and once again the VIP guests were more than satisfied.

In 1996 Masur moved from Leipzig to the New York Philharmonic, and was replaced as Gewandhaus Orchestra Chief Conductor by Herbert Blomstedt, with whom Masur was on bad terms – apparently Masur had taken serious offence over what he thought was a critical comment about his conducting by Blomstedt. Musical Leipzig was divided by this personality clash. One was either in the Masur or the Blomstedt camp. Musical Leipzig was eventually calmed after the 2005 appointment to the Gewandhaus Orchestra of Riccardo Chailly, with whom Masur got on well. Musical Leipzig could come together again.

After we had met at the Mendelssohn statue inauguration in 1997, Masur invited me to join his efforts to restore Mendelssohn's original house in the Goldschmidtgasse near the Gewandhaus. For some years Masur and colleagues had been working on a project to raise funds for this. I was seconded on to the Board, which Masur then led, of the Leipzig Felix-Mendelssohn-Bartholdy-Stiftung. The project eventually began to receive official financial support from the City of Leipzig for the restoration of the house, and for the subsequent establishment of a museum. The Mendelssohn-Haus Director, Jürgen Ernst, and his assistant, Christiane Schmidt, became close personal friends of Ruth and me – both when we visited Leipzig and staying with us when they visited London. They were especially supported by the approachable SPD Oberbürgermeister (Lord Mayor) Burkhard Jung, who was a music lover with an outgoing personality – and no doubt saw the political advantages of musical intervention in the 'Musikstadt' Leipzig, the home of Bach, Schumann and Mendelssohn.

The Gewandhaus Orchestra was founded in 1743 when it first performed in private homes before moving to the *Gasthaus* 'Zu den drei

Schwanen' (Three Swans Tavern), and in 1781 moved to its first concert hall – named Gewandhaus, because it was the building of the textile merchants. It has been for many years one of the world's great orchestras, and among its numerous distinguished Chief Conductors (*Kapellmeister*) was Felix Mendelssohn from 1835–1847. The second building, designed by Martin Gropius, opened in 1884 and was destroyed by bombing in 1944 during WWII. Masur led the project to have it rebuilt in its present location in 1981. The orchestra is both musically great and musically serious, as befits a top German orchestra, and its motto proudly displayed on the wall behind the podium is '*Res severa verum gaudium*' ('A true pleasure is a serious matter'), or more cheekily, 'You're not here to have fun'.

The Gewandhaus-Direktor (CEO), Professor Andreas Schulz, was perhaps initially somewhat cool to me because of the Blomstedt/Masur clash, where he naturally had to be in the Blomstedt camp. However, he subsequently became an excellent colleague, whom I see regularly in Leipzig and London – and I am privileged to receive a personal invitation each autumn to the opening concert of the Gewandhaus-Orchester season. The Prime Minister of the Free State of Saxony, Kurt Biedenkopf, whom I had first got to know in Bonn when he was CDU General-Secretary, was similarly a supporter of musical Leipzig initiatives, given the close links between Leipzig and nearby Dresden, the capital of Saxony.

Over the years the restored Mendelssohn-Haus with its Museum has become a wonderful addition to Leipzig culture, with chamber concerts every Sunday morning in Mendelssohn's own music room, and with many original artefacts, scores and documents. More recently it has developed an electronic conducting room (for aspiring conductors to try out), a Fanny Mendelssohn (talented sister of Felix) room and the International Kurt Masur Institute, as well as expanding the very user-friendly Annex in the garden, with many educational opportunities for young and old.

After Masur's death in December 2015, Ruth and I were invited to join family and friends at his moving funeral in Leipzig, with musical tributes by Leipzig's own Bach and Mendelssohn, and the subsequent dedication of a 'Kurt-Masur-Platz' and planting of a *Lindenbaum* in the park just behind the Gewandhaus.

In 2013 the UK Blue Plaques Panel decided to unveil a Blue Plaque to honour Mendelssohn's frequent visits to London. He stayed at the home of his friend Karl Klingemann, then Secretary of the Hanoverian Embassy, at 4 Hobart Place in Belgravia – within sight of Buckingham Palace, where he played music with Queen Victoria and Prince Albert; the house is now a private bank. Nicholas Kenyon, Director of the Barbican and member of the Blue Plaques Panel, the historian Howard Spencer and I were invited to speak to the assembled musical and political guests about Mendelssohn and his UK/German links. The violinist Dmitry Sitkovetsky played some solo Bach. And then in 2014 a group of music lovers from the Schleswig-Holstein Music Festival visited the UK 'in the footsteps of Mendelssohn in England and Scotland' and, in coordination with Leipzig, asked to see the Blue Plaque. I was able to arrange this for them and to say a few appropriate words to them in front of Mendelssohn's Plaque.

During the UK Government's 'Germany Panel 2000 Project' I persuaded the FCO to pay for some young chamber musicians (violin, viola, 'cello, double bass, piano) from the Royal College of Music (RCM), under Royal Philharmonic Society auspices, to give concerts in Berlin, Munich and EXPO 2000 Hannover – with an introductory concert in London kindly hosted by the German Ambassador Hans-Dietrich von Ploetz. The concerts included works by Bridge, Schubert, Shostakovich and a specially commissioned new work by Timothy Salter, who taught at the RCM. The three concerts were all successful and reasonably well attended, particularly in Munich and Hannover. In Berlin we were kindly supported by the British Ambassador Paul Lever (a fellow Queen's *alumnus*), my former CDU friend in Bonn, Berlin Senator Peter Radunski, and the Berlin Hochschule der Künste where the concert took place. However, although this initiative brought young musicians from the UK to Germany, I was disappointed that it was not supported by the local British Council Berlin representation, who commented that the concert was not sufficiently 'cutting edge'.

We also found UK funding in 2002 to send four young musicians from Leipzig to London to perform early authorised transcriptions for piano / two hands, violin and 'cello of Mendelssohn's 1st and 5th symphonies with the *Ruy Blas* and *Hebrides* Overtures. Again, Ambassador von Ploetz kindly hosted one of the concerts.

In 2005 the then-German Ambassador Thomas Matussek asked me to arrange a personal introduction for him to Kurt Masur, which I did over an intimate threesome lunch at the Athenæum. Matussek afterwards wrote to me:

> Dear Desmond, Thank you so much for the intimate lunch at the Athenæum. Maestro Masur was as impressive as ever ... let me say again how admirable I find your untiring efforts to promote classical German music in this country. After all, this music is not German, it belongs to all of us. Yours ever, Thomas.

Later that year Ambassador Matussek hosted a concert given by some of the young musicians whom we had earlier sent to Germany for the 'Germany Panel 2000 Project'. Kurt Masur and his wife Tomoko, as well as some key people from the UK and German arts and political worlds attended – thereby furthering the efforts to support music by young musicians in both countries.

In 2005 Ruth and I established the 'UK Friends of the Felix-Mendelssohn-Bartholdy-Foundation', a UK-registered charity of which Maestro Kurt Masur was President and HRH The Duke of Kent kindly agreed to become our Royal Patron. This Foundation organises fund-raising concerts 'to support the education of young musicians in the spirit of Mendelssohn'. I shall describe later how we work closely with our fellow Trustees and friends, Tom and Megan Tress, to support young musicians in the UK.

In the Germany context we were able to support the digitalisation of the Mendelssohn-Haus archive to enhance scholarship around the world and liaise between Leipzig and the Bodleian Library in Oxford on the exchange of Mendelssohn manuscripts. For the last seven years (at the time of writing) we have sponsored a young singer and pianist from the London Guildhall School for Music & Drama (GSMD) to participate in the annual International Mendelssohn Academy 'Meisterkurs' with the distinguished Kammersänger Peter Schreier in the 'Musikstadt' Leipzig. This has not only helped the young British musicians to understand German *Lieder* better from Schreier's scholarship, but to increase their knowledge of German culture, and for our German friends to see for themselves the benefits of such exchanges. We also sent one of our young GSMD pianists back to Leipzig to perform some of Mendelssohn's '*Songs without Words*', as once played by Mendelssohn's musical admirers Queen Victoria and Prince Albert – an appropriate British contribution to the 2019 Leipzig Bachfest.

In 2018 the recent German Ambassador, Peter Wittig, and I came up with the idea of combining the German Embassy's annual Christmas event with a concert given by four of our GSMD students who had visited Leipzig in the last couple of years. The students performed *Lieder* by Mendelssohn, Schubert, Schumann and Strauss, and fascinated the combined German/British audience with accounts of their seminal experiences with Maestro Schreier in Leipzig. The feedback from the audience was extremely positive – and the young musicians got paid (always important) by the Embassy, as well as having the chance to promote themselves to the assembled music lovers.

Before he finally returned to Berlin in April 2020 Peter Wittig wrote:

Lieber Desmond, It has been such a pleasure to get to know you and cooperate with you on some outstanding cultural events! Huberta [his wife] and I are truly grateful for your enthusiasm and commitment to our cultural bonds. I hope that our paths will cross again. Peter.

In 2018 we were able to co-organise a Leipzig visit by music-loving friends from the Athenæum Club, with personal invitations to the Mendelssohn, Bach and Schumann houses, as well as to the Gewandhaus – described later.

To conclude, we have found nothing but friendship, musical and personal, throughout our ventures into post-War Germany. The arts and especially music, as befits the country of so many great composers from Bach onwards, are especially respected and encouraged. Indeed, in the 'Musikstadt' Leipzig virtually every great composer who has lived there is honoured with a street name – which would not happen everywhere.

8

AUSTRIA

Variation: Vienna

IN 1985 THE TIME HAD COME FOR ANOTHER OVERSEAS DIPLOMATIC posting – in fact, it turned out to be our last. There was some talk of Rome, which would have appealed culturally, but the decision was taken to send me to the Embassy in Vienna where, by chance, the Ambassador Michael Alexander was a good personal friend from our time together in Geneva.

Having served at diplomatic postings in Bonn and then neutral/UN Geneva, we initially thought that German-speaking neutral/UN Vienna might be similar. A glance at a map showed Vienna lying to the East of (then) Communist Prague, at the far-eastern end of Austria, now separated from its former Austro-Hungarian Empire by the Iron Curtain. Vienna is divided into twenty-three Districts (Bezirk); Metternich is reputed to have said that the Balkans begin in the Rennweg (Third District) of Vienna.

On my first day in office I duly called on the relevant Permanent Secretary to pay my formal respects. I thought that I had said all the correct things in correct German, but somehow the *vibes* seemed wrong. When I got back to the Embassy the local staff apologised for not reminding me to take a bottle of the Embassy's finest duty-free cognac when paying my respects. I duly returned the next day with a fine bottle, which the Permanent Secretary, a perfectly honourable gentleman, took without a word and placed in his cupboard, which I saw was already well-stocked with similar bottles – almost unthinkable in most 'Western' European ministries, but quite acceptable in 'Balkan' Vienna. After that all was well. I began to understand how things worked and was warmly welcomed to Vienna.

While looking for a suitable family home, we stayed temporarily in various places until we found a spacious house in the hilly suburb of Ober Sankt Veit beyond Schönbrunn Palace in the west of Vienna. Above us was the Himmelhof with a small winter ski-lift. To the west of us was the Lainzer Tiergarten, formerly an imperial game-reserve, where we, like former Kaisers, loved to walk, and where there were still wild boar roaming – as there had been outside our house in Chavannes-des-Bois of happy memories, when I was posted to Geneva.

Our younger children: Andrew, fourteen, and Sarah, twelve, first attended a local Viennese school (Gymnasium) in the nearby Fichtnergasse for a year. However, there was a risk that they might have to repeat a year to catch up with the Austrian curriculum. So, we then moved them to the Vienna International School, rather than follow the usual diplomatic practice of sending them back home to an English boarding school. They made new and interesting friends, and developed into lively teenagers with many interests, especially sport, and passed their O-level exams. They added fluent German to their innate Vaudois village-school French. The elder children, Thomas and Nicholas, were by then studying in England, Thomas in his first year at Southampton University, and Nicholas in his final year at Tiffin Grammar School in Kingston, but both used their regular holiday visits to learn good German. They all skied with Viennese friends (see later), and Nicholas spent a university year teaching and being an ambulance man working in Innsbruck. He learnt that Tyrol, in the West of Austria, was culturally and linguistically very different from 'Balkan' Vienna.

As in Geneva, Ruth worked from the beginning of our posting, first as a nurse in the Neue Wiener Privatklinik in central Vienna and later in the International Atomic Energy Agency (IAEA) Medical Centre across the Danube. She also started working for *Caritas Socialis*, helping to set up the Austrian palliative care movement – not always easy in a largely

Catholic country. While listening to the radio at home she heard Dr Irma Schwarz, a psychotherapist, retelling her experiences of her visit to St Luke's Hospice in Sheffield. There was to be a meeting in a few days' time to explore the possibility of developing palliative care in Vienna. As a result of this meeting *Caritas Socialis* employed Ruth and Dr Schwarz to write the initial paper for the project. Today palliative care is well developed in Vienna – and Irma and Ruth remain very close friends.

Early on in Ober Sankt Veit we invited our Viennese neighbours round for a pre-Christmas drink. They expressed their delight at the neighbourly gesture, but somewhat to our surprise then asked us to introduce them to their other long-standing neighbours, whom they did not appear to know. Neighbourliness was apparently less prevalent in Vienna, in comparison with other places where we have lived. Our house was in a steep one-way street up on the Himmelhof Hill, which the children loved – although they hated the hundred-plus steps up from the local Ober Sankt Veit U-Bahn station.

In 1986, after the US bombing of Tripoli and subsequent threats to UK diplomats, for security reasons the Embassy senior staff relinquished their diplomatic car number plates. We were also given security guidance by the British Royal Military Police, who correctly advised us to 'vary our route from home'. When we explained that we lived in a narrow one-way street, so could not vary our route, they amplified their advice by saying that if we saw some suspicious people with guns at the exit to our street, we should 'put our foot down and drive like f*****g hell'. Fortunately, it never came to that. I was also instructed in 'defensive' driving techniques by the Royal Military Police. These included 'J-turns' and 'handbrake turns' (evasive manoeuvres, using sharp movements of the steering wheel/handbrake), which my children with delight ordered me to demonstrate in snowy open spaces.

Eventually, despite the charms of Ober Sankt Veit, the lengthy journey by car or U-Bahn to central Vienna became onerous for me and for Ruth's later medical job in the IAEA, and even more so for the children. So, after the usual searches, we found a magnificent renovated 'penthouse' apartment in the Bräunerstrasse just off the Graben, right in the very centre of Old Vienna with its wonderful historical buildings. Walking from our flat to almost anywhere was an architectural and historic experience: looking up at the dome of the Peterskirche, passing the Pestsäule (promised by Kaiser Leopold I as a mercy column for if the 1679 epidemic would end) or the Lipizzaner horse stables, and just down the street from the Josefsplatz where Harry Lime faked his 'death' in *The Third Man*. The flat had not only generous space for the family, but a splendid reception area which we used for Hauskonzerte, and stunning balcony views over the Stephansdom and the Hofburg. After our departure it was taken over by one of the UK disarmament ambassadors. However, given FCO economies and merging of roles, this did not last. When we visited Vienna in 2017, we found that our flat had become a luxury hairdressing and beauty salon – how the world moves on!

Vienna was and is an immensely charming and cultural city, but we had frequent reminders that its 'Balkan' legacy was never too far from the surface. As we searched for our various homes, we found that the Viennese property rental market could operate along flexible lines. The estate agent or owner might suggest an apparently modest price, with a strong hint that the deal could be facilitated by a separate cash payment. The locally employed Viennese lady at the Embassy, responsible for finding staff accommodation, was less than pleased when Ruth and I, as German speakers, took the initiative to look for properties ourselves, or even to help our colleagues. When I sold my car privately, I prepared for the purchaser a receipt stating the agreed price – he politely requested another receipt with the price left blank. When Ruth started working at the Neue Wiener Privatklinik, her nursing colleagues invited her to join their collection for an annual donation to the local Polizei Wache – and there were no parking fines if she parked her car in the street outside the hospital.

The nostalgia of the 'K und K – Kaiserliche und Königliche' Austro-Hungarian Empire was still very apparent in Vienna. Personal titles were usually upgraded by at least one rank in formal conversation. It was reputed that everything was for sale at the necessary price – certainly, tickets for sold-out opera/concert/theatre performances could usually be obtained through a discreet word with the Head Porter at the Bristol or Sacher Hotels.

The older monarchists would still refer to Otto von Hapsburg, a member of the European Parliament, as 'Majestät'. There was a well-circulated Austrian joke that, when he heard about a forthcoming 'Austria v Hungary' football match, he asked against whom 'we were playing'. When the ex-Empress Zita, the widow of ex-Kaiser Karl who had died in 1922, died in 1989 at the age of ninety-six, she was brought back from exile in Zizers in Switzerland to Vienna for burial in the imperial Kaisersgruft. The streets of Vienna were filled with parades of imperial uniforms from centuries gone by. Most of Europe's Royalty were present, apart from the British Windsors, who had historical Saxe-Coburg differences with the Hapsburgs, and declined to attend. We in the Embassy were asked to intervene with the FCO and Buckingham Palace, which we did but to no avail. After the Vienna funeral there was also a state memorial service in Budapest – ironically, despite the pre-war years of Admiral Horthy and the post-war Communism, Zita, although since 1918 no longer Empress of Austria, was still recognised as Queen of Hungary – long after the collapse of the Austro-Hungarian Dual Monarchy.

Shortly after we arrived Kurt Waldheim, with whom our paths had crossed at UN Geneva when he was Secretary-General, became Austrian President. There was international outcry about his alleged wartime collaboration with the Nazis and his alleged role in the deportations of Greek Jews – the US Ambassador Ronald Lauder (see below) did not attend his inauguration as President. SPÖ (Social Democratic Party) Chancellor Fred Sinowatz, no friend of Waldheim, resigned on Waldheim's appointment, with a coruscating reference to Waldheim's student membership of a Nazi cavalry corps, saying that perhaps 'only Waldheim's horse had been a

Nazi'. Waldheim's respected predecessor as Austrian President was Rudolf Kirchschläger, who, when a university student after the Anschluss in 1938 had refused to join the Nazi Party, and later was a judge and diplomat. When asked what he thought about the Waldheim issue, Kirchschläger avoided the question with '*Da bin ich überfragt*' – which can loosely be translated into the American, 'That's above my paygrade'.

However, there were also sinister voices in the other direction. ÖVP (the conservative Austrian People's Party to which Waldheim belonged) General Secretary Michael Graff had to resign after saying to a French magazine that it wasn't as if Waldheim had 'strangled six Jews with his own hands', which he later claimed had been misinterpreted.

Certainly, we found Austrian lingering anti-Semitism far more evident than in Germany. Perhaps, with a wife of German-Jewish refugee antecedents, I was unduly sensitive to Graff's and other clumsy remarks, an unfortunate Viennese slang word for 'ashtray', and dinner table anti-Semitic references in German, which perhaps a British diplomat at the far end of a table was not expected to understand – all quite disturbing, especially in the light of today's anti-Semitic and racial sensitivities. That said, I have found most of my Austrian friends and especially recent Austrian Ambassadors to London, absolutely and openly opposed to anti-Semitism and the terrible events of the Nazi years.

When Michael Alexander was replaced as Ambassador by Robin O'Neill, and we had to present his credentials to President Waldheim, I naturally had to shake Waldheim's hand. When I came home that evening, my children only half-jokingly told me to wash the hand that had shaken Waldheim's before they allowed me to touch theirs. Later, when Ruth and I attended a performance at the Vienna English Theatre, we were button-holed on arrival and asked if we minded having our seats changed. We had no objection and we found ourselves sitting next to Kurt Waldheim and his wife Elisabeth – presumably, the American Embassy had pulled out at the last minute. Needless to mention, the Waldheims were very congenial company for the evening.

Despite Metternich's 'Balkan' suspicions, the lingering anti-Semitism and Austrian neutrality under Socialist/Social Democratic Chancellors, the UK and the West benefitted from excellent cooperation from the relevant Austrian authorities – no doubt encouraged by Austrian aspirations to join the EEC. However, physical security for Western diplomats was always a concern, given the inevitable Middle Eastern presence in an open society. I recall a dinner which we gave at home for the US and British Ambassadors. The US Ambassador Ronald Lauder, son of Estée Lauder, was American, rich, Jewish and outspoken – a natural terrorist target – and before the dinner our house was surrounded with armed US security guards, with whom our children had great fun chatting and playing games.

While we were in Vienna in April 1986 the Chernobyl nuclear disaster occurred in the Ukraine. Since Chernobyl was not that far to the east of Vienna, the Austrian authorities took immediate action to advise against letting children play in sandpits and drinking unchecked milk. For the first few days after the accident the Soviet scientists at the International Atomic Energy Agency (IAEA) in Vienna continued to deny that anything serious had happened. It was only when the nuclear plume had gone far to the North over Scandinavia, and was even affecting Welsh sheep, that they were given authority to speak about it.

Then, once the Soviet embargo had been forcibly breached, the IAEA Soviet scientists became completely open overnight, and like good scientists everywhere were very keen to tackle the aftermath. Years later, when I was working on nuclear projects in Russia (see later), I was often reminded of these Viennese Chernobyl memories of nuclear pollution, initial Soviet denials, and subsequent positive cooperation with the relevant Russian experts.

Although we, as NATO diplomats, were not permitted to cross the Iron Curtain privately, in 1986 Ruth persuaded the FCO Security Department to allow a UK diplomatic wives' visit to Budapest. The first time our wives could not stay the night just in case they were seduced by Hungarian *cavaliers*. However, once they had returned, apparently unscathed and with their virtue intact, they were even allowed an overnight visit to 'hard-line' Prague. All went well and the wives had an enjoyable and interesting visit. Even so, a lunch invitation for the wives to meet Czech artists was 'cancelled' by the state authorities. Some months later a Dutch diplomat's wife knocked on our door in Vienna and delivered a package. It turned out to be a gift from the Czech artists of eight lovely musicians in Bohemian glass, which they had intended to give us at the lunch – and which grace our living room to this day.

In 1988 the Austrian Federal Chancellery announced a one-day visit to Hungary for Western diplomats and journalists, without any passports and visas being required. The Mayors of Haydn's Eisenstadt and Liszt's Sopron arranged for us to cross the Iron Curtain by coach, spend a pleasant day wandering around Sopron, and then return to Austria's beautiful wine-growing Burgenland by train, specially opening for us a railway border which had been closed for many years.

As the flow of refugees, especially from East Germany, through Czechoslovakia and Hungary to Austria became unstoppable, the Hungarian Foreign Minister Gyula Horn and the Austrian Foreign Minister Alois Mock agreed formally to cut the Iron Curtain at Hegyeshalom in May 1989. The Hungarian Deputy Ambassador, a friendly colleague, was present at the ceremony and kindly gave me a 'first-day' cut of the barbed wire (apparently of French manufacture). When we returned to England I went to the local sports shop and asked them to mount this piece of barbed wire on a sports shield with a brass plate saying 'Hegyeshalom, May 1989'. The sports-shop proprietor looked at me as if I were mad, but the shield remains a treasured memento of this transforming day in the development of a freer Europe. The recent Austrian Ambassador in London, Martin Eichtinger, had been Mock's Private Secretary in May 1989, and we shared our joint nostalgia of that historic day, comparing his photo of the event with my barbed-wire memento.

In early 1989 we so-called 'Soviet Bloc experts' predicted that Hungary might break away from Communism quickly, maybe followed by Poland, but that the other states, especially the GDR and Soviet Union might take a lot longer. Little did we think that within a year or so it would be all over and, except in Ceaușescu's Romania, largely without bloodshed.

Theme: Music

When we arrived in Vienna, I was delighted to find that my former pianist friend from Bonn, Raymond Adlam, was now the British Council Representative in Vienna. He lived in the very same apartment near Schönbrunn Palace where Beethoven had once resided. Naturally, we delighted in playing Beethoven violin and piano sonatas together in his circular music room, sensing the master's immediate spiritual presence. Michael Goppel, Head of the European Community (EC) delegation to the International Organisations in Vienna, was another very good pianist, with whom I regularly played violin and piano sonatas, including at our Hauskonzerte. A distinguished Austrian banker, Ferdinand Hain, a good amateur pianist, invited me to his home to play sonatas with him for Viennese friends in his Hauskonzerte. In London I had got to know the fine Austrian solo violinist Ernst Kovacic, and once played the Mendelssohn Octet with him – he wisely played second viola, while letting me struggle with the difficult first violin part. He lived in Bisamberg in the wine district north-east of Vienna, and we would meet to play duets and discuss violinistic questions.

I met an excellent Viennese/Hungarian 'cellist (also double bass and violin) from the Vienna Symphony Orchestra, and together with his Vienna orchestral colleagues we regularly played string quartets together. I was struck that, if they knew a piece well, they could play it brilliantly, sometimes tossing off a Paganini *Caprice* for fun. However, if they did not know a piece, their sight-reading could be quite limited. They would add as a back-handed 'compliment' that British orchestras were good at sight-reading…

It was noticeable that, while performances at the illustrious Vienna State Opera could be magnificent, on off-days when the top players were elsewhere, the standards could drop surprisingly. Then one would be better entertained at the Volksoper on the Gürtel, frequented by Viennese ordinary citizens – clad in respectful but ordinary clothes, rather than evening dress. It could offer splendid operettas by Lehár, Kálmán and others, but also fine performances of Mozart operas. The memory of a sparkling, typically Viennese, performance of *Così fan Tutte* with excellent soloists remains with me to this day.

Another fascinating musical colleague, Reinhard Öhlberger, a bassoonist in the Vienna Philharmonic Orchestra, was a world-leading collector of Baedeker guidebooks, whence developed our friendship (see later). He kindly passed to us his musician's tickets for the annual and rightly renowned Vienna New Year concert, where our whole family enjoyed a wonderful and unique cultural experience – which we are reminded of every time that we switch on the television on New Year's Day.

In 1988, with the help of the new British Ambassador in Prague Laurence O'Keeffe, a pianist with whom I had played when he was negotiating disarmament in Vienna, we got permission for a 'diplomatic' visit to Prague. We had the pleasure of playing the Dvořák violin and piano *Sonatina* together, while looking out of the Residence windows at Dvořák's own St Adalbert's church across the Prague Vltava river.

In 2008, when the London Philharmonic Orchestra was performing in the historic Musikverein concert hall, the then-Ambassador Simon Smith (with whom I had worked on nuclear environmental projects in post-Soviet Russia) kindly agreed to give a post-concert reception in his Residence. We invited, as well as the obligatory Viennese VIPs and LPO sponsors, all the orchestra musicians – who loved the hospitality and the opportunity to relax after their concert. During a rehearsal, our newly appointed Chief Conductor Vladimir Jurowski spoke of his awe in conducting for the first time in the Golden Hall of the Musikverein, with its excellent acoustics, in the footsteps of the greats such as Bruno Walter, Herbert von Karajan, Otto Klemperer, and the other distinguished Maestri.

One particularly memorable concert, which we attended in the Vienna Musikverein on the morning of Sunday, 23 April 1989, was what turned out to be Herbert von Karajan's last performance. He died three months later at the age of eighty-one. Already physically very infirm, he walked slowly on to the platform, getting support from the players' chairs, locked his lower body against the rail of the rostrum and conducted the Vienna Philharmonic Orchestra with only minute limited movements of his upper body. He gave us all Anton Bruckner's 7th Symphony quite magically. It was a wonderful musical experience – I still have the programme – and as it subsequently transpired, a historic occasion.

Yehudi and Diana Menuhin on a visit to Vienna joined us for a diplomatic dinner. Yehudi and I briefly discussed old Italian violins, but he was very much in his 'saving the world' mode, to which the ever pragmatic Diana raised the odd quizzical eyebrow.

On a later visit to Vienna, John Macgregor, a pianist with whom I and 'cellist Humphrey Maud had played piano trios in a 'celebrity' charity concert in the FCO Locarno Suite in 1995, had become Ambassador. We brought back happy memories, playing Beethoven and Mozart violin and piano sonatas together in the august surroundings of the British Residence – commissioned in 1871 by the then British Ambassador to the Hapsburg Court, Sir Andrew Buchanan.

My closest musical friend in Vienna was a Canadian, Gordon Murray, for many years the internationally renowned Professor of Harpsichord at the Vienna Universität für Musik und darstellende Kunst. He and his wife Ann, a teacher at the Vienna International School, and daughters Charlotte and Catherine, became close family friends for Ruth and me. We often shared congenial evenings in each other's homes. Gordon and I played music together many times privately in our homes, and publicly in the British Ambassador's Residence and in local Viennese concerts, not only baroque music with violin and harpsichord, but also classical and romantic sonatas with piano. Like many baroque specialists, he also loved 'lollipops', which we often played.

Tragically he was killed at the age of sixty-eight in a road accident on 12 March 2017, while getting out of a taxi in Vienna to help an ageing lady friend cross the road at midnight. Both were hit by an oncoming taxi and died as a result – Gordon shortly afterwards in hospital. When we heard the shocking news from Ann, we were both devastated. We attended the funeral in Vienna's Zentralfriedhof, where many famous musicians lie, together with Gordon's numerous family and friends. I had the sad duty and privilege of playing Bach on my violin (tuned down a quarter of a tone to match the pitch of the baroque harpsichord) in memory of our dear friend.

Once we had become acclimatised to the 'Balkan' nature of Vienna and did not look for yet another 'Western' European city, we became bewitched by its cultural magic – musical, architectural and historical. Music breathed out of every pore in the home of Mozart, Haydn, Beethoven, Schubert, Mahler, the Second Viennese School of Berg, Schönberg and Webern, and of course the masters of operetta such as Lehár and Kálmán – and many other great musicians.

Our departure from Vienna in 1989 was delayed by half an hour, as Ruth suddenly decided that she needed a souvenir of our four years in Vienna. She re-appeared carrying a brass wall candelabra, with a 'Doppeladler' (double eagle), which now hangs behind our dining table to remind us of the history of musical, cultural and Hapsburg Vienna. And, as everywhere, the real friendships, of which we had many in Austria, are much to be treasured.

9

CONSULTANCY

Variations

WHEN I DECIDED TO TAKE EARLY RETIREMENT FROM THE Foreign & Commonwealth Office in the autumn of 1995 and to move on from the 'safe' world of the civil service, where at least one was paid every month, it was with some trepidation that I faced the challenge of the commercial consultancy world – where one was paid if one delivered and not otherwise. Fortunately, the challenge turned out to be thoroughly worthwhile – with a series of fascinating projects and the happy development of interesting professional and personal friendships.

In my new role, much of the work dealing with foreign governments was similar to my past FCO experiences, but with the important proviso that the work was guided by commercial as well as by political requirements. Likewise, dealing with other UK ministries from a commercial, rather than another UK ministerial, perspective brought its own specific issues and challenges.

Variation: P&O

In the spring of 1992, I had just been given a promotion, but the FCO had not yet decided what to do with me. Accordingly, while I was waiting for my next job, I was sent on a three-week 'Senior Executive Programme' at Sundridge Park Management Centre in Kent. With half-a-dozen industry representatives, like me aspiring to move from 'middle-senior' to 'senior' executive positions, we were trained in modern management techniques, interspersed with team building and leadership exercises, intellectual and at times physical. Whether or not these 'modern' techniques made much practical difference, we all had a good time together, made friends and after three weeks emerged as embryonic senior executives.

Then in the summer of 1992, as a further part of my 'education' about the real world outside, I was seconded for two months with the Board of P&O European Ferries in Dover. The Managing Director Graeme Dunlop, who became a firm friend – also a fellow cricket-lover – took me under his wing and decided that, after a week of sitting in the various offices to see how things were run, I should do some 'useful' work for P&O. The big challenge facing the ferry industry would be the opening of the Channel Tunnel shuttle service, scheduled for 1993/1994. The London Business School (LBS) had written a serious study, citing the example of the Humberside Bridge and predicting that within a year of the opening of a 'fixed link', the ferry service would disappear. Graeme tasked me with writing my own analysis of the effect of the Channel Tunnel on the ferry industry.

He started by taking me with him round the various P&O units in the UK: Dover, Portsmouth and Felixstowe. I was particularly impressed, firstly, that he went through the finances in minute detail with the local MDs, inevitably spotted 'discrepancies', usually legitimate, which nevertheless pointed out operational issues that might otherwise have been overlooked. When I did some post-FCO consultancy for GEC/Marconi, Arnold Weinstock used a similar financial practice. Interestingly, my P&O colleagues were sceptical of some of the modern management theories which I had picked up on my 'Senior Executive Programme', saying that they were OK, but one still had to run a practical and effective business. However, the FCO and Whitehall did subsequently incorporate many 'modern management' theories – not always to their longer-term advantage, as later events have shown.

Next, I visited by myself the P&O and their competitor offices and staff in Hull, Larne and Aberdeen, Calais, Zeebrugge, Brussels, Düsseldorf, Rotterdam, and the relevant tourist and regional government offices in the UK and Europe. In short I was able to gather the information which disproved the LBS thesis, and which demonstrated that the ferry and shuttle offered different services to different customers, and that the costs of a ferry and a shuttle crossing the Channel were not that different. In particular, the ferry staff, as well as having their safety/management responsibilities, also ran a profitable duty-free business, which offset the costs of the actual ferry – and which the shuttle did not have. So, I concluded that, although the abolition of duty-free sales in 1999 would have an impact, there would still be serious business for the ferry industry in the long-term – *pace* LBS – which turned out to be the case.

I was invited to present my Report to the P&O Main Board under its Chairman Jeffrey Sterling, and my findings were incorporated into the P&O Five Year (1993–1997) Plan. The Report was also used by the Cabinet Office as a Eurotunnel Case Study for its 1993 Top Management Programme. Three years later, when I was looking for post-FCO outside employment, the contacts and advice from the likes of Jeffrey Sterling (by strange coincidence another violinist, who had studied with Max Rostal in London in the 1950s), turned out to be invaluable.

Variation: British Nuclear Fuels Ltd (BNFL)

By 1995 I had decided to take early retirement from the FCO, and having taken outside professional advice, set up my own Sole Trader Vat-registered business, acting as my own accountant and marketing agent, and learning how to use my new Viglen computer. I initially engaged a local accountancy firm to do my accounts, but later discovered that they had charged me a substantial sum for making a substantial error in favour of the taxman – and then decided to do it all myself, which, as well as saving money, turned out to be a useful discipline in money management and life generally. I enjoyed a courteous and pragmatic relationship with my HMRC tax office – occasionally they asked me to pay more tax, and occasionally they refunded some over-paid tax – all very reasonable.

I reported to the local Esher Job Centre every week, and while I was unemployed and job-seeking they kindly paid for my National Insurance and gave me the statutory weekly allowance. I recall that, since I had just started to receive my FCO pension, I felt that it was immoral to benefit twice from the UK taxpayer, and therefore donated this allowance to a worthy charity, the National Society for the Prevention of Cruelty to Children.

I wrote dozens of letters with what I thought was an interesting CV to the great and good of the business world, offering my 'international experience', and went to dozens of interviews. The replies were always polite, but nearly all negative. However, as often in life, the personal contact turned out to be invaluable.

I consulted a neighbour of ours in Thames Ditton, Curtis Keeble, a former Ambassador to Moscow. He suggested that I look to use my Russian language and kindly gave me a personal introduction to Norman Wooding, Chairman of the Russo-British Chamber of Commerce and a non-executive Director of the state-owned British Nuclear Fuels (BNFL), who later became a stimulating colleague on various industry and official visits to Russia. He said that BNFL needed help with their Russian nuclear clean-up projects. He put me in direct touch with the BNFL Commercial Director Graham Watts, who I subsequently learnt had checked me out with P&O Chairman Jeffrey Sterling, who apparently gave me a thumbs-up.

Anyhow, after various interviews BNFL offered me a short-term contract from February 1996. My first task was to visit Moscow for discussions with the relevant Russian officials, and to write a report for BNFL on their proposed nuclear environmental clean-up projects in NW Russia and elsewhere. My aborted chemistry studies of many years ago were helpful in providing a rudimentary understanding of the nuclear scientific jargon. I worked with the International Director Jeremy Rycroft and his colleague responsible for Russian projects, Paul Wilcox, who were both most helpful. After a couple of months, I presented them with the report, and then the BNFL management asked me to implement it, giving me a generous long-term contract as their 'Senior Adviser'.

My fascinating Russian experiences, working with international and British consortia to win nuclear clean-up contracts in Russia, particularly in the North-West, are described in detail later. I got a particular and personal satisfaction from working with Russian colleagues in far-flung places which I could never have visited in my FCO days, and we all felt that we were working together to address the challenges of a common European environmental threat.

The Contact Expert Group (CEG), including BNFL, was established under International Atomic Energy Agency (IAEA) auspices in 1996 to address Russian nuclear waste and clean-up issues. I was appointed as a delegate and attended meetings near nuclear sites in Russia (St Petersburg and Murmansk), the Scandinavian countries, France, the UK and the USA (Augusta – Savannah River Site), where we aimed for open international discussions about a common approach – with varying results. I also visited, as well as Washington DC for US Government discussions, the Westinghouse HQ near Pittsburgh, and the Holtec offices in Philadelphia.

Although we were not directly involved in Ukraine Chernobyl work, I visited Kiev for discussions with the Ukrainian government experts about potential nuclear clean-up projects. The Russian language (as opposed to Ukrainian in the telecoms authority and National Bank – which I visited for BT, see below) was still widely used by the nuclear authorities – and the visits gave me an excellent opportunity to see some of Kiev's magnificent cathedrals, monasteries, *lavra* (caves), the Great Gate of Kiev (actually surprisingly modest in size), historic architecture and streets for the first time – happily repeated on BT business and private occasions.

We also established an international consortium, entitled the International Group (IG), consisting of BNFL, the French SGN (later AREVA), Swedish SKB and Norwegian Kvaerner to work together on Russian clean-up projects, largely funded by the Norwegian Government, because of the environmental threat to the Barents Sea, or by international organisations – details in my Russian chapter later.

The Norwegians were also concerned about nuclear-waste pollution from Sellafield into the Irish Sea, especially technetium-99 for which BNFL developed a counter-process, although the BNFL calculation was that the actual radiation released was similar to that from brazil nuts (with their relatively high radium content). A Norwegian priest-led group from the Lofoten Islands and the Norwegian Environment Minister Børge Brende visited Sellafield for constructive discussions. I liaised on these with the BNFL Press Officer, an excellent colleague over the years, Jamie Reed. He was subsequently elected as Labour MP for neighbouring Copeland, promoted to Shadow Health Minister, and now – after disagreeing with the post-2015 Labour leadership over nuclear power and other issues, and resigning as an MP – is back at Sellafield as Head of Development and Community Relations.

The state-owned BNFL, under its then-CEO Neville Chamberlain, with whom I later worked as a colleague in my subsequent AREVA period, at the time regularly delivered hundreds of millions of pounds to the DTI/Treasury annually, mainly from its Sellafield-based nuclear waste/spent fuel management business. The UK Government was largely happy and let BNFL get on with its business. In 1998 BNFL bought US reactor producer Westinghouse for what seemed a reasonable price and set up the BNFL–Westinghouse complete nuclear cycle business – as the French did with Framatome and Cogema becoming AREVA.

The problems started when BNFL messed up two important contracts. Firstly, there was the 1998 fixed-price clean-up contract at the Hanford River site in the USA – fixed price is always unwise for nuclear clean-up projects when you do not yet know the future challenges. In 2000 the US

Government terminated the contract, and the UK Government had to bail out BNFL financially. Then, when the important Japanese customer Kansai Electric asked for manual certificates for its BNFL spent fuel contracts in 1999, the Sellafield middle managers, who thought that they knew better than their Japanese customers, produced 'virtual' certificates. These turned out to be in effect forgeries – although probably giving basically the correct information. However, as BNFL learnt to its cost, when the Japanese customers discovered what had happened, they were less than pleased – and the customer is always right!

The Government's attitude to nuclear power became less positive, given the then relatively low oil and gas prices. Some senior ministers, such as Patricia Hewitt (Trade & Industry) and Margaret Beckett (Environment), were equivocal about nuclear energy, and the nuclear section of the 2003 Energy White Paper, after re-drafting, was minimal. The then Government Chief Scientific Adviser, David King, who became another respected colleague and friend, told me that he had been officially reprimanded by the Blair Government for saying that climate change was a greater threat than international terrorism – he would have no problem saying this today.

Finally, the Sellafield THORP leak in 2005, when some twenty tonnes of highly radioactive liquid leaked, and was not reported for months, although fortunately it did not do any external environmental damage, was a turning point with the UK Government.

As a result, the complete UK nuclear business was broken up, with the newly created state controlled Nuclear Decommissioning Authority (NDA) (see below) taking over Sellafield responsibility, and Westinghouse being sold to Toshiba in 2006 for what seemed at the time to be a profitable price of £5bn.

The Blair/Brown government subsequently changed its attitude to nuclear power, both for reasons of climate change and of security of supply, when President Putin cut off gas supplies to Ukraine and Georgia in 2006, but by then it was too late to save BNFL. The tragedy was that we, the British, had been world leaders in civil nuclear power and we had some of the best nuclear engineers in the world, but the management/ government breakdown in trust by then was too great.

None of this significantly affected my work for BNFL in the early years. I left the UK Government relationship largely to the BNFL senior management, and worked with the Russian, Ukrainian, Chinese, Norwegian, Swedish, Finnish, French, German and Italian authorities to facilitate BNFL business with their governments and nuclear industries. I accordingly advised the then-Chairman the late Hugh Collum, with whom I subsequently developed a personal friendship outside the BNFL office, and accompanied numerous foreign VIPs, Ministers and Ambassadors to Sellafield. The BNFL senior management, having invited these foreign guests, would often become unavailable (usually for 'internal' or personal reasons) to host the visits themselves, and would ask me to stand in for them.

The journey from London, whether via Manchester, Penrith or Newcastle, was lengthy with picturesque but long drives over the Cumbrian fells, Sellafield being on the site of a WWII conventional arms establishment as far as possible away from the Luftwaffe – but the welcome by the Sellafield staff when one arrived was always enthusiastic. Once we read a critical article by the then Bishop of Liverpool, James Jones, whom I knew through our mutual membership of the Athenæum, about Sellafield's desecration of his 'green acres'. Accordingly, we invited him to Sellafield, and the sympathetic staff there worked their usual professional charm – if he did not become a supporter of nuclear energy, at least the critical articles eased off.

However, as UK Government confidence in BNFL declined, this started to affect the new business. The British Nuclear Industry Group (BNIG) representing BNFL, AEA Technology, NNC and Studsvik Rosyth had done all the work with the Russians and locally for a nuclear clean-up contract in Murmansk, but to general surprise the Department of Trade & Industry (DTI) gave the contract to another consortium, with German participation. The Russians, placing much stress on personal contacts and direct site knowledge, could not understand this – frankly neither could I, and I thought it very short-sighted. We persuaded the Chairmen/CEOs of the UK companies formally to protest to the relevant DTI Minister, but to no avail.

In 2005 BNFL was bidding for an Italian reprocessing contact, worth some £500 million, not huge, but significant not only for the money but for the renewed Italian interest in nuclear cooperation with the UK. With the enthusiastic help of the British Ambassador in Rome, my old diplomatic and skiing friend Ivor Roberts, we went to the top of the Italian Government and industry – for whom Ivor hosted a dinner, assuring them that the UK Government stood firmly behind us. Then the UK Government decided to pull out, no doubt influenced by a loss of confidence over the Sellafield THORP leak. One relatively junior DTI official, a good guy with whom I had worked over the years, was instructed by his superiors to order me to tell my friend Ivor to 'back off' – delicacy prevents me from revealing His Excellency's 'undiplomatic' response! A year later, when I was working post-BNFL for AREVA, my new French colleagues then won the contract which they thought that we had in the bag – and they teased me unmercifully. Again, I thought that this UK Government decision was short-sighted.

In 2004 the Energy Act established the Nuclear Decommissioning Authority (NDA), a non-departmental body which reported to the DTI, responsible for overseeing the decommissioning and clean-up of all the UK nuclear sites. While not responsible directly for the operational management of the sites, it oversaw the work and overall strategy through awarding contracts to Site Licence Companies – i.e. to bring in commercial experience, reflecting government frustration with BNFL management. In effect the NDA took over the role of BNFL, which then proceeded with the disposal of its assets and sites, completing this by 2009.

As 2005 drew on, despite the kind efforts of my colleagues to soften the blow by extending my contract on a limited basis, it was clear that my international role in BNFL was ending. I had also enjoyed some part-time work with BT – insights into telecommunications in the Baltic States, Poland and Ukraine, and with GEC/Marconi – possible developments in Russia. I gave some international political advice to Jim Ratcliffe's INEOS, and Oxford chemistry colleague David Marsh appointed me to the Advisory Board of his economic think-tank OMFIF (Official Monetary and Financial Institutions Forum) – but these were mainly short-term projects and, as a consequence, I began to look around for other possibilities. And, as before, through a personal contact.

Variation: AREVA

When we in BNFL had worked on Russian projects, a good colleague in the Paris end of the Industrial Group's French partner was Henri Zaccai of SGN, since integrated into AREVA NC. The AREVA CEO, Anne Lauvergeon, a graduate of the elite Corps des Mines and a former 'Sherpa' (personal preparatory work for summits, etc.) for President Mitterrand, had been CEO of the French waste-management equivalent of BNFL, Cogema. Anne Lauvergeon, later named by *Forbes Magazine* as the 9th most powerful woman in the world, in 1991 integrated Cogema with the Franco-German-US reactor company Framatome, to form a complete nuclear cycle company (like BNFL/Westinghouse), to which she gave the new name of AREVA (after a Cistercian abbey in Spain). AREVA was then sub-divided into AREVA NP (new build/reactors) and AREVA NC (fuel/waste management), and later added some renewables to its portfolio to create a low carbon 'circle'.

AREVA wanted to expand its UK business, partly in reactors which it constructed for EDF, but particularly in the waste-management and Sellafield areas. Accordingly, Henri Zaccai and I met in Paris to discuss possibilities, and he then introduced me in early 2006 to the Head of AREVA NC, Jacques Besnainou, and the AREVA International Director, Jean-Jacques Gautrot. Both became valued colleagues, especially Gautrot, a respected nuclear expert and later President of the World Nuclear Association, with whom I am still in regular personal contact. Both were admirers, if not of the UK Government's vacillating attitude to nuclear power, then certainly of the excellence of British nuclear engineers, and indeed of the wider UK industrial and political contribution to Europe.

After the initial formal interview, I was offered an immediate contract with AREVA from March 2006. I retained my self-employed status, but was given various 'honorary' titles, varying from 'UK Representative' to 'Senior Vice-President' and 'Expert Chair'. Other working friends in AREVA included Denis Hugelmann, Dominique Mockly, Rémi Coulon, Cécile Maisonneuve, Jean-Claude Lerond, and several others. As a mark of these new friendships, it was made clear to me that we should 'tutoyer' one another.

After initial 'familiarisation' visits to the Paris Head Office, the Reprocessing Plant at La Hague near Cherbourg and the Mélox MOX (Mixed Oxide) plant near Avignon, I started to build up relationships with the UK energy officials in DTI/BIS/DECC, and with the relevant ministers and MPs from the Conservative, Labour and LibDem parties, also regularly attending the party conferences – these were hard work but enjoyable, and offered direct one-on-one contact with ministers, who while at the 'political' conferences were not 'protected' by their civil servants. Generally, the UK reaction to greater French involvement in the UK nuclear scene was positive, especially as the engineers/technicians had long exchanged experiences and enjoyed mutual respect.

I accompanied visits by UK politicians – Shadow Energy Minister Charles Hendry, who was particularly good company, cross-party MPs, officials and trades unionists to La Hague, Mélox and the Le Creusot plant in Saône-et-Loire/Burgundy, which makes the components for the EPR nuclear power plant. The Mélox MOX plant was of especial interest to the UK visitors since it was able to make MOX fuel (from reprocessed uranium and plutonium oxides) on a commercial basis, while the UK over-sophisticated MOX equivalent at Sellafield never could. Every time that it broke down it took weeks or months to repair, whereas the French plant could usually be repaired within a few hours. This was perhaps a reflection on the UK fascination with technological brilliance, while some of our competitors preferred simpler but commercially more viable options.

In 2009 we opened AREVA's 'grandiose' new UK office in St James's Square London, to reflect our optimism at the time (pre-Fukushima). We had a well-publicised Franco-British opening ceremony, which our excellent press/media representative Martin Adeney organised in the Library of the Reform Club (he was a member) across the road. Captains of industry, politicians and senior officials attended. I made the opening speech introducing Anne Lauvergeon, who spoke eloquently about nuclear power, the Franco-British dimension and the vital contributions of the projects to the UK supply chain and UK jobs. She referred to me by first name as 'Cecil', rather than 'Desmond' – a frequent occurrence, which nevertheless generated good-natured teasing from some of my British friends.

Ed Miliband, then the Department of Energy & Climate Change (DECC) Secretary of State, spoke positively in response to Anne Lauvergeon's comments about nuclear power – which he might not have done in the past – and reinforced the message about the importance of the Franco-British dimension and the essential contribution to the UK industry supply chain and UK jobs. Happy times – when we were basking in a nuclear mini-honeymoon, until Fukushima changed everything.

From time to time we had meetings in No. 10 Downing Street to discuss the possible contribution of AREVA nuclear developments to the UK supply chain and UK jobs. My French colleagues were always impressed by the relative informality of No. 10, once past the tight entrance security. On one occasion we took CEO Anne Lauvergeon to meet the very influential, but approachable, then Chief of Staff Jeremy Heywood. After useful talks we were on the way out, when Anne mentioned that she had heard that one of my forebears had been Prime Minister. As we descended the main staircase, I pointed out the picture of Queen Victoria's PM, my illustrious great-great-grandfather, on the wall. 'Je ne comprends pas. C'est pas écrit Cecil, mais Sal-is-bu-ry,' said Anne, to which I had to explain the arcane British system of titles.

On another occasion we took Luc Oursel, in charge of AREVA nuclear new build, for similar talks with Nick Butler, then PM Gordon Brown's Senior Policy Adviser – a long-standing colleague and friend, previously Group Policy Adviser for BP, subsequently writer on energy for the *FT* and in the Athenæum management. As we came to the left-hand staircase, there was a lady waiting politely at the top. Luc, always forthright, zoomed up the stairs past the lady. I explained to Luc that the lady was in fact Sarah Brown, wife of the PM, and that the premises served as the PM's private as well as official residence. Luc was amazed and commented that this would not have been possible in the strict formality of the Elysée or Matignon.

While the AREVA top management generally dealt directly with their owners, the French state, I did have exchanges with Christine Lagarde then Trade Minister (whom I also knew as an Athenæum member) and later Managing Director of the IMF, and Arnaud Montebourg, an approachable socialist politician and later Minister for Industrial Renewal, whom I had met while accompanying UK MPs to Le Creusot in his Saône-et-Loire constituency. Later I was also invited to join a European Reform Round Table in London with the impressive young Emmanuel Macron, who of course later became President of France. He was easy to talk with, and afterwards we chatted constructively about nuclear energy. He then appointed as his Prime Minister Edouard Philippe, by coincidence a former AREVA colleague. Through music – we both attended Kurt Masur's eightieth birthday concert in Paris – I also met Claude Guéant, then Secretary-General of the Elysée.

In February 2010, Anne Lauvergeon, with her husband Olivier Fric (a charming man to chat with, but an unfortunate surname, given subsequent revelations about some of his Swiss financial dealings), was invited to a glamorous charity event hosted by HRH Prince Charles in Windsor

Castle. This was in aid of Armenia's 'Yerevan My Love Foundation' and consisted of a reception, classical and folk music and an elaborate dinner in the splendid and historic Waterloo Chamber. The international great and good were there, including from the Armenian side the former Prime Minister Armin Sarkissian and the Franco-Armenian musical star Charles Aznavour – a great supporter of Armenian restoration after the Soviet years. Anne (AREVA had a nuclear interest in Armenia) arrived at Heathrow by private jet, where I had to meet her – and, as often happened with her, she was inevitably late, touching down just as the reception was about to begin. From our car I had to telephone Windsor Castle with excuses for the delay and make last-minute arrangements for us to slip in later – which with the discreet help of the Royal officials, we just about managed.

Later that year Anne was invited to a dinner at the Institute for Strategic Dialogue in London, and at the last minute I had to stand in for her. It was hosted by George Weidenfeld (with whom I had later dealings over a Kurt Masur biography – Masur wanted the original German version to be published in English and asked me to liaise with Weidenfeld, who feared that it would not sell), and included philanthropist Ronald Grierson, Saxony Prime Minister Kurt Biedenkopf (whom I knew from Bonn political and Leipzig musical links), EBRD President Thomas Mirow, and others. The aim of the evening was for Jonathan Powell, Tony Blair's former Chief of Staff – whom I knew well from our diplomatic days together in Vienna – to introduce Catherine Ashton, then the EU High Representative for Foreign Affairs, to the assembled guests. I fear that they were not terribly impressed with what she had to say – but I found it an interesting occasion, nevertheless, observing their reactions.

Obviously, such industry/political informal meetings, to supplement the more formal official meetings, are an essential part of the whole two-way lobbying process – but on this particular occasion it was clearly less than successful.

Variation: Sellafield Contract

With the break-up of BNFL and the NDA's assumption of its legal responsibilities, the multi-billion Sellafield management contract was put up for open tender. AREVA, with the UK AMEC, and as lead partner the US Washington Group (later URS and then AECOM), formed the consortium Nuclear Management Partners (NMP). After intensive work and lobbying against fierce competition from rival international consortia, NMP was awarded the contract in 2008. The contract was potentially for seventeen years, renewable every five years. I was initially an Adviser to the NMP Board and did a lot of work behind the scenes until we won the 2008 award but was then replaced by an American nominee as part of an internal US deal ('stitch-up'). I was recalled as Adviser to the Board in 2014, ironically by our American partners under new leadership, but by then it was too late.

The NMP management ran into difficulties quite early on, exacerbated by some clumsy incidents from the lead Americans – for example, a well-publicised 'cat' incident when the consortium charged the NDA several hundred pounds to transport a family with its cat by taxi from Cumbria to Heathrow. Although this was subsequently repaid, NMP's reputation suffered. The consortium was savaged by the redoubtable Margaret Hodge's Public Accounts Select Committee, to some extent with justification. My own view was that the Americans had initially been 'high-handed', not respecting local sensitivities, but also that the junior UK and French partners AMEC and AREVA, who had a Board veto right and knew the local scene better, should have been more outspoken.

In 2013 NMP was awarded a five-year extension of the contract, although controversially and with much local opposition. We also had a more satisfactory second appearance before Margaret Hodge and her Select Committee. The American leadership of the consortium changed, in the view of many of us for the better. Once the early 'cat' incident and other difficulties had passed, NMP's performance improved very significantly, noticeably in safety, site management and morale, and cost savings for the UK taxpayer. But by then the UK official mood had changed. There was a move within the NDA, largely staffed by ex-BNFL people, to take back control of Sellafield, in effect to try to re-create BNFL, and ministers were over-focused on retaining their seats in the 2015 General Election – which some failed to do. The result was that the contract was taken away from NMP and handed, under overall NDA supervision, to Sellafield Limited, a managerial team which ironically had been set up by NMP.

The future will tell whether this 're-creation of BNFL' was a wise move – just as the future will tell whether the 2006 sale of Westinghouse, the UK's only nuclear-power asset, and indeed the original break-up of BNFL in parallel were wise moves.

Shortly afterwards the NDA was subject to severe legal criticism for its 'mishandling' of the large 'Magnox' decommissioning contract – the High Court Judgment used words like 'fudging' and 'manipulating'. The National Audit Office referred to 'serious questions' about the NDA's ability to manage such large complex procurements and estimated that it had cost the taxpayer 'upwards of £122 million'. The NDA's senior management was subsequently replaced from outside the nuclear industry.

I was naturally disappointed about the ending of the NMP contract, not just because a lot of work had gone into it, but also because of the excellent cooperation which we had enjoyed with many of the Sellafield staff, and with NMP colleagues such as Duncan Guy and Clive White of AMEC and Ian Hudson and Kevin Tebbit of AECOM. When I had left BNFL in 2005, I thought that I would never again have the long picturesque drive over the Cumbrian fells to reach Sellafield – until the NMP involvement revived this scenic pleasure.

Variation: AREVA – Nuclear New Build

The other aspect of AREVA's UK interest was its role in the construction of the EPR (European Pressurised Reactor) for EDF. We took UK senior government visitors to Olkiluoto in Finland where the first EPR was under construction, and, as mentioned above, to the Le Creusot plant where the components were made. After the opening of the AREVA London office in 2009 we worked hard to demonstrate the advantages which the EPR would bring to the UK supply chain. I was able to organise UK-French meetings, including with Labour, Conservative and LibDem ministers – John Hutton, Ed Miliband, Peter Mandelson, Charles Hendry, Jonathan Marland, Greg Clark, Chris Huhne, Ed Davey, all of whom listened carefully to questions about nuclear energy. Even if some of them were cautious about nuclear as such, reflecting the positions of their parties, they all recognised the potential value of its contributions to the UK supply chain and UK jobs.

Former Conservative Energy Secretary Patrick Jenkin was an enthusiastic supporter of new nuclear power, and became a good ally, joining Labour MPs on a useful cross-party visit which we took to the French nuclear sites. The Labour MPs came from rival areas of Scotland and argued non-stop among themselves. However, they all conceded that Patrick was quite a good guy 'for a Tory' – they would obviously have to send him to the *guillotine* in due course, but not yet!

We also took Luc Oursel, Anne Lauvergeon's successor as AREVA CEO, to Edinburgh to meet the First Minister of Scotland, Alex Salmond, to discuss with him potential energy and supply-chain benefits for Scotland of AREVA's offshore-wind initiatives. Salmond kept us waiting for an hour in his official Residence, Bute House, but when he turned up, he was very entertaining company. He said that he was not against nuclear power as such, and demonstrated an impressive knowledge of the subject, but explained that Scotland was going down the renewables route because it had plenty of wind and was surrounded by water. We had a follow-up meeting (early morning when Salmond was clearly not at his best) when he came to a conference in Paris, and again had a positive discussion – although in the end nothing constructive transpired.

In the margins of the Cameron-Sarkozy Paris Summit in February 2012, the new Energy Secretary LibDem Ed Davey, who had just replaced the displaced Chris Huhne, met his French colleagues for talks on energy and nuclear issues. Davey, who knew well my journalist son Nic (we are similar in appearance) from the *Evening Standard*, came up to our AREVA nuclear group, took one close look at me and said: 'You must be Nic Cecil's father.' No DNA test required.

I regularly briefed successive British Ambassadors in Paris, John Holmes, Peter Westmacott and especially Peter Ricketts, who had dealt with energy matters when in London. They and their staff were always positive colleagues. The FCO in London, who although helpful, were less involved, many of their responsibilities having been taken over by the home departments such as DTI, subsequently DECC and BIS (and then merged into BEIS). My view was that UK/France energy issues were politically and diplomatically sensitive, and I was surprised that the home departments did not always keep the FCO and the Ambassadors fully briefed.

As related, in No.10 we dealt with Jeremy Heywood, later Cabinet Secretary, who was always very approachable, especially on the crucial role of the UK supply chain and UK jobs. In 2012, at the UK-French Cameron-Sarkozy Summit in Paris, we signed a 'key' MOU with Rolls-Royce offering them a significant share of the supply chain and jobs benefits. Sadly, the subsequent nuclear-energy setbacks negated these.

The well-publicised Olkiluoto delays and cost-overruns, and the falling oil/gas prices did not help the case for nuclear new build. However, the crucial blow was the Fukushima disaster on 11 March 2011. I can recall a working lunch with Anne Lauvergeon, French Ambassador Maurice Gourdault-Montagne and Jean-Jacques Gautrot in London that day, just before she made a 'keynote' speech at the Royal Society of Engineering.

Over lunch we heard news about 'something in Japan', but did not immediately appreciate its gravity.

Although it was not a 'nuclear' accident as such, the tsunami destroying the conventional generators for the cooling systems, something which would not affect more modern designs, the repercussions had grave implications for the nuclear new-build industry, including in the UK. Shortly afterwards, CDU Chancellor Merkel announced that Germany would be pulling out of new nuclear power. She was no doubt influenced by the forthcoming Länder elections in Baden-Württemberg, which the anti-nuclear Green/SPD coalition won anyway. As a result of the pull-out, the German energy companies RWE and E.ON lost billions and had to undergo major restructuring. The over-optimistic 2007 prediction by EDF Energy's then-CEO Vincent de Rivaz, that the British would be cooking their Christmas dinners with EPR electricity by 2017, backfired. The latest predictions are for some time after 2025, and the other UK new-build projects are suffering equally.

In France, Anne Lauvergeon was sacked in June 2011, we understood by President Sarkozy personally. She was replaced by her deputy Luc Oursel, who tried to introduce structural reforms and cost-cutting. He resigned for health reasons in October 2014 and died a couple of months later. Because of the massive cost overruns in Olkiluoto and nuclear setbacks generally, the French Government broke up Lauvergeon's dream of a complete nuclear company, as had happened with BNFL/Westinghouse ten years previously. The French state, AREVA's principal shareholder, had to deal with reputed overall losses of some 11bn Euros. AREVA NC became the fuel/waste company ORANO under Oursel's deputy Philippe Knoche. The reactor company AREVA NP reverted to the original name Framatome, under a new CEO Bernard Fontana who had been brought in from outside, and is now owned by EDF.

The initial AREVA optimism about developing its UK new-build activities evaporated. Inevitably my role with AREVA came to an end, as it had done with BNFL ten years before. Kind colleagues in Paris kept my contract going for another year, but the writing was on the wall, and my formal role ended in 2016. I keep in touch with personal friends in Paris, especially Jean-Jacques Gautrot, and together we monitor nuclear developments. Once the initial 'Franco-British' ice was broken, I was privileged and lucky to enjoy mutual friendship and respect with my French colleagues, who as well as being expert nuclear engineers, were often highly cultured people with whom one could enjoy fascinating discussions about a wide variety of issues.

Variation: Nuclear Industry Association (NIA)

In 2010 I was appointed as AREVA Director to the Nuclear Industry Association (NIA), the UK Trade Association representing some 270 companies, UK-based, if not all UK-owned, and to the NIA Nominations Committee. With the demise of AREVA in 2016 I offered my resignation from the NIA Board; my Board colleagues asked me to leave the room for two minutes, and then kindly re-appointed me to the Board as an 'Independent Director', which I remain to this day – and which allows me to give something back to the industry.

As a member of the Nominations Committee, I and two other colleagues, a real 'nuclear expert' Terry Gilbert as Chair, were responsible for the appointments of Labour ex-Business Secretary John Hutton and then ex-DECC Expert Chair Tim Stone (and fellow musician – double bass player) as successive NIA Chairmen – as well as Labour ex-Shadow Business Minister Tom Greatrex as NIA CEO. In each case we chose people who were natural supporters of the nuclear industry and future nuclear power, had good political connections and understanding – essential in a government-dominated industry world – in addition to their strong personal qualities.

We in the NIA are all trying to get across to successive UK governments, pre-occupied with Brexit and internal political issues, the important value of nuclear as an essential, continuous and secure part of the low-carbon energy mix, and of course of the UK supply chain and UK jobs – even more relevant in the current climate-change debate.

Whatever the uncertain nuclear future holds, I look back with great pleasure and some satisfaction on my ten years with BNFL and then the ten-plus years with AREVA. I am a strong believer in the long-term climate-change and security-of-supply advantages of nuclear power, given the move from fossil fuels to clean electricity – notwithstanding the Windscale, Three Mile Island, Fukushima, and especially the disastrous Chernobyl, nuclear accidents. I believe that the negative environmental consequences of nuclear power can be contained, especially with the continuing development of used-fuel recycling. In these more than twenty years I learnt a great deal about industry, energy and recycling, made many friends, and I was generously paid – which certainly helped my musical life, and the practical and much-needed contributions which I could make to support the musical world.

In an ironic way my aborted diplomatic postings to Moscow and Paris were later realised, and probably in rather more integrated and satisfying incarnations.

*

As I write, a major US company has been in touch with me through mutual nuclear contacts, asking for advice on a business move into the UK – which could have significant economic and political consequences. We shall see what transpires, but it is always flattering to be asked to make a modest contribution.

10

RUSSIA – SOVIET AND POST-SOVIET 'WINDOWS'

Variation: Soviet 'Window'

MY FIRST INTEREST IN THE RUSSIAN LANGUAGE AROSE WHEN I was a violinist in Switzerland in the late-1960s. I had already picked up the Swiss languages – German, Swiss German/Bernese, French, Italian – and following in the linguistic footsteps of my musical inspiration Yehudi Menuhin (whose family was of Russian origin from Odessa – like many other great violinists), decided that musical erudition required a knowledge of Russian. Accordingly, I started to study the basics of the language, including an elementary Migros (a Swiss supermarket chain) language course.

A strange episode occurred when I received a telephone call from the Soviet Embassy in Berne inviting me to give them lessons in English and German. English I could understand but was mystified by the request to a Brit for German lessons in a German-speaking country. However, as an impecunious violinist, who needed the money, I did not ask any questions and accepted the offer. My main pupil was a young Soviet diplomat, whom by coincidence I later got to know well when we were both Counsellors in Vienna in the late-1980s. Nothing untoward happened, although I later learnt that the Swiss authorities had alerted the British Embassy in Berne about this young Englishman visiting the Soviet Embassy. The British Embassy belatedly tried to contact me, but by then I had left Switzerland and was talking to Oxford University about possible future jobs. To this day I still have no further idea why the Soviet Embassy approached me as a German language teacher.

My next Russian experience was in 1970, when the FCO having seen the high results of my language aptitude test decided to prepare me to be posted to the British Embassy in Moscow. Accordingly, I was sent to the illustrious FCO Language School then in Palace Chambers opposite Parliament to enrol with the head Russian teacher, the formidable White Russian Countess Shuvalova. Beneath a daunting classical Russian aristocratic exterior, she was an excellent but demanding teacher, who either made or broke her pupils – I determined that with me it would be the former. At our very first lesson she instructed me to give her, despite my very basic Russian at that stage, a full account of the news in that day's newspapers – which she corrected mercilessly. However, and as a result of her strict discipline, both my spoken and written Russian improved quite dramatically during the next few months. I was told later by Soviet friends that my Russian was both grammatically correct and with a pure Northern 'St Petersburg/pre-Baltic' accent. Indeed, at a nuclear energy meeting in Moscow many years later, when the UK BNFL team asked our Russian Muscovite hosts which of them spoke the most correct Russian, our hosts grinned and nodded in my direction.

My serious Russian language studies also gave me the wonderful privilege of being able to re-read the masterworks of Russian literature – Pushkin, Tolstoy, Dostoyevsky, Pasternak, Solzhenitsyn and others – no longer in English translation, but now in the original Russian.

I have related how my planned Moscow posting was aborted, as a consequence of *Operation Foot* in 1971. However, as the years went by, I continued to use my Russian in diplomatic postings to UN Geneva and to Vienna – and interestingly once on holiday when visiting Israel with its influx of Russians. I have to say that, whatever official reservations my Soviet counterparts may have had about the UK, and *vice versa*, I always enjoyed good personal relations with them. For example, as the Cold War drew to an end, Vienna was the setting for exploratory meetings

between the Soviet and British Foreign Ministers, Eduard Shevardnadze
and Geoffrey Howe – and the Soviet Ambassador and his colleagues were
happy to use me as a local intermediary.

In 1988, seventeen years after *Operation Foot*, I finally visited the Soviet
Union for the first time, coming from our Vienna Embassy to discuss with
the Soviet Foreign Ministry the possibility of Austria joining the then-EEC,
given Soviet concerns about Austrian neutrality – as I have related. A personal objective of this visit, of course, was finally to gain direct experience
of the country and system which I had studied for years. I was allowed
to take my wife Ruth, which perhaps perplexed the Soviets. On arrival
at Sheremetyevo Airport the KGB surveillance – which we understood
was normal for Western diplomats – was immediately apparent, as it was
throughout the visit, but always without unpleasant incident. Indeed, when
we were visiting the Pushkin Museum and our taxi got lost, a surveillance
car – presumably aware of our plans from listening to a conversation in a
British Embassy flat the night before – kindly indicated the way.

In Moscow we were privileged, both then and on subsequent visits, to
explore some of the magnificent sights, such as the Kremlin, Red Square,
St Basil's Cathedral, the Bolshoi Theatre, the Tchaikovsky Concert Hall,
etc., etc., to admire the spacious parks, and simply to wander through the
wide main streets, the lively Arbat and the many other varied districts,
along the Moskva River, and wherever – to experience for ourselves the
deeply impressive history and culture of the Russian people.

We were able to visit Leningrad by overnight sleeper, during which
we were wakened with sweetened tea served from a samovar. We were
lucky enough to visit the magnificent Hermitage for the first of several
times, the Fabergé eggs making a lasting impression on us, as well as
some of the city's other historic places, including the cruiser *Aurora*.
She had served in the Russo-Japanese War in 1905, and then in 1917 her
crew joined in the Russian Revolution, and a blank shot from the cruiser
signalled the launch of the attack on the Winter Palace. We ended the
day, after wandering along the canals, in an empty cafe, where a string

quartet was playing. That evening we attended at the Kirov Opera a *Don Giovanni*, with the alternate ending after the anti-hero descends to hell, conducted by the young Martyn Brabbins, a future musical acquaintance when we were together on the Royal Philharmonic Society Council. In Leningrad we were subjected to a standard KGB illegal money exchange proposal (to try to entrap foreigners), but it was clear what was happening from the grins of the occupants of the black van across the road, and we ignored it.

For some reason we were not allowed to visit Kiev, but at the last minute we got Soviet Foreign Ministry permission to visit Tbilisi in Georgia. The flight was due to leave Moscow after midnight, but we dozed off at the airport and just missed the flight. I was able to persuade airport officials to put us on the next flight in the small hours, which they did, although no doubt off-loading some unfortunate locals.

When we arrived at Tbilisi, by chance with a goodwill delegation from New Zealand, there was no official 'reception party' – given the change in flight – so we walked out of the airport and flagged down an unofficial taxi which took us belatedly to our hotel. There was visible consternation at the hotel, who demanded to know where we had been, as we had clearly been off the radar screen for some hours. Maybe as a result, surveillance in Tbilisi was particularly close, but never hostile. Interestingly our local *surveillant*, a young man in a plaid shirt, waited outside, but did not enter the ornately decorated Orthodox church where we listened to a magical chant from two choirs opposite each other. Our Georgian hosts were especially charming, in comparison with Moscow formality. It was immediately noticeable that, whereas in a Soviet Moscow restaurant one might look at the menu and then be told that the item was not available, in a Tbilisi restaurant, they would tell us not to bother with the menu, but just say what we wanted – which was usually provided with a smile. Georgia was very much the 'food and wine store' of Moscow, with daily flights carrying the ample Georgian supplies there.

In 2019 we revisited Georgia and Tbilisi privately, by then dramatically separated from the Soviet Union and Russia, and saw the many changes thirty-one years on – as I relate later.

Overall, I found the whole visit fascinating and deeply satisfying, having studied the language and having prepared for a Moscow posting seventeen years previously. However, when we were leaving Moscow with our diplomatic visas, the airport officials waved my wife almost through, and then said that there was a problem with my visa, requesting me to accompany them to an adjoining office. My wife in a loud voice explained to the officials and the other passengers that she was not leaving without her husband – at which the officials giggled and waved me through.

We experienced a similar incident many years later in the early Putin era, when relations were starting to worsen again. With a new BNFL CEO, who had never been to Russia before, we were held up for some time at Sheremetyevo Airport – the officials claimed that this was for 'visa checks' – while our CEO became increasingly irritated. Eventually I went into the appropriate office, explained in my 'St Petersburg' Russian to the uniformed official that we had a meeting with a minister in Moscow shortly – and if we were late we would tell the minister that he (quoting his badge number) was personally responsible. Just as in the Soviet days he giggled and waved us through. Games, whether old or new, do not change much!

After the breakdown of the Iron Curtain and the Soviet Empire the UK Government arranged a series of visits to formerly hostile states with the aim of building up relationships to address mutual concerns. Among a series of counterterrorism 'Roadshows' to states such as Poland, Hungary Czechoslovakia and Bulgaria, we also participated in an inter-Service visit to post-Soviet Moscow, including a visit to the infamous Lubyanka KGB headquarters and prison. Again, we were received with courtesy and civility. Again, I had no personal problems or embarrassments, although when the then MI5 Head Stella Rimington had official exchanges with her Russian opposite number Vladimir Kryuchkov, I apparently featured in an unpublished list of UK officials which he gave her as an 'Expert on Soviet Affairs' – whatever that means?

Variation: Post-Soviet 'Window' – Nuclear Environmental Clean-up

When I was preparing to leave the FCO in 1995 and looking around for possible future activities, my Russian was an immediate selling point, and I was taken on by BNFL as their 'Senior Adviser'. My initial task for BNFL was to write a report on their proposed nuclear environmental clean-up projects in NW Russia. After a couple of months, I presented them with the report, and they then asked me to implement it, subsequently with Norwegian, Swedish, French and Russian partners – as I have described.

When I initially applied for a Russian visa at the London Embassy, the reaction was cautious but not unhelpful. A 'specialist' diplomat interviewed me, and presumably checked out the project with Minatom (the Russian Ministry of Atomic Energy). I happened to know personally through music the Russian Ambassador in London, Yuriy Fokin, which may have helped. In any event, after the initial visits Minatom then sponsored me with a multiple-entry official Minatom atomic energy visa, which entitled me to go anywhere in Russia as often as I needed – a far cry from my post-*Operation Foot* seventeen-year visa inertia.

In the course of the developing projects I visited Russia several dozen times over the next few years, Moscow and St Petersburg, but often Murmansk in the Kola Peninsula and also Archangelsk on the White Sea, with the 'secret' nuclear sites such as Severodvinsk, Polyarny, Nerpa and Zvezdochka. As another indication of our cooperation we were also taken as guests to the first Soviet nuclear reactor, the Kurchatov, which was built in Moscow in 1946 – and which certainly for many years would have been a top-secret establishment totally out of bounds for foreigners. I travelled initially with BNFL colleagues David Wilkes, Richard Acton and the BNFL Moscow Representative Andrei Mooshtai, who all became good partners.

Later (as related earlier) we set up both an international consortium, the International Group (IG) consisting of UK, French and Swedish nuclear experts financially supported by the Norwegian Government, and also the British Nuclear Industry Group, (BNIG) representing BNFL, AEA Technology, NNC and Studsvik Rosyth. For both consortia I acted as the Russian-speaking 'Foreign Minister', negotiating with senior officials and making and interpreting the 'official' speeches and (many) toasts. At an official dinner, the first toast was given by the senior host for the visitors, the second by the senior visitor for the hosts, the third toast was always for the ladies present, there was usually a silent toast for the departed colleagues – and then the floor was open to everybody. We often learnt that a Russian nuclear colleague had died at a youngish age, for example late-fifties or early-sixties, and surmised that vodka rather than nuclear radiation may have been the cause.

In the harsh cities and nuclear sites of NW Russia and the Kola Peninsula we were warmly received by the local Russian colleagues. They were grateful for Western technical and financial support in tackling common Northern European environmental challenges to the Barents Sea posed by the waste from the Russian nuclear submarine and ice-breaker fleets. To clarify, we were helping with the nuclear waste from the propulsion reactors in the vessels, which was either left in the decommissioned vessels or stored on shore in inadequate containers, with the eventual aim of transporting it to the *Mayak* site beyond the Urals (of which more later), the Russian nuclear-waste treatment equivalent of Sellafield. However, in the meantime the Norwegians, especially, were concerned by the potential threat from this untreated nuclear waste to their extensive fishing industry in the region – hence their major financial support for our nuclear environmental projects.

The citizens of NW Russia and the Kola Peninsula also had a special welcome for the British, remembering with gratitude the wartime Murmansk convoys – which of course had cost many lives in the British ships sunk by the Germans. Although Stalin and the official Soviet attitude for many years had played down the importance of these convoys, the local people had not forgotten. Indeed, it was touching to experience after the collapse of the Soviet Union how British Murmansk convoy veterans, by now elderly, were invited to Russian National Day receptions at the Russian Embassy in London, when their sacrifice was officially recognised by successive Russian Ambassadors.

On the shores of the White Sea near Archangelsk we were also shown a monument to the British Captain Richard Chancellor, who in the sixteenth century had developed initial trade routes from Britain to Moscow via the Arctic, the direct land routes being impracticable at the time. In 1553, when Chancellor landed on the shore of the White Sea, he was invited to Moscow by the Tsar, Ivan the Terrible, and travelled some six hundred snowy miles by horse-drawn sledge to get there – he was impressed with Moscow, which he noted was bigger than London, and he was entertained to lavish dinners by the Tsar in his luxurious palace.

Life was certainly harsh during winter in the Kola Peninsula, with less than an hour of greyish 'daylight' and extremely low temperatures. I recall that after a visit to a nuclear submarine plant at $-40\,^{\circ}$C our Western team literally cuddled together for sheer warmth during the coach journey back. When we could finally chill out at the post-visit dinner with our Russian hosts, we all reached out for the ubiquitous vodka bottles as a source of warmth – although medical advice said the opposite – but needs must when recovering from $-40\,^{\circ}$C.

In December 1999 the Murmansk Shipping Company (MSCO) celebrated the 60th anniversary of the Russian nuclear ice-breaker fleet (Atomflot) at a big event in Murmansk. There were many speeches and toasts – including a compulsory one from me as the Russian speaker for our Scandinavian Industrial Group. Our Russian colleagues persuaded me to be photographed with Atomflot Director-General Vyacheslav Ruksha, and with the Commander of the Russian Northern Fleet Admiral Vyacheslav Popov, which would have been unlikely in the old Soviet days.

We worked closely with the Norwegian and Swedish Government Agencies, especially the Norwegian Foreign Ministry. Our Industrial Group used the Norwegian Consulate (which also served as the Swedish Deputy Consulate – the UK not being represented there) in Murmansk as our convenient and hospitable 'diplomatic' working base.

The Norwegian environmental Bellona Foundation were also useful collaborators. In the early 'free for all' days following the collapse of the Soviet Union, they had obtained access to several of the 'secret' nuclear sites in NW Russia, and had published their findings – which gave us all useful background information for our environmental projects. While Bellona were clearly opposed to nuclear environmental pollution from the NW Russia sites, and potentially from Sellafield, they were not anti-nuclear as such. Years later a Bellona colleague, Nils Bøhmer, approached me about the possibility of reprocessing used fuel from the Norwegian research reactor at Halden, and we jointly visited the AREVA reprocessing plant at La Hague.

With our Scandinavian Industrial Group, we also visited the 'secret city' *Mayak* (literally *'lighthouse'*), the huge Russian equivalent of the Sellafield reprocessing and waste-management site, situated near Chelyabinsk beyond the Urals in Western Siberia. As a 'distinguished' visiting delegation we were received with great hospitality, including a lavish lunch with, as usual, many mandatory toasts.

I had the pleasure of sitting next to a stolid-looking but very alert Russian nuclear scientist, who displayed his very Russian love of culture by seeking my views on contemporary British authors – would such a position be reversed in a reciprocal visit to the UK? At the same time, a Norwegian diplomat whispered in my ear that, to her amazement, my neighbour had drunk fifteen (literally) vodkas during the lunch and many toasts, before going back to work. (This may have had a connection with why Chernobyl happened, when a low-temperature experiment was not closed-down sufficiently promptly – at Sellafield, a single beer on duty would be a sackable offence). That evening over dinner with the *Mayak* senior management we collected from our Western team modest personal donations to enable a local student to be sent on an essential course to St Petersburg. The father, a *Mayak* worker, was summoned to join us and unsurprisingly looked worried when confronted with his bosses and us foreigners. When we explained about the collection to enable his son's studies, he was reduced to tears – as were some of us…

Given my medical wife, I was always told to be careful about potential nuclear radiation in the Russian sites. Indeed, we once saw a dog running out of a nuclear-waste enclosure – needless to say, we did not stroke it. However, in *Mayak* for example, despite the obvious signs of dilapidation around the site, the actual radiation level recorded by our Scandinavian nuclear technicians was lower than that to which we had been subjected to at 30,000 feet on the Lufthansa flight there.

En route to *Mayak* we were able to visit historic Ekaterinburg, formerly Sverdlovsk, named after Yakov Sverdlov, who coordinated the execution of the Tsar and family, although this has been later disputed. His statue there, with its pointing finger, is locally reputed to be indicating the royal hiding place. One of the great pleasures of our Russian nuclear work was the ability to visit historic sites, museums, art galleries and palaces in many cities, and to do this with our local friends and gain their perspectives on the past, present and future. Once, after an event in St Petersburg, we were all sitting together in a very Russian restaurant, when our Russian friends started toasting Leningrad, not to reject the restoration of the name St Petersburg, but to remember the heroism of Leningrad during the Second World War.

We were well supported by the British Embassy in Moscow, by successive Ambassadors Andrew Wood and Rod Lyne, and their helpful scientific and economic staff. They commented that we would probably have better direct access to Russian Ministers, Governors and Admirals than the Embassy, which would be obliged to go through the various foreign-relations departments of the ministries – which indeed turned out to be the case. As well as the Atomic Energy Ministry, we also visited the Foreign and Defence Ministries, and the Duma (Parliament) to discuss nuclear clean-up issues with the relevant Russian MPs.

In 1998 we were most grateful to HRH The Duke of Kent who, during a St Petersburg World Monument Fund (WMF) visit, kindly agreed to speak at a BNFL event. We hired the Vladimir Palace, once the home of the Duke's great-grandfather the Grand Duke Vladimir, and now the 'Home of Scientists', a magnificent building on the banks of the Neva. The overall cost of hiring the Palace for the day, including food and drink, was probably less than the cost of a bedroom at a smart St Petersburg hotel. All the local VIPs, Governors, Ministers and Admirals turned up, delighted to meet a direct royal descendant of their Romanov imperial heritage (his grandmother was the first cousin of the last Tsar Nicholas II). The Palace staff were also delighted, asking the Duke to pose for a photograph at the desk of his great-grandfather, and pointing out a portrait of the Duke's maternal grandmother as a little girl. Some years later the Duke, also a sincere music lover, kindly agreed to become a committed Patron of our UK Mendelssohn Foundation, as I shall relate.

The night before the nuclear event in the Vladimir Palace, HRH and his son George, the Earl of St Andrew's, kindly joined the whole BNFL team for dinner at a local St Petersburg restaurant. The Duke's UK security team had told us beforehand that we must find a restaurant that had no connection with the Russian *mafia*. When we consulted our Russian colleagues, they laughed and said that probably no such restaurant existed – and if it did, it would be likely to be attacked by the *mafia*. So, we would all be much safer in a restaurant with *mafia* protection. In any event we all enjoyed a very pleasant and peaceful evening.

We were privileged to join the Duke's visit to some of the historic sites, such as the Peterhof, Tsarskoye Selo, and of course the magnificent Hermitage Museum, with its wonderful collection of paintings by the great masters – I was particularly fond of the Dutch Golden Age collection, including Rubens and Rembrandt. I had visited the Hermitage in the Leningrad/Soviet days as related, and later one of the pleasures of nuclear business, when flying from Murmansk back to London via St Petersburg, was to fit in yet another visit to the Hermitage while transiting the city.

My Russian colleagues later told me that I must have met Vladimir Putin in the St Petersburg administration during the early stages of negotiating this VIP visit, but I cannot recall it. Perhaps he forgot to tell me that he would soon be President of Russia…

We also participated in Russo-British Chamber of Commerce meetings, under its Patron HRH Prince Michael of Kent, who with his beard looked even more 'Romanov Tsarist' than his elder brother The Duke of Kent. Meetings in places like Nizhny Novgorod, with its sixteenth-century Kremlin and views over the busy Volga, and Samara, as well as Ekaterinburg and St Petersburg, gave us further insights into Russian life outside Moscow.

Relations with Russian Ministers and their senior officials in Moscow also developed positively. When the submarine *Kursk* sank in the Barents Sea in 2000 – a great personal tragedy for many of our Russian friends in the Kola Peninsula/Murmansk area – after the initial anti-Western accusations, e.g. that a US or UK submarine exercising nearby might have rammed it, the nature and repercussions of the tragedy struck home to the Russians. I recall being in the Minatom (Ministry of Atomic Energy) headquarters in Moscow when senior Russian nuclear officials asked me to pass on requests for advice on nuclear leakage from a sunken nuclear submarine. I was able to put them in direct contact with one of our British specialists in the BNIG nuclear consortium – and our Russian friends were personally visibly grateful, notwithstanding the wider politically motivated anti-Western suspicions.

We recognised the importance to senior Russians of not losing face in front of their officials. From time to time Western colleagues, especially the Americans, would lecture a Russian Minister in public, nearly always producing a negative reaction. We preferred to invite the Minister to dinner, usually a fairly liquid one, the night before, and present the hard facts of our arguments. He would not necessarily agree with them then, but often the next morning he would present them to his somewhat surprised officials as his own ideas.

Our Russian friends told us that they were disappointed when a new British Foreign Secretary (I forget which one) first met his Russian counterpart for a breakfast meeting at Moscow Airport, rather than getting to know each other personally beforehand over a convivial dinner the night before.

I developed a good relationship with the Minatom Deputy Minister and State Secretary, Valeriy Lebedev, who discovered that we had been born within two days of each other during the Second World War, and concluded that 'Fate' (a very Russian concept) had brought us together. He explained that, if twenty years previously he as a top Soviet nuclear expert had developed a friendship with a former Western diplomat, he would probably have been in serious trouble. Yet here we were, all working together to tackle a common European environmental challenge. To celebrate our joint sixtieth birthdays in 2001 he organised a birthday dinner with wives at the renowned 'Tsarskaya Okhota' (Tsar's Hunt) restaurant outside Moscow, with appropriate speeches and toasts.

Valeriy Lebedev also sent me a very warm personal letter (translation).

Dear Desmond, With all my soul I congratulate you on your 60th birthday. We in Russia greatly value your contribution to our common work, which makes the world a safer place, environmentally cleaner and more stable. I hope that this work will continue successfully. I am also taking this opportunity to send you congratulations from all your Russian colleagues. We all think with great pleasure of our meetings with you – a true partner, an interesting person and a wise interlocutor. I wish you robust health, success in your difficult work, and a lively spirit for the next 60 years.

With best personal wishes, V. A. Lebedev

P.S. I thank you for your congratulations and I look forward to our next personal meeting soon.

Again – a long way from *Operation Foot*.

Incidentally, in my ten years working in Russia for BNFL, there was only one 'provocative' reference to my FCO past. At a formal conference

25. At Sarajevo Airport by RAF Hercules, 1990

26. 'Latino' music session with the locals in Quito at 2,850m in the Andes, 1993

27. Batting in Sri Lanka, 1995

28. HM Queen Elizabeth II awarding the 'Companion of the Distinguished Order of St Michael and St George' – CMG. London, 1996

Claygate cricketer honoured by club and country!

Text book stuff. Des Cecil CMG pulls for four in Sri Lanka.

THERE were joyous New Year celebrations at Claygate Cricket Club last week as the players toasted the success of their club captain **Des Cecil**, who was among those recognised in the New Year's Honours List, writes Tim Cotton.

Although Mr Cecil, 54, of Palace Road, East Molesey, had his most successful season ever with the bat last year topping 500 runs and he led Claygate with distinction on their tour to Sri Lanka 11 months ago, he was not honoured for his cricketing prowess.

Des was appointed to be a Companion of the Order of St Michael and St George (CMG) for his services to the diplomatic service. He recently retired after a distinguished career in the Foreign Office, at the UN Mission in Geneva and on Her Majesty's Service in Vienna and Bonn.

Mr Cecil, who is married to Ruth, a volunteer at the Princess Alice Hospice, Esher, and has three sons and a daughter, has been a keen member of Claygate Cricket Club for 15 years and told the News & Mail last week that being asked to captain his club a year ago was almost as big a thrill as receiving his New Year Honour.

All three of his sons have played for Claygate and Des, who has lived in Molesey for the past five years after spending 20 years in Esher, is looking forward to the forthcoming season in which he hopes to surpass his record runs tally of 1995.

29. *Esher News & Mail* – 'Claygate cricketer honoured by club and country!' January 1996

30. Dedication of new Mendelssohn statue at Leipzig Gewandhaus. Kurt Masur with DC, 1997

31. Athenæum Wine Committee trip to Burgundy. L to R: DC, Ken Warren, Ralph French, Brian Gilmore. 1997

32. 60th Anniversary of Russian nuclear ice-breaker fleet (Atomflot). L to R: Commander of the Russian Northern Fleet Admiral Vyacheslav Popov, Atomflot Director-General Vyacheslav Rushka, DC. Murmansk, 3 December 1999

33. Felix Mendelssohn Bartholdy Foundation in front of Mendelssohn-Haus Leipzig. L to R: Volker Stiehler, Kurt Masur, Jürgen Ernst, Siegfried Herr, DC. 1999

34. Playing music with Leslie Howard, *c.* 1995

35. Gypsy music with Martin Neary, Athenæum Ball, 1997

36. Memorial to Captain Richard Chancellor (1553) on the shore of the White Sea, Archangelsk, 2000

Уважаемый г-н Десмонд!

От всей души поздравляю Вас с 60-летием!
Мы в России очень ценим Ваш вклад в нашу совместную
работу, которая делает мир более безопасным,
экологически чистым и предсказуемым. Надеюсь, что
эта работа будет успешно продолжена.
Пользуясь случаем, передаю Вам поздравления от
Ваших российских коллег. Все мы с огромным
удовольствием вспоминаем встречи с Вами – надежным
партнером, интересным человеком и остроумным
собеседником. Желаю Вам крепкого здоровья, успехов в
Вашей трудной работе, бодрости духа на следующие 60
лет.

С наилучшими пожеланиями,

В.А.Лебедев

P.S. Я благодарю Вас за Ваши поздравления и надеюсь
на скорую личную встречу.

37. Russian State Secretary and Deputy
Minister of Atomic Energy Valeriy
Lebedev's personal congratulations
on DC's 60th birthday (translation
on page 152), October 2001

38. With Gio Batta Morassi and
his 1974 violin, Cremona, 2004

39. With Mstislav Rostropovich and the 1974 Morassi violin, Cremona, 2004

40. Swiss mountain accident 1 – Strapped up by helicopter crew. Col du Pillon, July 2006

41. Swiss mountain accident 2 – Suspended from helicopter *en route* for hospital operation. Col du Pillon, July 2006

42. Menuhin Museum Curator Dr Rolf Steiger interview. 'Der Brite Desmond Cecil CMG als International Representative des Festivals'. *'Anzeiger von Saanen'*. August 2011

Der Brite Desmond Cecil CMG als «international Representative» des Festivals

43. Family, including all children, grandchildren and daughters-in-law. L to R: Sarah, Nicholas, Jo, Thomas, Alison, Andrew (top); Jemima, Tobias, Christopher, Matthew, DC, Tara, Christine, Ruth, Alexandre (bottom). East Molesey, 2012

44. Distinguished Friend of Oxford University Award. Procession to Sheldonian Theatre. L to R: Vice-Chancellor Andrew Hamilton, DC, John Poynter, Ivor Agyeman-Duah, Catherine Roe, Rosalind Hedley-Miller, Public Orator Richard Jenkyns, Nicola Ralston, Louisa Service. September 2012

45. Ruth's 70th birthday dinner at the Oxo Tower. L to R: Nicholas, Thomas, DC, Andrew, Ruth, Sarah. 2013

46. 1724 'Cecil' Stradivari violin. Photo by Hiroko Umezawa

47. Bust of 'Nefertiti' (copy) with Ruth and DC. James-Simon-Galerie, Berlin, 2019

48. Chalet 'Les Ruisselets' in winter, Les Diablerets, 2014

dinner in St Petersburg a well-vodked Russian referred to me as a foreign subversive, and was immediately and publicly rebutted by a senior Russian naval officer who corrected this to 'deputy minister' – the equivalent in Russian to a UK 'under-secretary'.

When in 2000 the UK Parliament Select Committee on Foreign Affairs issued a 'Report on Relations with the Russian Federation',* I was among the UK industry representatives invited to give evidence on personal experiences of dealings with Russia and the Russians.

What did become noticeable however, round about 2003–2004, no doubt connected with Putin's presidency, was a diminishing Russian enthusiasm for Western involvement in the NW Russia nuclear projects. At the same time, we noticed increasing problems with visas, although not for me personally, airport delays and problems with site access. Many of the joint projects were simply blocked. This was a negative environmental development after the openness of the 1990s, when we all started to work together for common objectives, and of course such cooperation has continued to decline rather more dramatically in recent times.

Violence was never far away – fortunately never for us personally. However, the Russian local representative of another Western nuclear company, whom we knew, disappeared one day. We subsequently understood that he had been dabbling in the *mafia* black market, and that something had gone wrong. His frozen body was discovered in the snow a week later.

Our Russian friends told us privately at the time, always when they were abroad – never in Russia – that 'they', i.e. the FSB/ex-KGB, were warning their compatriots, 'We were weak, but we are now becoming strong again.'

*

Recently at an international nuclear dinner, I was approached by a former diplomat at the British Embassy in Moscow who was now working on

---

* https://publications.parliament.uk/pa/cm199900/cmselect/cmfaff/101/10103.htm

international environmental funding. We had not seen each other for years, but he just wanted to say to me that the Russian nuclear clean-up work which we had initiated with our international partners more than twenty years ago was continuing to bear fruit – despite the obvious current political difficulties. He went on to say that the relevant officials, international funders and environmentalists, especially the Russians, were grateful for our early work, which had prepared the way for future progress.

In return, I was grateful that he had taken the trouble to tell me this.

Theme: Music

Much as the example of Yehudi Menuhin first inspired me to study the Russian language, Russian culture and especially its music and musicians have been a lifelong inspiration to me. In my youth many great violinists were of Russian-Jewish extraction, often with family ties to Odessa – which my wife and I visited recently, staying next to the 'David Oistrakh Suite' in the Londonskaya Hotel.

As described earlier, while awaiting a Moscow diplomatic posting in 1971, I liaised with the then British Ambassador, Duncan Wilson, father of 'cellist Elizabeth Wilson and father-in-law of pianist Radu Lupu, about musicians with whom I might play in Moscow. However, because of *Operation Foot* this came to nothing at the time.

In 1998 I visited in Moscow's Arbat quarter the home of the International Music Charity 'New Names', with its formidable founder lady Ivetta Voronova, which did excellent work in promoting the careers of young musicians. With the help and support (such as visas, travel and accommodation) of Ambassador Andrew Wood in Moscow, Ambassador Yuriy Fokin in London and the Russo-British Chamber of Commerce, we were able to bring a group of outstanding young musicians to the UK for concerts in the Athenæum Club (see later) and Wellington College.

Olga Adamishina, wife of a former Ambassador to London and a good personal friend, persuaded me to become a Trustee of her 'Russian Arts Help' Charity in Moscow, which likewise has done excellent work over the years in supporting young Russian artists and musicians. Rossotrudnichestvo, the Russian cultural office in Kensington, regularly puts on interesting music and arts events, often with young Russians, and of course vodka. These events continue, despite increasing UK/Russia political tensions.

I only played the violin once in Russia, at a BNFL VIP ministerial reception, when an excellent string quartet from the Tchaikovsky Academy was performing. When the musicians were told that I was a violinist, the first violin lady 'dragged' me to her chair and thrust her violin into my hand. Normally I make it a firm rule never to touch alcohol before playing in public – in this case not possible because of the various vodka toasts in which I had been obliged to join. The music fortunately in front of me was a Mozart *Divertimento*, with which I was reasonably familiar, so I managed to get through it without any serious mishaps.

I have worked on cultural matters with successive Russian Ambassadors in London, Yuriy Fokin, Grigoriy Karasin (as related, whom I first met in Moscow on diplomatic business in 1988), Yury Fedotov, and most recently Aleksander Yakovenko. They have generously provided their Residence for concerts by our musicians which we have arranged – for example, in partnership with the London Philharmonic Orchestra and its Russian-born Chief Conductor Vladimir Jurowski, and with other young UK/Russia musicians.

Despite worsening political relations between Russia, the UK and the West generally – because of criminal poisonings, military incursions, and all the other recent such developments – the informal advice from the British Council and the FCO is to keep the cultural dialogue and channels open. We do what we can to follow this advice, given a love of Russian culture.

Let us hope that relations will improve again one day.

Back in the UK – Musical Developments

Theme: UK Music and Arts Charity Support

M Y DEEPLY REWARDING *pro bono* PARTNERSHIPS WITH FOREIGN arts charities and organisations such as the Leipzig Felix-Mendelssohn-Bartholdy-Foundation, its UK partner the UK Friends of the Felix-Mendelssohn-Bartholdy-Foundation, the Gstaad Menuhin Festival & Academy, and the Moscow Russian Arts Help Charity are described in the earlier chapters on Germany, Switzerland and Russia.

Through my Australian pianist friend Leslie Howard (see below), in 1996 I joined the Council of the Royal Philharmonic Society (RPS), which has done outstanding work since its foundation in 1813, supporting composers such as Beethoven, Mendelssohn and Dvořák in the nine-teenth century, continuing this work into the twentieth and twenty-first centuries supporting young musicians and new compositions. Like most arts organisations, it looks for outside funding to enhance its activities, through generous sponsors, and through the initiative in 2002 of the then-Chairman Tony Fell to sell to the British Library the historically rich RPS archives covering two centuries of UK musical activity. My position on the Council was given the venerable title 'Honorary Co-Treasurer', also 'Chair of the Sponsorship Committee'. I was able to help by finding sponsors for some of the annual RPS Awards, and by negotiating useful discounts for RPS members with shops and concert promoters. I stood down from the Council for personal reasons in 2005, although remained an RPS member, recognising its valuable work for the musical world.

Fellow RPS Council member and amateur horn-player Laurie Watt introduced me to the London Philharmonic Orchestra (LPO), and in 2005 I was appointed to its Trust – later Board and Council. My Leipzig friend Kurt Masur, as related, was Chief Conductor at the time, and shortly afterwards he was replaced by the brilliant young Russian-born, Berlin-based, rising star Vladimir Jurowski. The combination of Masur's 'German' discipline and Jurowski's 'Russian' inspiration, astutely managed by the orchestra's quiet but effective CEO Tim Walker, served to make the LPO one of the best orchestras, if not the best, in London – and indeed one of the best in the world. It is also a very friendly orchestra, as several 'defectors' to the LPO from other top London orchestras observed. Before the concerts and during the intervals many of the players came to the 'Beecham Bar' (named in recognition of the LPO Founder in 1932) in London's Royal Festival Hall to chat with the orchestra's supporters and potential supporters. This created a happy spirit of partnership, which benefitted the orchestra both socially and financially – the latter has become even more important in these days of cuts in public funding for the arts.

A small but dedicated LPO administrative team led by CEO and Artistic Director Tim Walker, with General Manager David Burke (who subsequently succeeded Tim Walker as CEO), Development Director Nick Jackman and his successor Laura Willis, coordinated the overall management and the essential fund-raising work. While I am by no means one of the wealthier supporters, I was able to provide useful introductions to future sponsors. Through my diplomatic contacts I was also able to negotiate British ambassadorial receptions when we accompanied the LPO on tour, for example to Vienna, Beijing, Stockholm and Mexico City. In Beijing we were the first foreign orchestra to play at the new 'National Centre for the Performing Arts' for the opening of the 2008 Olympics. We offered our Chinese hosts a choice between our star young (36) Principal Conductor Vladimir Jurowski or his eminent (81) predecessor Kurt Masur – unsurprisingly, the Chinese with their respect for age elected for Masur. Also, I regularly helped to resolve numerous international visa problems, for example Russian, Chinese, Korean, often at the last minute. Many of the players, who knew of my youthful experiences as a professional oboist/ violinist with the associated challenges, became good friends, especially violinists Geoff Lynn, Martin Höhmann, Tom Eisner, Pieter Schoemann and double bass Kevin Rundell.

Through my diplomatic contacts, I was able to arrange LPO and charity musical events in London, especially at the German and Russian Embassies. The German and Russian Ambassadors were happy to host such events, for example with Kurt Masur talking about Mendelssohn with performances by young musicians from London and Leipzig, or Vladimir Jurowski at the piano performing chamber music with LPO musicians. We were also able to arrange for Jurowski to speak at the German Ambassador's Residence about forthcoming LPO major productions of Beethoven's *Fidelio* and Wagner's *Die Walküre*, accompanied by performances from the star opera singers. As well as furthering international musical cooperation, they provided valuable events, hosted by the Embassies, for the LPO to invite their sponsors and financial supporters to, as a much appreciated thank-you for their loyalty over the years.

The LPO was the first major London orchestra to merge its Trust and its Player Board, following a serious fraud problem with a former Finance Director, when the Player directors realised that they needed external skills. At a Player AGM, despite some concerns mainly from the brass section, the Players voted for the merger, giving the Non-Player directors a majority on the Board for the first time, although with the clear understanding that they would not 'meddle' unduly with artistic matters, which remained the preserve of the Players. Fortunately, the generally excellent relations between players and supporters, which continue to this day, greatly facilitated the merger. The Board is chaired by Victoria Robey, with the players represented by the orchestra's President, principal piccolo Stewart McIlwham, now succeeded by first violin Martin Höhmann – all working harmoniously together for the overall benefit of the orchestra.

For years I had been aware of the excellent musical work of the Park Lane Group (PLG). For more than sixty years, under the dedicated leadership of ex-Royal Opera House violinist John Woolf, it has supported young musicians (PLG Young Artists) – both performers and composers. John and I had chatted over the years, and in 2015 he invited me to join the PLG Advisory Council. While the actual musical programmes are coordinated by the PLG Artistic Committee, I'm able to provide 'external' ideas and support, and very much appreciate the friendship with John, whose musical memories go back for well over half a century.

The PLG regularly arranges concerts at Central London churches, such as St James's Piccadilly, St Martin-in-the-Fields or St Margaret's Westminster, to give young artists initial publicity in their careers – which is much appreciated, as this is often a difficult time for them. We always try to put on enterprising programmes, whether with living or past composers. A current PLG project (although under threat from Coronavirus) is the farewell concert at the Queen Elizabeth Hall in October 2020 for Tasmin Little, the outstanding British violinist – who also studied at the Yehudi Menuhin School, of which she has just been appointed Co-President with Daniel Barenboim. For this final concert before her retirement from the concert platform we are organising a programme of only women composers, such as Clara Schumann, Amy Beach, Ethel Smyth and Roxanna Panufnik, all distinguished in their different ways – but not regularly performed in standard concerts. This concert is already attracting public, media and sponsorship – and of course any profits will be recycled into much-needed support for future PLG Young Artists. We recently arranged a PLG fund-raising concert at the Riverside House home of PLG Vice-President Camilla Panufnik, widow of Polish composer Andrzej Panufnik and mother of British composer Roxanna Panufnik, also an Athenæum member. Over the nearly sixty years under John Woolf's leadership, the PLG has supported the initial careers of some 1,600 PLG Young Artists, many of whom have since become household names.

Other UK arts organisations with which I did short-term *pro bono* work included the Jupiter Orchestra, Voices for Hospices and the Norbert Brainin Foundation, all of which went their separate ways. In 2017 I talked with Marios Papadopoulos, the enterprising pianist and conductor of Cypriot origin, who with his wife Anthi had founded and then managed the Oxford Philharmonic Orchestra (formerly Oxford Philharmonia) for twenty years. This was the 'professional' orchestra of Oxford, bringing in many first-rate players from the London orchestras, with stars such as Maxim Vengerov, András Schiff and Anne-Sophie Mutter as soloists. Marios would conduct many of the concerts himself, often directing concertos from the piano, interspersed with distinguished visitors such as Valery Gergiev. In addition to the inevitable financial challenges which all professional orchestras have, the OP's were exacerbated by the lack of Arts Council funding, and the small box-office returns from the Oxford 'concert hall' – the historic Sheldonian Theatre, which only seats about 800 people. With laudable initiative, Marios gathered together a group of wealthy and influential supporters, who worked to fill the financial gaps. Marios invited me to join his Trust as a *de facto* director, which I did out of admiration for Marios's enterprise and for the love of Oxford, my hometown. Initially I was able to provide practical advice to his team on orchestral matters and fund-raising, although I subsequently stood down from the Trust, albeit reluctantly, because of other personal demands.

A colleague from the nuclear world, Tony Cleaver, encouraged me to join the Worshipful Company of Musicians, of which he was Master at the time, and I recently progressed to become a Liveryman. The Company does excellent work supporting musicians of all ages, but especially young-sters at the beginning of their careers, and I look forward to becoming more involved with their charitable work.

The chapter on Germany describes the work with the Leipzig Felix-Mendelssohn-Bartholdy-Stiftung and the establishment of its UK partner, the UK-registered charity 'UK Friends of the Felix-Mendelssohn-Bartholdy-Foundation' (UKFFMBF). As always, even modest funds raised by charities are of immense value to largely impecunious young musicians starting out on an uncertain career. However, we also tried to give the young musicians more than just money – for example, the seven successive years, in which we have facilitated young British musicians from the London Guildhall School of Music & Drama (GSMD) participating in Leipzig master-classes with the great tenor Peter Schreier has given them direct personal experience of the German language and culture as well as a deep understanding of German nineteenth century *Lieder*.

With our UKFFMBF fellow Trustees, friends and neighbours Tom and Megan Tress, themselves the parents of talented young professional musicians, we regularly arrange fund-raising concerts with young musicians – some of whom we have supported, like the Guildhall/Leipzig students, and to whom we always insist on paying a reasonable fee – in our own homes. We are both able to seat 40–50 people for 'house concerts' in our 'music rooms' (borrowing extra chairs from the local church) and have built up a loyal and generous list of supporters. In addition, the internationally acclaimed Maggini Quartet has regularly given fund-raising concerts for us, either in local churches or in the nearby historic eighteenth century Hampton Course House. We invite our audiences, rather than to buy tickets, to make 'suggested donations' which enables us to claim Gift Aid, and we always include an informal supper (at our expense) with the musicians after the concerts.

With the accumulated proceeds we have been able to support young musicians with initiatives around the country, setting up annual 'Mendelssohn Awards' with the Royal Welsh College of Music & Drama in Cardiff and the Royal Northern College of Music in Manchester – always relatively modest amounts, but of great value to young musicians starting out on their careers.

We have supported such educational projects for young children as the Multi-Story Orchestra in a Peckham carpark, the Arensky Orchestra in Merton and the Cambridge Micro-Opera. In London we have supported young musicians in 'Foyle's Future Firsts' at the Southbank Centre, the LPO 'Junior Artists and Composers', the GSMD's 'Rediscovering Mendelssohn', and the music and poetry 'Odyssey Project' about WWI. Further afield we have worked with the Vale of Glamorgan Festival, commissioning works from contemporary composers, with young musicians at the Sevenoaks International Chamber-Music Festival and with the Consone Quartet, bringing classical music to new audiences in Bolivia and helping a young British composer in Brazil. We also regularly help the 'mentoring' of young musicians, for example with the Dante and Maggini Quartets, and with the Chilingirian Quartet in 'Mendelssohn on Mull', the island which of course Mendelssohn himself once visited.

We all feel strongly that as we have gained so much pleasure from music throughout our lives it is both a duty and a privilege to give something back to music by helping young musicians – who need all the help that they can get.

Theme: Chamber Music

In 1972, while I was awaiting a diplomatic posting to Moscow (which turned out to be Bonn), I played a few sonatas with a London-based Italian pianist, Noretta Conci, herself a pupil of the great Arturo Michelangeli. She mentioned that she was giving lessons to a 'brash young Australian' who had just arrived in the country and suggested that I play with him. This turned out to be Leslie Howard, a distinguished solo pianist, and also a great Liszt scholar, who has made the biggest solo recording (ninety-nine Liszt CDs with Hyperion Records) of all time – which earned him a place in the *Guinness Book of Records*. Leslie and I met in a Commonwealth hostel near Cricklewood, and I recall that the first piece that we ever played together was the César Franck Sonata. He gave Ruth and me most helpful practical advice some forty years ago, when we bought an externally faded but fine-sounding second-hand Steinway 1924 Model O grand piano, which accompanied us to Vienna and back to the UK. We became firm family friends, meeting very regularly to play sonatas, listening to Wagner operas including the complete Ring cycle, interspersed with playing snooker in our cellar or Five-Hundred (an Australian bastard offshoot of Whist) with his then-partner Douglas Copeland, who sadly died in 1989. Years later Leslie became the godfather of our granddaughter Jemima.

Over the years Leslie and I have played together most of the violin and piano repertoire from Bach to Bartók, both privately and in local concerts, and I have learnt an immense amount musically from him. While no longer 'young' – in April 2018 we celebrated his seventieth birthday with many friends at our house – I am pleased to say that he still retains a little of Noretta's 'brash' description. We all must grow up but let us hope not completely.

While at Oxford I was fortunate to play not only much chamber music with excellent musicians, but also concerts with chamber orchestras, often leading from the first violin desk. In the Oxford University Orchestra my fellow oboist was Penny Warren, who married the distinguished conductor/organist Martin Neary, later at Winchester Cathedral and, controversially, Westminster Abbey – a well-publicised 'church versus music' dispute with the Dean of Westminster, which resulted in Martin losing his job there, many thought unjustly. Martin invited me to lead a couple of his professional orchestras in local concerts, and we often still play violin and piano duets.

Penny's younger sister Amanda, a fine pianist and later opera librettist/translator together with her then-husband Anthony Holden – distinguished journalist and author, subsequent poker grandee and good friend – was another regular sonata partner over the years. Through the Holdens I met Stephen Walsh and his wife Mary. Stephen was then music critic of the *Observer*, and we played sonatas and chess – the latter with great passion. He then moved to become Professor of Music at Cardiff, and erudite biographer of Stravinsky and others.

Through the Nearys, when Martin was at Winchester, we met the renowned arts/music photographer Clive Barda and his wife Rozzie, who have been close friends over the years. Through them we have also met various serious musicians, amateur and professional – including David Whelton, the then Chief Executive of the Philharmonia Orchestra, who became a good friend and pianist with whom I have the pleasure of playing music, and Philippe and Martina Monnet, the French/Dutch makers of inspirational films about music.

Ruth's 'Aunt' (cousin of her mother) Emmie Hess was an accomplished 'cellist and chamber musician. We often played quartets together, including with the renowned solo violinist Maria Lidka – a fellow Rostal pupil. Emmie had also commissioned a quartet of instruments from the top Cremonese maker, Gio Batta Morassi, and she very kindly gave me one of his lovely violins – see later. Apart from Emmie, the remarkable three other Hess sisters were: Dorothy, a renowned piano teacher; Steffi, a viola player whose Lake District home provided post-war hospitality for Peter Schidlof the distinguished viola player, a member of the Amadeus Quartet for many years; and Alice, a composer from Southwold.

In the Foreign & Commonwealth Office we established a resident string quartet. John Boyd, later Ambassador in Tokyo, played first violin – he would not claim to be the best player, but as he was the most senior of us as FCO Chief Clerk and with a gentle personality, we were all happy to 'defer' to him. Michael Arthur, a future Ambassador in Berlin, played second violin, and Richard Manning, a senior DFID official and local musical friend, the 'cello. I was content to play viola *à la Mozart*.

Richard Coulson, the organist at the local churches in Esher, Christ Church and sixteenth century St George's, was an excellent musician and pianist. We often performed sonatas, Bach and Händel obviously, but also later classics and romantics, in the local churches and school to support local causes. I recall one fascinating evening in 1971 when we participated in a 'words and music' performance at a friend's flat in Wandsworth. Timothy West and Prunella Scales, already very well-known in the theatre world, treated us to *A Short Battle of the Sexes* and our Imber Park Road acting neighbours John Abineri and Hilary Bamford gave us *The Waste*

Land. Richard and I contributed with a Bach sonata, and Grieg's vibrant second sonata for violin and piano. It was a fine evening, with the words and the music working together in real partnership.

Ruth worked in a hospice charity with Sheila Hurton, an excellent pianist with whom I played many sonatas and charity performances at the nearby hospice. The local Kingston & District Chamber Music Society (KDCMS) contains some good professional and some remarkable amateur chamber musicians, with whom I had much joy in playing over the years. These included the 'cellist Sylvia Palmer, with whom I was privileged to lead a complete cycle of the Beethoven late quartets – one of the most daunting and satisfying of all chamber music challenges. Sheila and Sylvia are no longer with us, but the happy musical memories remain strong.

John Wilson, a world-leading authority on autographs and historical documents, and a close Athenæum friend, is a dedicated pianist and harpsichordist, with whom I enjoy playing 'lollipops' and sonatas. We meet regularly in our home in East Molesey and his home in Cheltenham – where he and his wife Gina were energetic supporters of the Festival, often providing accommodation in their house for the performers. They also stayed with us in our Swiss chalet, where our violin and piano contributions would ring across the valley. Every year John and I perform the carols, supplemented with Bach and 'lollipops', for the Athenæum annual Christmas lunch – the only time (apart from the 'vodka incident' in Russia which I have related), when I would mix violin playing and alcohol. We assume that the critical judgement of the lunch audience might have been lessened by their enjoyment of Christmas hospitality. In April 2018 I was privileged to play Elgar and Mozart with John in the Cheltenham Pittville Pump Room, in tribute to his greatly missed late wife Gina.

A neighbour, Julian Callow, organist at the nearby early nineteenth, but originating in the fifteenth, century St. Peter's Church, a successful economist by profession and a dedicated musician, often invites me to play with him serious music in his church and 'lollipops' at street parties – which I do with pleasure.

An especial friend from KDCMS is Lawrence Caun, a barrister and part-time judge by profession, a lover of horse-racing, but at the same time an extraordinarily fine chamber music pianist. He can sight-read anything, often better than many professionals. With 'cellists Julian Ogilvie, Richard Manning, Michael Southgate and Rosalind Laher, and violist Liz Hart, all of them fine and inspiring musicians, we work on the piano trio and piano quartet repertoire. Indeed, having played all the standard works, such as Mozart, Beethoven, Schubert, Mendelssohn, Schumann, Brahms, Tchaikovsky, Dvořák, Bruch, Fauré, Strauss, Ravel, Elgar and Walton, we are now exploring Chausson, Bliss, Bax, Arensky, Rimsky-Korsakov, Taneyev, Enescu, Beach, Clarke, Huber, Rachmaninov, Turina, Lekeu and Bridge – among many other fascinating compositions.

From time to time we also assembled small chamber orchestras for charity concerts in local churches, and I was happy to revive my earlier practice of directing from the first violin desk. As I have said, often the ensemble is better if we all listen to each other 'internally', rather than try to follow an 'external' conductor.

More recently I was invited to play in a local piano quintet with the then Head of Music at the Royal Opera House, David Syrus, who coached the musicians at the ROH and at times stood in for Antonio Pappano and other stars, conducting the opera performances himself – also a very sensitive professional pianist and accompanist. For various reasons the quintet slowly faded, but David and I replaced it with regular violin and piano sonata sessions. We have since worked through much of the literature, often playing half-a-dozen major sonatas – enough for two full concerts – in the course of an evening. Apart from the odd cup of coffee, and occasional glass of wine, we simply play without a break, both of us inspired by the excellence of the compositions and by the joint music making – each creating musical ideas for the other.

Even more recently, I was encouraged to speak Russian to a local lady of Russian origin who attended one of our Mendelssohn charity concerts.

It transpired that Elena Landon, born in Russia but for years now living here with her UK family, was a first-rate pianist who had studied at the Rimsky-Korsakov Academy in St Petersburg – and the Russian influence is still noticeable. We started playing regularly together, with Mozart, Schubert and Beethoven violin and piano sonata performances at KDCMS, and Grieg and Schumann sonatas at the 'PlayFest' of the internationally renowned Wimbledon Festival. No doubt because of her Russian professional training, she is a strict observer of rhythm and detail, and according to 'severe' critics such as my wife Ruth, she has brought some necessary discipline back into my own playing. She, through natural talent and sheer hard work, has become an excellent musical partner in the various concerts where we have performed together.

Together with some of the above musical friends I have been privileged to perform at charity concerts, both locally and further afield in the UK, to support a range of charities – such as Médecins Sans Frontières, Brain Tumour Charity, Princess Alice Hospice and Oxford Home Start – when the audiences generously donate valuable charity funds.

To this day I know of no greater pleasure, and count myself lucky despite the advancing years, than to be able to continue with the joy and inspiration of making chamber music with such friends – and if we can also make a modest contribution to worthy charities, the pleasure is doubly enhanced.

…and when chamber music with friends is not possible, as for example during the 2020 Coronavirus 'Lockdown', there are always the wonderful and technically extremely demanding six solo Bach violin sonatas and partitas, and his six equally wonderful but technically less demanding six 'cello suites. These latter lie well for the viola, played in the same key as on the original 'cello but an octave up, except for the sixth suite, which requires a fifth string which our four-stringed violas no longer have…

Variation: Hearing Aids

A few years ago, like many people *d'un certain âge,* I noticed that my hearing was weakening, especially in the upper registers – one specialist told me that I should not be able to hear the upper notes on the violin, but fortunately a knowledge of fingerboard geography combined with the brain's innate 'wiring' largely resolves this, although there is an inevitable loss of sound quality. Accordingly, I took appropriate advice about hearing aids, both via the NHS and then privately – given the wider options. As far as speech is concerned, I find that hearing aids are useful although not essential for one-on-one conversations, but invaluable for large committee/board meetings and family Zoom meetings, especially in rooms with indistinct acoustics.

Music is rather more complicated than speech, especially so for violinists, as Kreisler, Menuhin and other greats discovered in their later years. After much searching I came across a Swiss 'channel-free' technology, which although no more expensive than some of the other standard makes, is reasonably compatible with violin playing – I select the 'music programme' (no doubt designed for loud concerts) and then tone it down several clicks according to music and mood. I still play my viola without aids, given its lower register, and oddly enough also my bright-sounding 1974 Morassi violin. However, the 1724 Stradivari violin appears to lose quite a bit of its tonal subtleties, which the discreet setting of the aids largely solves – and the other players in a chamber group do not appear to notice any loss of tone or intonation.

I am indeed fortunate to be still playing, especially my Stradivari violin, without noticeable negativities, in my late seventies.

12

VIOLINS AND BOWS

Theme: The 'Cecil' 1724 Stradivari – and Other Instruments

I HAVE DESCRIBED MY EARLY DOLMETSCH DESCANT TREBLE AND tenor recorders, and my subsequent Boosey & Hawkes 'Imperial' Conservatoire-system oboe, with additional keys added by the redoubtable Charlie Morley.

When I switched to violin, having been bewitched by Yehudi Menuhin's solo Bach and Bartók in the Oxford Sheldonian Theatre, I initially borrowed a serviceable violin from my school. As my technique improved, over the years I bought and resold various modestly-priced violins, including an Italian Gagliano-School of the late eighteenth century – heavy and unresponsive, a French Claude Pierray of c.1730 – sweet but small tone, an Erich Sandner of Mittenwald modern violin, and an early nineteenth century French Didier Nicolas violin – more powerful, but my later teacher Max Rostal commented that it sounded 'like a trumpet'.

In 1968 I ordered a Stradivari model from Bert Smith, an interesting British maker who lived in Coniston in the Lake District, working in his attic, just as Antonio Stradivari had done. He was recommended by Ruth's 'Aunt' Steffi Hess, who had looked after Peter Schidlof from the Amadeus Quartet, and who lived nearby (as already described). Bert Smith had a reputation for excellent varnish, which he had researched at length. This reputation turned out to be justified, but as he only made four violins or fewer a year I had to wait for a long time before it finally arrived. I still have it, and it is a quality modern English violin, with a clear distinctive sound.

When I moved to Berne and Max Rostal, given his comments on the sound of my Nicolas violin, I looked around for something better, and found from the Swiss dealer Henry Werro (see earlier) a Tomasso Balestrieri of Mantua violin of 1750–1760, with a label 'Petrus Guarnerius 1720'. This was an excellent old Italian violin, with a sought-after authenticity certificate from the renowned Hill family, and with a sweet rather than powerful tone.

Before I finally left Rostal and Berne, I exchanged the Balestrieri violin with Werro for a top-class Giovanni Battista Guadagnini violin labelled Milan 1754. This had previously belonged to the well-known German soloist Saschko Gawriloff who had exchanged it for the 'Spohr' Guarneri del Gesù violin. My Guadagnini featured in Karel Jalovec's learned compendium *Italienische Geigenbauer* of 1957 (no.179, p.189), and was certified as authentic by Hamma (1941), Möckel (1934) and Neuner (1872). It had been played by Konzertmeister Hanske of Heidelberg in 1952, before that by Direktor Kühne in 1941, and in the late nineteenth century was played by the second violinist in the well-known Müller Quartet, contemporary with the famed Joachim Quartet. The violin was in very good condition, despite having been well-used over the years, and a distinguishing feature was an *Eisenmal* (iron marking in the wood) on the two-piece back. Although there was some (inevitable in the violin trade?) speculation that the violin might be composite, bringing together parts from Guadagnini's Milan and Parma adjoining periods, we could never clarify this, despite expert but inconclusive photo-analysis. At any rate, all the violin experts agreed that the violin is a 100 per cent authentic Guadagnini, and a fine concert violin. When I eventually sold it privately thirty-five years later, it went to a Swiss Foundation which lends out fine instruments to star young players, so its voice is still being heard today.

My violin bows purchased over the years, all beautiful in their different ways, and which I still play to this day are:

- a fine and very practical Albert Nürnberger of Markneukirchen Germany bow (silver and ebony with an octagonal stick) acquired from Beares of London, made in the late-nineteenth century with a rare early photograph of the maker in the nut. It is powerful and direct to play – David Oistrakh played one.
- a beautiful Albert Caressa bow (gold and tortoiseshell) acquired from Pierre Vidoudez in Geneva. It is stamped 'Caressa', being from his workshop in the early twentieth century, and was made either by Alfred Lamy – according to Vidoudez, or by Victor Fétique – according to Beares, both of whom were bow experts working for Caressa. It is very flexible, and produces a rich warm tone.
- a rare early Dominique Peccatte bow (silver and ebony c.1840) with a light-coloured stick (*baguette claire*) acquired from Vidoudez. Peccatte's bows have greatly increased in value in recent years. I tend to use mine for playing baroque music.
- a much-sought-after Eugène Sartory bow (silver and ebony early twentieth century) acquired from Werro. It is both powerful and flexible to play.

My excellent viola bow is by John Clutterbuck (c.1960 gold and tortoiseshell with an octagonal stick and stamped with his 'bow name', 'J. S. Rameau'), who worked for Hill – also acquired from Werro. This bow, being slightly heavier than a standard violin bow, matches the viola's deeper sound and physical qualities well.

It goes without saying that these bows, all still in good condition, while purchased for relatively modest prices many years ago, would cost vastly more today. I vary the use of my violin bows according to the nature of the music and to my mood of the day.

As described earlier Ruth's 'Aunt' Emmie Hess kindly gave me a violin made by the *doyen* of Cremonese makers, Gio Batta Morassi, in 1974. It is modelled on the Stradivari 'Cremonese' 1715 violin, now in the Cremona Museo del Violino. In 2004 I was in Cremona and showed it to Morassi himself. He was pleased to see one of his original larger instruments, having in recent years made smaller ones for the Japanese market. Gio Batta died in 2018. A couple of years ago I was passing through Cremona and met his son Simeone, who has taken over his father's *lutherie* business. I had a couple of tiny scratches on the violin, and Simeone told me to come back an hour or so later – I returned to find the scratches impeccably repaired with the same varnish which his father had used in 1974. The violin is still in lovely, virtually mint condition, the tone is bright and resonant and improves all the time with playing.

When in October 2004 I was with Morassi father at the annual 'Mondomusica' Fair (the string instrument and accessory 'Mecca' for makers, dealers and enthusiasts from all over the world) in Cremona, we were joined by the great Russian 'cellist Mstislav Rostropovich, who was due to perform Haydn's 'cello concerto there later that day. We started chatting, and Rostropovich very kindly agreed to be photographed with me and the Morassi violin.

Many years ago I had a viola made by the well-known maker Clifford Hoing of High Wycombe. It was a good instrument, but on the large side, which I found challenging at times when switching between viola and the smaller violin. In 1977, while living in Geneva, I found from Jean Werro (who had taken over from his father Henry) a fine early viola made by the great French maker J. B. Vuillaume in 1828 – signed on the inside of the table and back by the maker, who numbered it 99, and certified by the leading French expert Etienne Vatelot. It was relatively small (385 mm), which made the violin / viola switch easier. Despite the belief that bigger violas sound better, it has a very warm full tone. I play it with pleasure to this day and consider myself truly fortunate to own it.

After many happy years with my Guadagnini I decided to make one final change in my violinistic life, before old age finally set in. The Guadagnini was indeed a fine instrument with a sweet singing tone. However, it was relatively short in length, 354 mm, which I found a slight disadvantage with my long arms. Accordingly, in 2001 I started to look around the violin dealers of Europe, many of whom I had known over the years. I saw and tried many fine instruments, including the Stradivari violins (named after previous owners): 1720 'Rochester', 1669 'Clisbee', c.1718 'Szekely', 1716 'Milstein' and 1722 'de Chaponay' (which I had known half a century earlier when it had belonged to my fellow Rostal pupil, American Larry Homolka, son of the illustrious actor Oscar), as well as violins by Bergonzi, Guarneri, etc. – most of which were way above my price range.

Finally, I saw at Beares a 1724 Stradivari, which was little known, not in any of the major reference books, and which had not been played seriously for many years, having been with a family in Northern Italy since early in the nineteenth century. Accordingly, the sound was somewhat dead – a well-known soloist had played it with only limited results – but I thought that I could remedy that in time. In addition, because it had lain in a wooden case for so many years, it had been attacked by woodworm, as often happened with such old instruments, mainly in the table, but fortunately hardly at all in the back.

However, the beautiful golden red varnish, especially on the back, and the cut of the woodwork – corners, purfling, f-holes, edges and scroll – were all still amazingly 'fresh' and pure. It was of especial note that the varnish had not been polished or retouched, as happened to many great violins, especially in the nineteenth century, but remained very much as the master had finished it. The scroll particularly showed very clear signs that the violin had been made entirely by Stradivari himself – even with a few slips of the chisel for which we can forgive the eighty-year-old Antonio – rather than completed by his sons Omobono or Francesco, as often happened with some of his instruments in his later years.

The violin was fully certified by the *doyen* of the violin trade, Charles Beare, as 'absolutely authentic', including Stradivari's original 1724 label *'Antonius Stradiuarius Cremonensis Faciebat Anno 1724'* – and his later corrected 'spelling mistake' with a 'u' rather than a 'v'. We also had papers of authenticity from Alfred Hill of the leading Hill family of violin experts, who described it as *'bien authentique'*, and from the renowned French *luthier* Charles-Eugène Gand of Paris, who had expertly restored the woodworm damage in 1887 and very clearly describes this 1724 violin in his *Catalogue descriptif des instruments de Stradivari et Guarnerius del Gesù (Vingt années d'expertise d'un grand luthier parisien; 1870–1891)* – 'Fond de 2 pièces. Jolie tête. Vernis rouge doré'.

We also found a likely reference to this violin in the *Catalogo* of 1808 by the renowned Italian collector Count Cozio di Salabue, who praised its construction and varnish, and its 'very strong voice, almost tenor – for its rare voice [it is worth] 140 *luigi*'. The Count's writings are always notoriously complex to interpret, but nevertheless we have so far found no other 1724 Stradivari which matches his description.

In addition to Charles Beare, respected UK *luthiers* such as John Dilworth had no doubts about its purity and its authenticity, which was also largely confirmed from expert dendrochronological analysis by the authoritative Peter Ratcliff. He stated that the wood of the table came from the same period as well-known 1723–1726 Stradivari violins, such as the 1723/1725 'Duke of Edinburgh', 1725 'Hammig', 1726 'Hilton' and 1724 'Abergavenny', and indeed probably came from the same tree. The violin was from Stradivari's later period, when he was eighty – and he still had thirteen years of his working life to go – with the slightly darker tone of that later period which is greatly sought after by the great soloists. It was made from his PG (*più grande*) model and at 356 mm, was of a comfortable length for me.

Very few 1724 Stradivaris are known to exist, most famously the great Spanish violinist Pablo de Sarasate's favourite Stradivari which is now on permanent display at the Paris Musée de la Musique – and which we think that Cozio refers to in his later *Catalogo* of 1818, with a yellow varnish and valuing it at the slightly lower price of 130 *zecchini*. It is similar in appearance to mine, although some experts, for example John Dilworth, say that mine is better preserved – woodworm restoration notwithstanding. Of the two 1724 Stradivaris described in his *Catalogo*, Count Cozio preferred the one which we think refers to my one.

Because of the somewhat dead tone, the restored woodworm damage, and it being relatively unknown, the price was less disastrous than it might have been with a more famous instrument. Accordingly, after the inevitable financial juggling, including extending the mortgage on our house, I took a risk and bought it in 2004. As I had hoped, after a couple of years the sound came back to its original glory. The G and E strings had always been quite strong, but the upper reaches of the D and A strings less so. I put on lower tension strings, to allow the old wood (a violin is made of some seventy separate pieces of wood) to vibrate more fully, and a respected local *luthier* David Hume put on a slightly more resonant bridge. Otherwise I did nothing other than play it very regularly – and of course learning the technique of how to coax, rather than force, the sound out of a Stradivari. The full resonance was restored across all the strings, and it re-found the astonishing *Nachklang* (lingering tone) for which such instruments are renowned.

In 2017 I was invited to play solo violin in a charity concert in Oxford Town Hall, and my wife Ruth, always my strongest critic, and other listeners commented how the *pianissimo*, especially in the upper notes, had sung out across the large spaces of the hall. There were similar comments about the sound of the violin when in 2018 I had the sorrowful duty of playing Mozart and Elgar in the spacious Cheltenham Pittville Pump Room, together with my good friend John Wilson, at a memorial concert for his late lovely wife Gina.

Fuller details of the violin can be seen in my monograph 'A Violin by Antonio Stradivari 1724', with a personal preface by Charles Beare, and exquisite high-quality photographs taken by Hiroko Umezawa of Beare Violins. I describe in detail the history, construction and the remarkable tonal qualities of the violin, and my personal experiences of playing it. The monograph was published in 2017, and signed and numbered copies, in standard or deluxe vellum-bound editions, are available from the author directly or from Abebooks: www.abebooks.co.uk.

The Strad, the widely respected international violin-trade magazine, which was launched in 1890, published a full-page lead 'poster article' about the violin in November 2018, with text by John Dilworth and photographs again by Hiroko Umezawa. The article is entitled 'An Overlooked Wonder', and likewise describes in detail the history, construction and tonal qualities of the violin, together with a full-size poster* of it.

Since Stradivari violins traditionally have names, and mine did not, given its obscure history, *The Strad* also formally gave my violin a name for the first time – the 'Cecil' Stradivari of 1724.

I continue to play it very regularly in chamber music and charity concerts and consider myself to be an extremely happy and lucky person to be so privileged.

---

* available from www.thestradshop.com

13

THE ATHENÆUM

Variation: Exploration

A FTER I HAD RETURNED TO THE UK FROM THE VIENNA EMBASSY in 1989, I was encouraged by the FCO to join a London Club, partly to entertain visiting foreign VIPs as I became more 'senior'. While the Traveller's Club was somewhat regarded as the 'FCO canteen', and I preferred to seek somewhere not full of my FCO colleagues, I liked the aesthetic academic reputation of the Athenæum. Since its foundation in 1824, its membership over the years had included many leading writers, musicians, statesmen, and more than fifty Nobel Prize Winners. It is still in its original 1827 building, designed by the young Decimus Burton, in London's Pall Mall.

Accordingly, an FCO colleague, who was already a member, put me up for membership. Unfortunately, although he had a fine mind, his hand-writing was notoriously illegible. When I had heard nothing for many months, I nervously rang up the Athenæum Secretary and asked him what was happening. He replied that he was pleased that I had rung, since they had been unable to decipher my name. Finally, with this clarification they were able to proceed with candidature and I was duly elected in 1991.

Despite the reputation of being populated by bishops and judges, I found the Athenæum's membership to be much more varied – with cer-tainly some clerics and lawyers, and quite a lot of medics, but an interesting cross-section of writers, musicians, academics, scientists, civil servants and serious journalists among its 2,000 members. It had no particular political leanings, unlike some of the other London clubs, and those few politicians who were members were of the more arcane variety.

I was uneasy about the lack of women members, which was common to nearly all London clubs at the time, but we were soon to change this. There were regular formal and informal talks, discussions, library evenings, wine-tastings and later concerts. Despite their reputed 'eminence', most members were quite unstuffy and very human. I felt quickly at home and made friends. Among these early friends was the government scientist and adviser Alcon Copisarow, who gave me helpful career advice when I was thinking of leaving the FCO – by coincidence I succeeded him as a Trustee years later.

As well as the sociability and good company of the members, the staff, under the excellent leadership of Secretary Jonathan Ford and House Manager Avril Shorland, make a great contribution to the life of the Club. They know the members, strengths and weaknesses, and look after them very well. When our son was seriously ill, as described earlier, the staff could not have been more sympathetic – indeed for at least five years after our son had fully recovered, one long-standing lady staff member kept asking me how he was getting on.

My first 'window' into the Club 'hierarchy' was due to Peter Meisner, a cultured Hungarian member, a cardiologist who had left Budapest in 1956, and who had been given the task of organising a Club Ball – maybe that's what the Club management thought that Hungarians were good at. Anyway, we met one evening by chance in the 'gods' at Covent Garden during a performance of *Götterdämmerung*, got chatting and he invited me to join his newly constituted Ball Committee – although I am no dancer. At the Ball I played 'popular' dance tunes for violin with at the piano my friend Martin Neary, then Organist of Westminster Abbey – and the rest followed...

Early on I wrote to the Chairman of the Wine Committee, Ralph French, who with his wife Rosie were to become close family friends, somewhat overstating my European wine experience – and was delighted to be invited to join this much-sought-after body. Later the then Club Chairman, John Cuckney, invited me to take over from Ralph the chairmanship of the Wine Committee, giving me wise advice and brushing aside my relatively limited knowledge – 'experts should be on tap, not on top,' he said. The Athenæum benefitted from extensive wine cellars stretching underneath Waterloo Place outside, with stocks of several hundred thousand pounds' worth of excellent quality wines at a wide range of prices. Inevitably, as in most clubs, while the majority of members favoured the Club Claret (a nicely matured *Cru Bourgeois*) and the Club White Burgundy (including a flinty *Chablis 1er Cru*) at reasonable prices, our efforts to expand the cellar to include quality Italian, Spanish, Lebanese, New World and other wines met with only a limited membership response, given their established wine loyalties.

We, under the guidance of retired Treasury official Brian Gilmore, introduced a transparent wine-pricing formula, based on actual cost of purchase, storage, service and the cost of money invested – a pragmatic formula which gave the members quality wines at a realistic and fairer price than many restaurants with their 100–200 per cent mark-ups. Nevertheless, when one member said that he had seen the same wine in Tesco at a lower price, the fact-based answer had to be that he could have his next dinner in Tesco. We were able to reduce stocks, but not quality, significantly, often by purchasing a few years after *en primeur* (for example the 2000 clarets, which we felt that the French had over-hyped) when prices had dropped, thereby reducing investment costs. We also introduced temperature controls in the cellars, which helped to preserve the wines better. We, including fellow wine and music lovers Michael Hockney and Michael Oppenheimer, also made several trips – always at our own expense, rather than the Club's – to Burgundy, Bordeaux, the Rhône, the Moselle, Languedoc, Tuscany and further afield to learn about their wines at first hand.

Our first Wine Committee trip in 1997 was to Burgundy, staying at a charming family hotel in Aloxe-Corton. One of our members, Ken Warren – former senior Tory MP and distinguished engineer – offered to drive us there in his spacious Mercedes, which seemed a practical solution. However, it went wrong on the first morning when Ken found that the tasting wines were 'too good to spit out'. Inevitably the new boy on the Committee (yours truly) realised what was happening, drank as little as possible and took over the driving duties in the afternoon. For the rest of the trip we wisely hired a small van and local driver, who, we were assured, would stay strictly sober. However, we noticed during a splendid last-night dinner at Chagny, that our driver was sitting at the bar enjoying himself – when we queried this, the response was that in Burgundy the local wine doesn't really count as alcohol.

Ken was a great joker, for which he was renowned in Parliament, and regaled us with numerous anecdotes – one particularly hilarious and rambling (i.e. none of us were ever sure about the punch line) one involving a South African gentleman 'van der Merwe' and his dog. For our final Saturday morning we had arranged to visit the renowned winery of Robert Groffier – but we were warned to be on our best behaviour, because Mme Groffier objected to her Saturdays being disturbed. All was fine until we heard a dog barking nearby. Ken inevitably interjected that this reminded him of the 'van der Merwe' story, and we all collapsed in laughter – with Mme Groffier very distinctly unamused.

Needless to add our follow-up Wine Committee trips around Europe always provided lively companionship – while, of course, not distracting us from the key 'professional' business of identifying good-quality and good-value wines to purchase for the Club's members and guests to enjoy.

In 1996 I was nominated to join the General Committee, the elected governing body, which provided fascinating insights into the workings of the Club. While the Secretary runs the catering, staffing and management aspects very efficiently, a series of membership sub-committees run the 'membership' and 'cultural' aspects. My particular duties on the General Committee included: the appointment of honorary memberships for distinguished foreign ambassadors, mainly the major European, Commonwealth and Asian representatives, but also from smaller countries, with positive personal recommendations: the establishment of reciprocal arrangements with like-minded clubs, mainly in Europe – Paris, Brussels, Rome, Madrid, Berlin, The Hague and beyond. I was also invited to join the Executive Committee, which being smaller and more focused, looks after the financial and managerial detail on behalf of the larger General Committee.

Theme: Music

With a fellow music lover, David Cooper, we established an Athenæum concert series, consisting of three professional concerts a year – mainly chamber music, either with top established musicians or young rising stars, singing, and occasional jazz – supplemented with an annual 'St Cecilia's Day' concert in November, for members both amateur and professional to perform/sing/entertain without fee. The professional costs during the rest of the year were supplemented by a generous legacy from the late-Leonard Halcrow (after whom the concert series was named), so we could always keep within budget for the artists. We were also able, drawing on the Halcrow legacy, to negotiate with personal contacts at Steinway London the purchase at a reasonable price of a top-class Steinway Model B grand piano for the Club, thereby providing a high-quality instrument for high-quality artists.

We opened the concert series in 1999, with 'Music and Words from the Twentieth Century to Mark its Passing'. With my pianist friend Lawrence Caun, I contributed Elgar, Bartók, Hindemith on the violin, and the last movement of Shostakovich's Viola Sonata, his final work, to close the series. We brought over young musicians from overseas, for example 'New Names' from Moscow in 1999, as described earlier – of whom the violinist Alena Baeva has risen to the top, performing the Tchaikovsky Concerto with the LPO at the Royal Festival Hall in December 2018, and in 2008 the solo 'cellist Sol Gabetta from Switzerland, who has since become world-renowned – she played the Elgar Concerto at the 'First Night of the Proms' in 2016. For these overseas artists, we negotiated financial/logistic support from the relevant ambassadors and national sponsors, so staying within budget.

Ruth and I, together with John and Gina Wilson, formed a musical friendship with Derek Wiblin and his wife Pam. Derek was a retired senior civil servant, and his passion was making violins, which he did with great enthusiasm. At the 'St Cecilia's Day' concert in 2001 I was listed in the programme as playing with Leslie Howard two pieces for violin and piano by Fritz Kreisler. At the end of the first piece (*Liebesleid*) I stopped, put down my violin, and told the audience that they had just heard a violin made in 1754 by Giovanni Battista Guadagnini of Milan. Now they were going to hear a violin made in 2000 by Derek Wiblin of Watford. I picked up Derek's violin, and we gave them *Schön Rosmarin* – which the Wiblin violin conveyed most impressively.

In February 2005 we organised a Celebrity Concert to raise funds for the Tsunami Disaster – Thomas Allen, the Choir of Westminster Abbey conducted by James O'Donnell, the Belcea Quartet, Leslie Howard, Fiona Kimm with Stephen Wilder, all generously gave their services, and we were able to raise many thousands of pounds for the 'Child Victims of the Tsunami'. After managing the concerts for twelve years, David Cooper and I decided that the time had come for us to step aside, leaving a solid base for our successors to build on.

Variation again: Development

I mentioned above my unease that, when I joined the Athenæum, its membership, like most London Clubs at the time, was men-only – no problem with Jews, Catholics, Muslims, ethnic minorities and others among the membership, but no women. For years, there had been a simple majority of members in favour of women membership, but according to the Club statutes we needed a two-thirds majority. Interestingly the original 1824 establishment defined itself as '*association of <u>individuals</u> known for their scientific and literary attainments, etc.*' Nowhere did it state that women were excluded, and we understand that mention of '*gentlemen*' may have meant people of '*gentle*' persuasion, rather than exclusively males. However, 'men-only' was and remained the accepted practice.

As the twentieth century was drawing to its close, there was often heated debate of the issue between the 'reformers' (among whom I proudly count myself), and those who maintained that they had joined a 'gentlemen's club'. I recall one stormy AGM chaired by the then-Chairman John Cuckney, when the Committee was accused (even by some reformers) of trying to subject the Club to outside 'political correctness'. Subsequently, we conducted a written survey of members, seeking their views on a variety of Club issues, including women membership – for which a clear majority wrote that they were in favour.

The new Chairman, Brian Gilmore – my predecessor – wisely recognising that the one thing which united most Athenæum members was a belief in the expression and validity of their own arguments (or to put it more bluntly – the sound of their own voices), organised a series of Open Meetings on the subject in 2000. Equal air-time was allowed to both camps, and to counter the 'political correctness' suspicion the Committee itself did not take a position – although individual Committee members, mostly pro-reform, could and did – as I most certainly did, arguing passionately against discrimination.

Over the series of three meetings, the anti-women lobby gradually lost its convictions – one leading spokesman privately admitting that he had listened to the debate and changed his mind – 'but don't tell my friends'. After the final meeting, since there was little new to be said, we all, from both camps, adjourned for an amicable glass of champagne. Rather than have a show of hands from those present, we arranged for the Electoral Reform Services (to counter any possible suspicion of internal pressures) to conduct a written ballot of the whole membership. We got their sealed response at a General Committee meeting on 26 March 2001, and, not knowing the result, we opened the letter and immediately pinned it to the Club notice board. The result was quite categorical – 70.35 per cent of the votes in favour of 'full and equal' membership for women and only 29.65 per cent against – a clear two-thirds majority. I was personally delighted that liberalism had prevailed.

That evening a group known as 'The Traditionalists' (unsurprisingly against women membership) had organised a dinner, either as a celebration or a wake. Brian and I went up to their table and said that we hoped that we all remained friends. They replied touchingly that of course we remained friends – the Club had spoken, and the result was overwhelming; they insisted that we sit down and share a glass of wine with them.

There was a minor attempt to say that, while women were now admitted as members, they should not have access to the Club Table or certain hitherto men-only public rooms. The Committee firmly rejected this, stressing that 'full and equal' meant exactly that. In the end there were only some half-a-dozen resignations, a few of whom might have left anyway because of not paying their subscriptions. Unlike in some similar organisations, there was 'no blood on the carpet'. One of the leaders of the anti-women campaign, Alfred Goldstein, later wrote the history of the debate, and did so in such unbiased terms that you could not tell which side he had been on. The new women members were an enrichment to the Club and were almost universally accepted by both camps. There were a couple of instances of rudeness to them, but these were firmly jumped upon. As a result, not only was a lingering sore peacefully removed, but the Club has gained hugely, intellectually, socially and financially, from the change. The Athenæum now benefits greatly from the contributions of women members in key cultural, financial and literary positions, including the current Chairmanship of the General Committee, Jane Barker, distinguished in the financial and voluntary fields.

In January 2003 I received a telephone call from the Senior Trustee Basil Hall – would I take over as the next Chairman of the General Committee – in effect the Chairman of the Club? Although I was much surprised to be offered this at the relatively tender (for the Athenæum!) age of sixty-one, and was still busy with my nuclear work, I decided that I would never get a second offer and accepted. Then followed three years (the maximum tenure) of fascinating involvement in the Club's management. Apart from chairing the monthly meetings of the Club's main board, the General Committee, chairing the AGMs and Open Meetings and being the Club's external representative, it also meant being visible and readily available to the members. I would sit at the Club Table at least once a week and attend many Club events, regularly being approached by a member with, 'Have you a minute?' – which usually turned out to be rather longer. Most of the questions and requests were interesting, pertinent, or both, and more than compensated for the few predictably tedious ones.

One memorable event which I had the pleasure of chairing was a formal dinner in 2004 to celebrate the centenary of the Entente Cordiale. HRH The Duke of Kent, an Honorary Member, proposed the toasts to the two Heads of State. Speakers included the French Ambassador to London Gérard Errera and the British Ambassador to Paris John Holmes (against whom by chance I had played cricket – see later), with Francophile and Anglophile members and guests from both sides of the Channel. The wine served was a vintage Château Palmer, in honour of Roundell Palmer, Lord Selborne, a former member, whose portrait hangs in the Club (note; subsequent research suggests that he may not in fact have been related to Charles Palmer, the nineteenth century owner of Château Palmer). Attendees came from both sides of the Channel, including Mary Soames, daughter of Winston Churchill and former Ambassadress in Paris, and the Prince de Broglie, the chair of our Paris reciprocal Club the 'Nouveau Cercle de l'Union', founded in 1835.

As related earlier – I was also invited to speak at a Formal Talk Dinner on Athenæum Prime Ministers, and unsurprisingly the subject was my illustrious ancestor the 3rd Marquess of Salisbury, three times Prime Minister under Queen Victoria. During my research I discovered, as described, several surprisingly liberal for the time aspects of the Prime

Minister, which were then unbeknown to me. Harry Kinloch, a loyal friend, my successor-but-one as Chairman and a formidably knowledgeable historian, kindly chaired the meeting. I invited my cousin, the current 7th Marquess of Salisbury, to join us, and in the discussion after the actual talk, we shared the responses to the many and varied 'learned' questions about our mutual great-great-grandfather.

There was occasional need for adjudication by the Chairman between the Club membership committees and the management, but surprisingly little. Likewise, there were very occasional (but inevitable among 2,000 members, all human beings, notwithstanding their 'eminence') disciplinary incidents, when 'naughty boys' (I never had any 'naughty girls', but understand that this has since changed), usually after too much of the excellent Club wine, had committed some indiscretion. This resulted in them being invited to a 'cup of tea with the Chairman'. In most cases an appropriate sincere apology in the relevant quarters served to end the matter. These rare incidents apart, the Chairmanship offered enriching familiarity with the intellectual and cultural aspects and traditions of the Club. It was a great privilege to be the Athenæum Chairman.

All our children, and now grandchildren, enjoy the hospitality of the Athenæum – old-fashioned dress code notwithstanding, and Brussels-based son Andrew has been an overseas member for many years – in fact when he was elected at the age of twenty-four he was the youngest of all the members.

When our eldest son Thomas reached fifty in 2016, he proposed a joint 50th (for him) and 75th (for me) party to celebrate our combined 125 years. We looked around local hotels and found that the Athenæum at its weekend rate was both cheaper to hire, and infinitely more stylish. Accordingly we went ahead for a Saturday evening dinner/dance for some hundred-plus guests (family, personal friends and Tom's medical colleagues), with music (Vivaldi, Bach, Monti) and words in poetry and prose, all performed by the family, and an after-dinner traditional jazz band for the youngsters and the middle-aged. Everyone enjoyed the evening greatly, noticeably many of those who had never been there before. One highlight of the evening, which the staff still talk about, was the sight of our young blonde-haired Brussels granddaughter Tara shooting down the wooden bannisters of the august central stairs – the Prime Minister Marquess of Salisbury might have been shocked, but I suspect amused.

Finally, in 2008 I was invited to become a Trustee of the Athenæum, by chance succeeding Alcon Copisarow. The five Trustees, as well as being formally responsible for the assets and liabilities of the Club, attend General Committee meetings with speaking and voting rights, and offer their advice and experience to the Chairman and Committee members when appropriate. They also have the unwritten duty of recommending senior appointments such as the Chairmanship. Rather like the Conservative Party in the old days, the candidate 'emerges' after appropriate consultation among the members, rather than being selected by a popular vote. One of our well-known politician members tried to argue for a popular vote (perhaps he had himself in mind as the lead candidate!), but this did not get anywhere with the membership, who perhaps distrusted the inherent 'politicisation'. The Athenæum practice may not be 'democratic', but so far it seems to work.

For the last three years (ten being the maximum) of my tenure as Trustee, I acted as the 'Senior Trustee', responsible for coordinating the responsibilities and advice of the Trustees. At this time, they included the literary agents Bruce Hunter and Mike Shaw, who gave me valuable advice about publishing this memoir and my earlier Stradivari monograph.

Other Athenæum good colleagues and friends include finance expert Michael Fowle, eminent virologist Jangu Banatvala, medical-school administrator Julian Axe, dentist and researcher Malcolm Bishop and former FCO colleague Nick Adamson – with their wives kind attendees at our home charitable events – fellow Oxford 'Distinguished Friend' Louisa Service – of the seven Oxford 'Distinguished Friend' awards in 2012 (as related) we discovered that four were for Athenæum members – Camilla Panufnik, eminent photographer and music supporting colleague, Jane

Newell, pensions adviser and widow of my 'mentor' John Cuckney, successful author Ken Follett and his Labour politician wife Barbara, whom my literary and poker friend Anthony Holden introduced us to, Carl Jackson, Director of Music at the Chapel Royal, Hampton Court, where we enjoy beautiful local music at Christmas, Paul Tempest, ex-Bank of England and compiler of the membership's literary compendium *The Athenian Heart*, David Morphet, whom I first met in Vienna IAEA atomic energy days and who has brought poetry to the Club, Christopher Wright, distinguished librarian and neighbour in East Molesey, Nick Butler, energy expert with whom I had worked when he was adviser to Gordon Brown in No. 10, distinguished immigration lawyer Libby Watkins, and Graham Nicholson, former legal adviser to the Governor of the Bank of England and also a dedicated violinist. These friendships, and many others, have all enhanced my life at the Athenæum.

Eventually, at the June 2018 AGM, I stood down as a Trustee after twenty-two years of being involved in the Club management and was elected to Honorary Life Membership. While I felt greatly privileged to have been involved, I am now much enjoying the 'real' activities of the Athenæum, the many personal friendships and the intellectual and cultural stimulations. One of the delights is chatting, while seated in the famed green leather chairs, with fellow members, whom one may or may not know – as I said the supposedly 'eminent' ones remain surprisingly modest – about any topical, intellectual or cultural subject, and both enjoying the lively discussions and developing good friendships.

*

However, when I thought that I had finally left the General Committee in 2018, I was invited back on to it, once again with responsibility for honorary membership for distinguished foreign ambassadors. The member of the Committee who was due to take over this role declined because of a potential conflict of interest, and somewhat to my surprise I was invited back. As well as being an important element of the Athenæum's structure, there were also musical and other cultural benefits in maintaining personal links with the London diplomatic world.

Variation: 'Study Tours'

Recently, in 2018, an Athenæum friend, Julian Axe, with his wife Mary, asked me whether I would join him in organising a 'musical study' tour to Leipzig. Julian was happy to do the administration at the London end, while I handled the Leipzig end. When we circulated the concept to the Athenæum membership, instead of the expected half-dozen applications to join us, we had over one hundred – which involved a ballot to bring the number down to a manageable twenty. I was able to use my personal musical Leipzig contacts, and the German language, to manage the Leipzig programme.

This involved visits with concerts to the Mendelssohn, Bach and Schumann establishments (museums / churches / houses), the Altes Rathaus and the Gewandhaus concert hall – usually guided by long-standing personal Leipzig friends, such as Mendelssohn House Director Jürgen Ernst and Gewandhaus Director Andreas Schulz, which added something very special to the tour. In the evenings we were able to relax in Germany's oldest coffee house, Zum Arabischen Coffe Baum at Schumann's own table, at the historic Auerbachs Keller of Goethe's Faust notoriety, and – wine being integral to any Athenæum 'cultural' activity – to visit the Klaus Böhme Saale-Unstrut Weingut. What made the tour an especial pleasure was the friendship, intellectual interest and personal courtesy of the Athenæum members in the group.

As a follow-up to Leipzig, Julian was prevailed upon to arrange another 'study tour' in 2019, this time to Armenia and Georgia. Along with Julian and Mary Axe, Ruth and me, happy survivors from the Leipzig trip were Alan and Caroline Crockard, Hubert and Sue Lacey, David Thompson and Jerry O'Sullivan, together with very sympathetic newcomers, and once again the team spirit made a splendid overall contribution. In fact, the tour started badly with our Ukrainian Airlines flight via Kiev to Yerevan delayed by over twelve hours at Gatwick. When we eventually arrived in Kiev, we had missed our onward connection to Yerevan, and, with no 'official' or airline local help, our in-house Russian speaker (yours truly) had to organise a daytime hotel at Kiev and a new connection via Istanbul's striking new airport to Yerevan – where we eventually arrived in the small hours a day and a half late. Nevertheless, team spirit remained totally undamaged.

These two neighbouring early-Christian countries were similar, but often different – Armenia noticeably isolated with both the Turkish (genocide denial) and Azerbaijan (Nagorno-Karabakh dispute) borders closed, although supported by the Armenian *diaspora*, e.g. the French-Armenian star singer Charles Aznavour – and Georgia opening up rather more, although still dependent on their recent Russian invaders. Post-Soviet influence, economic, energy, cultural and architectural, was evident in both Armenia and Georgia, with the older generation still speaking official Russian in addition to their local languages – but the younger generation, especially in Georgia, was clearly replacing this with 'international' English and a strong Westward-looking European vision.

Highlights of the Armenia visit included the ancient Khor Virap Monastery with its eternal view over the closed Turkish border to Mount Ararat, and the incredibly moving Genocide Memorial. We then drove north, past bullet-marked buildings near the Azerbaijan border –a reminder of the recent fighting – over the border into Georgia. At the border we changed coaches and moved on to Tbilisi, with study visits to churches, fortresses and the magnificent Caucasus scenery – naturally interspersed with local wineries. On the final evening we all took the Tbilisi funicular railway up the local mountainside (as Ruth and I had done in the Soviet days thirty-one years ago), where we had a lovely team dinner in the restaurant overlooking the dramatically lit-up city.

Happy memories.

14

MORE VARIATIONS –
CRICKET, TRAVEL, LANGUAGES,
SKIING, CHESS, POKER,
SHERLOCK HOLMES, IRELAND,
ANTIQUARIAN TRAVEL BOOKS

Variation: Cricket

AT SCHOOL I HAD PLAYED CRICKET AND ENJOYED THE GAME although I was not particularly good at it – a stolid opening batsman, a floating leg-break bowler and an above-average slip fielder. I then gave it up because of my violin career and potential damage to my fingers – although the only person who ever broke one of my fingers was my lovely wife Ruth, as described earlier.

When I arrived at the British Embassy in Bonn, I was 'invited' as a 'senior' diplomat to form and then captain the Embassy team – composed of a few Brits with a selection of Aussies, Kiwis, Indians and Pakistanis scattered around Bonn in various non-diplomatic capacities. The healthy cross-grade exercise of digging a net in the Embassy garden under the wary eye of the Ambassador brought a group of us together, and one of the security guards and I decided to translate this teamwork into a formal British Embassy Cricket Eleven. We played against the RAF bases and occasionally won, and against the British Army in Rheindahlen and always lost. The RAF teams were quite informal, sometimes addressing their officer-skipper by his first name on the pitch, with an expletive not deleted if he dropped a catch, and only reverted to 'Sir' after the game. In contrast, the Army was rather more formal, with the skipper, usually a half-colonel, instructing the sergeant to 'send Private Smith to third man'.

Back in the UK I joined Esher Cricket Club, which was smart and of a standard rather higher than mine. Our next-door neighbour, the *Sun's* sports journalist Brian Woolnough, wisely persuaded me to move to nearby Claygate Cricket Club, more down-market and much more fun. Rather than being a small fish in a big pond, I became a medium fish in a medium pond – a good move.

We moved in 1976 to Geneva, which incidentally has one of the oldest cricket clubs in Europe, founded in 1872. At the time the club played on a matting wicket at the Stade de Richemont, an athletics ground, against local rivals from Berne and CERN, interspersed with visiting teams from around the world. From the UK came Sheffield Cricket Lovers and the Law Society, and from further afield came Barbados and Kuwait. I can recall some distinguished UK lawyers seriously letting their hair down with the lively Swiss wines, as opposed to the Kuwait Select Wanderers staying strictly sober for religious reasons, and yet thrashing us on the field.

Our President, the late Dr David Barmes, the Australian Director of Oral Health at the WHO, opened the batting with me and we became close family friends. His only transgression was in a Commonwealth-against-the-UK match, when he was wicket-keeping (standing up) to my batting and suddenly shouted, 'Well bowled.' However, as I trudged off, I noticed that the bails had fallen forwards rather than backwards. All's fair in love and cricket – for an Aussie against a Pom!

We took Geneva on tour to Barbados in 1979, when it was not as touristic as it is today, and we had a wonderful family holiday and made local friends. When Bob Bailey our wicketkeeper was hit on the head, the local players rushed him to hospital and looked after him until he was released. However, on the cricket field our results were disastrous – in one match the locals even declared with ten overs to go in a limited-over match, because they were so far ahead. Our Bajan friends, calling themselves 'Rick's Cavaliers', came to Geneva the following summer, renewing both the warm friendships and the cricketing humiliations. Over the years we have kept in touch with some of them, such as batsman Winston Haynes, journalist Louis Brathwaite and bowler Norman Holder – both when we visit Barbados and when they come to the UK – Winston even made a guest appearance for Claygate, scoring a sparkling fifty.

Every summer we also went on tour to Paris, who have played cricket at the Standard Athletic Club in Meudon since 1890. The matches were more evenly balanced than in Barbados, although I recall John Holmes, a future Ambassador to Paris with whom I later worked on nuclear matters, getting me caught-and-bowled second ball for a 'duck' and celebrating with an undiplomatic whoop. Dining and then exploring Paris in the evening after the Saturday game was always fun, including midnight cafe music in Montmartre, and we usually got to bed very late. I recall a Sunday morning game when we were still almost waking up and seeing through my bleary eyes the very first ball of the day being edged towards me at first slip. Probably because my eyes were still too bleary for me to react, to everyone's amazement, especially mine, I held the catch.

We also visited The Hague, where the Dutch play serious cricket. More exotically, every summer we travelled to Porlezza on the shores of Lake Lugano in Italy, to play against Milan Cricket Club – which did include a few Italians. The matting wicket, in the middle of a farmer's field, was surrounded by fairly-long grass, which favoured the lofted shots rather than the ground strokes – the latter unfortunately my speciality. This seemed a minor disadvantage by the evening, when in the very Italian hotel restaurant David Barmes regaled us all with his renowned renderings of Australian ballades and colonial songs, usually well lubricated with *grappa* as the night progressed.

Geneva CC also toured England, playing on various charming country-side grounds, including Hambledon, originally on Broadhalfpenny Down in Hampshire. Hambledon CC, founded in 1756, once claimed to be the 'most powerful' cricket club in the world, responsible for developing the laws of the modern game.

After David Barmes died in 2001, with some loyal Geneva cricketers led by Nigel Tickler and Hascal Gollop, we organised a 'sing-song' in London in his memory. Later 'Cricket Switzerland', of which David was the first President, established a 'David Barmes Memorial Trophy', which the various Swiss clubs now compete for annually.

In our next diplomatic posting to Vienna in 1985, I joined the local cricket club the 'Five Continents', which was run by a wealthy Indian restaurant owner, Sushil, who managed to smuggle in outstanding sub-continental players as 'temporary staff' for his restaurant. Shortly after we arrived, he appointed me as his captain, no doubt because of my British Embassy label rather than any cricketing reputation. At my first appearance as 'Five Continents' captain I won the toss, and on a dubious wicket invited the opposition to bat first. 'No, no, Desmond, we always bat first,' said Sushil. However, I stuck to my guns, which I fear was the beginning of the end of a beautiful friendship.

We played against local sides from the UN and other embassies, our 'Five Continents' team often being reinforced by my own growing-up children. A highlight was a visit to the International Cricket Festival at Zuoz in Switzerland, where a British schoolteacher in the 1920s had constructed four proper cricket pitches in the rarefied air at a height of 1,700m. We participated as 'Austria', and I was invited to captain the side – my only 'international' captaincy appearance. In our first 'Austria' game in Zuoz, the umpires complained that excessive appealing from our team was holding up play. I duly resolved to exercise my 'international captaincy' authority and ruled that only those close to the wicket should appeal. However, in the very next over, the ball struck an opposition batsman's pad, to be challenged by a loud lbw appeal from the fielder at deepest square-leg – my own teenage son, Nicholas. Collapse of any 'captaincy' authority.

In Vienna we also had an annual 'Ashes' match between the British and Australian Embassies – sharp rivalry on the field, but warm fellowship afterwards. We had one especially muscular and clear-eyed security guard in the British Embassy. Although he only had one stroke – over 'cow corner' – I usually asked him to open the batting. Even if he only survived for four balls, we already had twenty-four runs on the board.

Back in our quiet Surrey village of Claygate after Vienna, we also became infected with the touring bug. In 1995 our resident Sri Lankan Suranjam Cooray, a lovely outgoing guy partnered with the daughter of the local Claygate doctor, persuaded us to visit Sri Lanka. We played seven matches and lost them all, one 40-over match against Kalutara by a staggering 243 runs. In Kurunegala near Kandy, when it was my turn to captain, we saw the names of English Test players posted in the changing room, with Mike Atherton as my 'captain' predecessor – but could not live up to their performances. Visiting English village clubs were quite a rarity in those days, and the locals at first assumed that we were all professionals, and indeed may even have played for England – they were quickly disabused. Cricket apart, it was a wonderful opportunity to see the beauties of Sri Lanka – Galle, Colombo, Kandy and others. Ruth and I took a two-day hire-car trip away from cricket, limited by the continuing unrest in the north-east, visiting Sigiriya and the magnificent Buddhist temple sites. The British Deputy High Commissioner Ronald Nash, a colleague from Vienna days, very kindly hosted a reception for us and local cricket lovers.

Inspired by Sri Lanka, we toured Barbados in 1997, and unlike the Geneva tour eighteen years earlier actually won three matches – perhaps reflecting a decline in West Indies cricket. Our first overseas victory ever was against the 'Entertainers XI' in St Michael. They were perhaps complacent, letting their youngsters open their batting and only achieved 130 in their 35 overs. Our two opening batsmen, Ian Darke, sports commentator of *Sky Sports* fame, and I, knew that we only had to stay in to win, which we did doggedly, collecting runs wherever we could from outside edges and leg byes. I finished 'not out', exhausted from the heat but undefeated and happy with the win – and the 'man-of-the-match' award for the only time in my cricketing life.

The news of our surprise victory got quickly round the island. Late one night we were in the Bridgetown's lively Baxter's Road, where tourists were at the time advised to be on their guard in the evenings, and we were asked by none-too-friendly locals who we *'honkies'* (an abusive term for whites) were. When we explained the cricket, they relaxed and welcomed us with smiles, knew all about our matches and invited us to share some beers. Years later, on a diplomatic mission to the Caribbean, I entered a very local bar near the Kensington Oval in Barbados to look for an old Bajan friend, Louis Brathwaite, then sports analyst of *The Barbados Advocate*. I was the only white face in the place and was given suspicious looks – until a voice shouted out, 'Hi Dessie!' and again it was beers all round.

After we had played against Windward in St Philip, then still a whites-only club, that evening around the swimming pool we 'Surrey liberals' complained about the whites-only practice. Our black Bajan friends politely corrected us, saying that, although they didn't like the local whites, they had been in Barbados as long as the blacks and had the same rights as they did to be there – 'Surrey liberals' were put politely but firmly in their place. Once again, the British High Commissioner kindly hosted a reception for us and the locals.

In 1999 we toured Goa, with its historic Portuguese links. Ruth and I hired a Vespa scooter to be able to see more of the beautiful countryside, scenic coastline and the many imposing churches, although driving on Indian roads with their enormous lorries was an experience. Needless to write, we lost all our matches.

In 2001 we toured South Africa, where we played along the Garden Route from Cape Town: in Hermanus, George, Mossel Bay, Knysna for our first ever day-night game and venturing inland to play the Army in Oudtshoorn. In conversations with the locals we experienced both apologies and non-apologies for apartheid. Four of us hired a car and visited the townships to explore them for ourselves, to talk with the locals and get their frank views on post-apartheid developments. Of course, we visited Robben Island and Mandela's prison cell, the refreshing winelands, Cape Town's Table Mountain and Newlands Cricket Ground. Surprisingly, we did actually manage to win one game, in George, the home of South African captain Hanse Cronje – which the locals didn't appreciate.

My final Claygate tour was in February 2003 to Tobago with its relaxed atmosphere, lovely scenery and unspoilt beaches – including the famous 'Nylon Pool', named by HRH Princess Margaret in 1962. We crossed over to Port of Spain in Trinidad to play on the celebrated Queen's Park Oval Test Ground, where we were welcomed, although we were amused to see that women were not allowed in the ground floor of the pavilion – when even the MCC had relented by then. One of our players had the 'temerity' to venture without his shirt into this hallowed area of the pavilion and was politely but firmly told that 'bareback' was not permitted there.

I only scored a few runs but felt proud to have done even this on a Test Ground, where I also had the privilege of captaining (again following in the awesome footsteps of Mike Atherton and others). In Port of Spain the British High Commissioner Peter Harborne, a former diplomatic colleague, once again kindly hosted a reception for the Claygate visitors, as had his counterparts in Sri Lanka, Barbados and Goa. We had to advise the Claygate village youngsters to go easy on the drinks, and not to leap fully-clothed (or even un-clothed) into the High Commissioner's swimming pool – they all behaved impeccably – and we had the great pleasure of meeting local Trinidadian invitees, including distinguished cricketers.

Back in Claygate, I continued to play most weekends despite the advancing years. I never scored a century for them, my highest score being 95 – although, as the press secretary writing the weekly reports for the local *Esher News* (still with pen and paper in those days), I was able for several weeks to add 'fresh from his 95' to compensate for the lack of runs. Our children, sons Thomas, Nicholas, Andrew and sporting daughter Sarah, firmly putting any latent gender prejudice in its place, all appeared for Claygate over the years. They usually contributed more runs than their father – Nicholas and Andrew both scoring centuries.

When I first played for Claygate the captain and subsequent president was David Milner, Yorkshireman and dour opening bat, but, underneath the 'Yorkshire' exterior, kind and sympathetic. He was succeeded as president by Steve Wells, a middle-order batsman and LibDem councillor and great supporter of local charitable causes, and then by Nigel Abbott, former British Oxygen communications director and medium-fast bowler, an outgoing personality who handled all the publicity for the Club. Other all-round players included Rufus Legg, now handling FCO Protocol, Alan McKinley and Andrew Spector (whose great-great-grandfather came from Russia in about 1900 – *en route* for the USA, he got off at Tilbury by mistake, and, speaking little English, said that his profession was 'inspector', hence the derivation of the name) – fun colleagues on and off the pitch, and great stalwarts of our overseas tours.

In 1995 I persuaded the MCC Secretary Roger Knight, for whom I did some *pro bono* work helping the Librarian, and also as 'European Cricket Adviser' – using my diplomatic and other official European contacts to help local cricket grow across the continent, which it certainly did over the years – to let me play a few games for the MCC. We played against smart local schools and clubs, nearly always winning since we usually had a couple of ex-professionals in the team. Unsurprisingly, although I enjoyed the company, I did not score many runs. The one exception was a 'needle match' against my former club Esher in appalling weather. It was always going to be a low-scoring game, and, as against the 'Entertainers XI' in Barbados, I realised that we would win if I didn't get out – so I boringly resisted everything they flung at me, including from their West Indian professional fast bowler, until the victorious end.

Finally, in my sixty-fifth year I decided that it was time to call it a day. I was then opening the batting with an eighteen-year-old, and if he shouted 'run three' we were lucky to manage one. The once elegant cover drives would now only trickle a few yards, and the formerly effortless slip catches would hurt and drop. A Swiss accident provided a natural excuse for retirement.

In July 2006 I fell on a summer walk at the 'La Cascade' waterfall near the Col du Pillon – I heard a big ripping noise in my left leg as I fell. Ruth came round the corner, and told me firmly to get up, but it was not possible. She summoned the Swiss First Aid and a helicopter arrived – I was winched up and flown to Monthey-Chablais Hospital down the valley. The local orthopaedic surgeon Dr Pierre Berruex, who was very used to such accidents, insisted on operating immediately (a correct decision – confirmed after family medical telephone calls). I was given an epidural, was conscious throughout, chatting with the theatre staff – the pain came later. Dr Berruex drilled holes in my left kneecap and sewed up the severed tendons. A family relay team, Andrew from Dijon to Paris, and Nicholas from Paris to London, helped Ruth to drive the car with its immobile passenger back from Switzerland to the UK.

The next few days were very painful, but I was soon walking on crutches, helped by physiotherapy in a Wimbledon Parkside hospital pool with a charming young Canadian girl. I was determined not to be denied a planned August visit to Rome, where I hobbled painfully on two crutches down the Spanish Steps. As promised by Dr Berruex, although regular cricket was over, I was skiing again next winter, albeit cautiously – and in time, aided by ongoing physiotherapy, made a near-complete recovery, although I still feel the injury when walking downhill.

After retirement I made a couple of brief appearances for Claygate against Surrey Over-60s and was honoured when Claygate elected me as their Life Vice-President. I had loved my time at Claygate, the cricket, the fresh air, the exciting tours with Ruth, the good company and the friendships.

One particular and pleasing characteristic was that, whereas comments from Whitehall colleagues about the political developments of the day were usually predictably cautious, the honest Claygate village 'lads' said exactly what they thought, albeit 'undiplomatic' – which I much appreciated, getting a feel for the views of the wider British public, rather than just of the metropolitan elite.

One 'antiquarian' cricketing spin-off is my collection of *Vanity Fair* 'Men of the Day' cricketers, bought years ago when they were somewhat cheaper than today, complete and all original except the 1913 'Dillon', of which I only have a copy. This, being the last of the set and published just before the demise of *Vanity Fair*, is extremely scarce, and on the rare occasions when it comes up for sale can fetch several thousand pounds. Perhaps one day...

Variation: Travel

In addition to our 'diplomatic', 'nuclear' and 'cricketing' travels, we have been fortunate to visit much of Europe. The joy of travelling for me is not just about visiting the tourist sites, but wandering through the streets, getting lost, smelling the fresh fish markets and using my languages to chat with the locals.

This is especially true for Italy and Sicily, where we feel very much at home: Canaletto paintings, Stradivari violins, Frascati wine, and overarching Italian culture; magical Venice, sitting on the terrace of our favourite small hotel behind the Palazzo Ducale listening to the church bells, and exploring the myriad churches, canals and squares; Cremona, with the third-highest brick campanile in the world, in the footsteps of Antonio Stradivari where his first married home, the Casa Nuziale, still stands; Verona of *Romeo and Juliet* fame, which we visited on our honeymoon, hearing from outside the music of the open-air opera in the Arena, and on later visits could afford tickets; magnificent historic Rome, Bologna, Urbino, bustling and *Last Supper* Milan, extraordinary Pisa, and of course wonderful artistic Florence. I recall exciting visits: from Naples via Pompei to Positano; through Calabria over to Sicily, and then through Taormina and Caltanissetta to exotic Palermo; from Bari and Brindisi through Puglia via Monopoli and Gallipoli to architecturally rich Lecce – being some of my unsurprising favourites.

I have described in earlier chapters our diplomatic and musical travels through Switzerland, Germany, Austria and Russia.

– Switzerland: Berne the capital, Geneva and the UN, Lausanne, Neuchâtel, Basel, Zürich of 'gnomes' fame, musical Lucerne, Arosa, St Moritz, Gstaad / Saanen with the Menuhin Festival and concerts in the charming old churches in the Bernese Oberland, the ski resorts – and now of course our lovely Les Diablerets second home in the Vaudois Alps.
– Germany: Leipzig, home of Bach, Mendelssohn, Schumann and others, with Saale-Unstrut vineyards, Dresden, Berlin, Bonn in my youth the capital, Bremen, Lingen for the wedding of my schoolfriend Roland Needham, Hamburg, Stralsund and Caspar David Friedrich's Greifswald, Cologne, Düsseldorf, Mainz, Trier and the vineyards of the Moselle, Frankfurt, Heidelberg and the Neckar, Nuremberg, Karlsruhe, Munich, Goethe's Weimar, Wagner's Bayreuth – from Bavaria through the Rhineland and Saxony to Baltic Rügen.
– Austria: 'Hapsburg' Vienna, 'Tyrolean' Innsbruck, Salzburg – Mozart's birthplace, Melk with its ornate baroque Abbey, the Neusiedlersee in the flat wine-growing Burgenland – once part of Hungary, Haydn's Eisenstadt, Graz and Styria, the Ossiacher See in Carinthia, Mauthausen – and of course the famed ski resorts, such as Kitzbühel and St. Anton am Arlberg, as well as those closer to Vienna.
– Russia: the cultural glories of Moscow and St Petersburg, and then especially the remote Kola Peninsula, Murmansk, Archangelsk with the various 'secret' nuclear sites where we worked together with Russian colleagues tackling the nuclear environmental challenges, further afield to historic Ekaterinburg, Nizhny Novgorod and Samara.

Through nuclear-energy work I often visited the Nordic countries with their stunning landscapes and scenic coastlines: Norway – Oslo, Grieg's Bergen, Trondheim, Tromsø; Sweden – Stockholm and Malmö; Denmark – lovely Copenhagen, Aarhus; Finland – Helsinki, Olkiluoto, and once, in transit to Murmansk, the original 'Father Christmas' village of Rovaniemi.

France was a frequent destination, again through nuclear and diplomacy as well as privately – obviously extraordinary Paris, which I visited for the first of very many times at the age of ten, as related earlier, Brittany and beautiful Dinan where my late brother Tim had lived, Lille, Alsace-Lorraine, including Albert Schweitzer's historic birthplace Kaysersberg, horse-riding in the Camargue, 'Mediterranean' Marseille, stylish Lyon and Dijon, Cherbourg and Le Havre with nuclear sites, papal Avignon – near the Mélox nuclear recycling plant, Aix-en-Provence with annual opera visits thanks to my French nuclear colleagues – and naturally the wine regions of Bordeaux, Burgundy, Alsace, Loire, Rhône and Languedoc.

Elsewhere in Europe including: Belgium – Brussels where son Andrew lives, picturesque Bruges, Ghent and Antwerp; Holland – Amsterdam and the Hague; Luxembourg; former Yugoslavia – Zagreb, Ljubliana, Mali Losinj and the lovely Croatian islands, a family wedding in Belgrade, Split and Sarajevo by RAF Hercules; Turkey – exotic Istanbul, diplomacy in Ankara and a relaxed holiday in Antalya; Greece – Athens, Piraeus, Thessaloniki; Spain and Portugal – Madrid and Lisbon; Hungary – Budapest, Liszt's Sopron; Czechoslovakia – Prague and Bratislava; Poland – Krakow and Katowice – from where Ruth's family originated and where we could still find family graves, Auschwitz-Birkenau, Gdansk, Gdynia and Sopot – again where Ruth has family links; the proudly independent Baltic States, Estonia, Lithuania, Latvia, where I did research for BT; Bulgaria – Sofia; Macedonia – Skopje; Albania – Tirana and World Heritage Site Berat; Cyprus – Nicosia, Larnaka and 'diplomatically' across the Turkish dividing line to scenic Kyrenia.

More recently we visited Ukraine – from spectacular Russian-speaking Odessa on the Black Sea, via overnight railway sleeper to Ukrainian-speaking

Lviv (formerly Polish Lvov and Austro-Hungarian Lemberg, reflecting its turbulent past) in the West, and then to Kiev – already well known through my nuclear environmental work. I have already related the fascinating Athenæum 'study visit' to beautiful Armenia, isolated and cultured, and to lively, historic Georgia, which we had the experience of visiting thirty-one years earlier in the Soviet days.

Further afield we enjoyed the glories of Rajasthan, learning about another history and culture – Delhi candlelit at night during Diwali, Agra and the wondrous Taj Mahal, Jaipur, Udaipour, Varanasi, bustling Mumbai; and of course cricket tours to Goa and Sri Lanka; the West Indies – Barbados, Jamaica, Antigua, Dominica, Tobago and Trinidad, again strongly influenced by cricket, as well as Aruba and Puerto Rico; Havana in Castro's Cuba, where, as described, I was 'mugged' for the only time in my life.

On FCO duty I briefly visited Lebanon during the hostage crisis, and we later relaxed on a post-hostage private visit, appreciating the outward-looking people, despite the troubles around them, and extraordinary historic Baalbeck. Similarly, I also briefly visited Syria and Damascus – 'cradle of civilisation', Egypt – Cairo and the glories of the Pyramids and Sphinx, Jordan, Algeria, Morocco and Israel. Post-FCO we privately visited Israel, where we stayed in kibbutzim and visited northern settlements where Russian was becoming the *lingua franca*, Palestinian areas and all of Jerusalem, which would have been impossible in FCO days – and were received both with kind hospitality, being invited into a private home in Jericho for coffee during Ramadan, and with hostility, with stones thrown at our Tel Aviv-registered hire-car in Nablus.

In Africa, in addition to our South African cricket trip, we also visited Kenya on holiday, staying with friends in Nairobi, with an exhilarating trip to the game reserves, expertly guided by local wardens, followed by a week on the lovely coast South of Mombasa.

I went all over Latin America on FCO business: Venezuela – Caracas; Columbia – Bogotá and the oilfields, always under diplomatic protection; Belize – with an RAF-helicopter flight over the magnificent Caracol pyramid;

Guatemala; Honduras; Mexico – Mexico City and also later with the LPO; Brazil – spectacular Rio, bustling São Paulo and artificial Brasilia; Chile – Santiago, Valparaiso, the wonderful Torres del Paine National Park, and all the way down South to dramatic Punta Arenas and across the Strait of Magellan to wild Tierra del Fuego; Argentina – Buenos Aires with a concert at the imposing Teatro Colón and La Recoleta cemetery with the grave of Eva Perón. As related, I visited Ecuador – Quito at 2,850m for my intensive '*Latino*' Spanish course and the 'Mitad del Mundo' on the Equator; later with Ruth, 'backpacking' from Lima, historic Cuzco, magnificent Machu Picchu, and across the Andes via Lake Titicaca to La Paz at 3,640m in Bolivia. And, of course by RAF TriStar to the beautiful, windswept Falklands.

In North America: Canada – Ottawa, Montreal, Halifax. In the USA – as well as diplomatic Washington, New York and Miami Airport, Boston where Ruth has relatives, and Augusta with the Savannah River nuclear site. We travelled privately down the West Coast from Seattle via never-sleeping Las Vegas to the magnificent Grand Canyon and Death Valley, then back up to the *Big Sur* with its *Citizen Kane* Hearst Castle, and to multicultural and hilly San Francisco which we loved – before joining up with the LPO for musical business in Mexico City.

The furthest East that we went was to China, again on musical business when the LPO was the first foreign orchestra to play in the new Beijing National Centre for Performing Arts before the opening of the 2008 Olympics, and we arranged diplomatic support – then we went on privately to the fascinating East / West metropolis of Shanghai, exploring the French Concession, the rich Museum of Fine Art, the Bund and Pudong.

Who knows what travels the future will bring?

Variation: Languages

I think it worth saying something about the value and the joy of languages. Although as a schoolchild I only had the usual basic spoken French and

German, I have mentioned benefitting from the excellent teaching of English language and structure by our inspiring Music Master Christopher Bishop at Magdalen College School. This understanding of the language structure, together with Latin – with a similar grammatical declination basis as German and Russian – later turned out to be invaluable.

I was very fortunate that as a young violinist I learnt the Swiss languages – German, Swiss-German (for practical purposes another language, given the grammatical and vocabulary divergences from 'High' German), French and Italian – while living there as a virtual Swiss. While I obviously spoke English with Ruth, otherwise I spoke the Swiss languages with all the locals. No doubt being a musician helped – even today, if I am not quite sure how to phrase something in another language, I try to imagine the correct sound, and then the correct structure and vocabulary will click in. When I learnt Russian a couple of years after the Swiss languages, the acquired Swiss linguistic experiences, combined with the Latin structural knowledge, and of course the complete immersion course with the formidable Countess Shouvalova, all paid off – resulting in grammatically correct Russian, with a 'St Petersburg/pre-Baltic' accent as described. I am fortunate in that the four Swiss languages and Russian are for me in separate 'boxes', not translated from or to English, and which can be switched from one to another without confusion.

When I learnt Spanish at the age of fifty, the three-week total family immersion course in Quito brought quick results, but the age gap since my earlier youthful Swiss experience meant that the process was less natural and considerably harder work. This is my one language which fades, although it was noticeable that the few days in Mexico City recently with the LPO did start to bring it back relatively quickly.

I cannot stress too highly the importance of conversing with foreigners in their own language whenever possible, notwithstanding the pragmatic 'international' English which is becoming more and more widespread. Not only does this avoid interpretation limitations, but even more importantly, it facilitates cultural communication and getting on to the same personal wave-length, both to transmit and receive, as one's interlocutors – who then may almost forget that they are communicating with a 'foreigner'.

Variation: Skiing

In our first Swiss incarnation in Berne in the late 1960s my Swiss friends tried to entice me to ski. Frankly, on long 2.25m wooden skis with rigid cable bindings, I found it difficult and painful. Subsequent family holidays in Igls and Kandersteg were likewise not great skiing successes.

When we arrived in Geneva in 1976, despite my earlier reservations, we looked up from our house in Chavannes-des-Bois towards the La Faucille pass in the Jura mountains half an hour away and decided to give it a go. On Boxing Day, the family set off with the *Sunday Times* 'Teach Yourself Skiing' guide, and uncertain expectations.

I took the lift to the top of La Faucille, and with more modern and user-friendly skis descended easily – admittedly only a blue run – and loved it. As they say, I never looked back from that moment. Our four children, all in the village school with their *vacances de ski* high in the mountains and often off-piste, took to skiing like young Swiss. Ruth and I could only do our best to keep up. Apart from the immediately nearby Jura, we were only a relatively short drive from major French and Swiss resorts like Flaine, Megève, Chamonix, Argentière, Les Gets, Portes de Soleil, Avoriaz/Morzine, Verbier, Gstaad, Schönried and, even further afield, Zermatt, Tignes and Val d'Isère – these latter with their huge and very challenging skiing possibilities.

Although these villages can be full of skiing visitors in high season, one only need look upwards to experience the magical views of the surrounding mountains. Then, when up there skiing amongst the mountains, I found that I could quickly get away from the most crowded pistes, and revel in the glorious scenery and the extraordinary possibilities to move swiftly and effortlessly over long distances. I would look at a distant mountain slope some miles away, and then within a relatively short time be almost surprised to discover that I was already there.

With our children and our Swiss friends, we went everywhere, on- and off-piste. Once, when we had arrived at some daunting resort, Ruth asked the children not to take me on a black run on the first morning. At lunchtime they smilingly told her that they had obeyed her instructions and kept me off the black runs – we had spent the whole morning off-piste.

The same family tradition continued when we arrived in Vienna in 1985. Our eldest, Thomas, went on a summer glacier course near Kaprun and found that he was skiing with the son of a UN contact of mine, the late Barry Crowston. We and the Crowstons became close family friends – a friendship which continues to this day, despite the sad death of Barry – and we often went on skiing holidays together. Apart from the smaller resorts near Vienna such as Semmering and Lackenhof, we often went to the major resorts like Kitzbühel, with its famed 'Hahnenkamm' descent and St Anton am Arlberg, and skied everywhere.

Our children, thanks to the skills which they had picked up at their earlier Swiss schools, were able to work as 'junior' ski guides/instructors in Kitzbühel and Val d'Isère. Sarah, as a fifteen-year-old at the Vienna International School, won a slalom race against all the boys and girls in the school. Naturally, the boys, most of whom were aged seventeen, complained that there must have been a timing mistake if they were beaten by a fifteen-year-old girl. The instructors re-checked the timings – and there was no mistake…

When we bought our chalet in Les Diablerets in 2000, this gave us access not only to the local village Isenau and Meilleret runs, but further afield to the Villars, Gstaad, Schönried and Zweisimmen areas, and also to the nearby 3,000m Tsanfleuron Glacier with its steep 7km 'La Combe d'Audon' black descent. Our long-standing friends from the FCO days, Ivor and Elizabeth Roberts, now in Oxford, join us every year for a week of 'sensible' skiing. With our children, and now especially with our fast-growing six grandchildren, it can be less 'sensible' when they all try to compete together with each other, but it still provides enormous fun.

Fortunately, we have had no major accidents during all these years. Ruth broke a collar bone crossing her skis while racing with son Andrew in Lackenhof and fractured her pelvis in Les Diablerets – but both mended. I hit a snow drift in thick cloud at the bottom of the 'Diamant Noir' in Flaine and ripped a calf muscle, and once stuck a ski-stick into my leg in Gstaad, both painful but without permanent damage. Andrew, being the most cavalier of our skiing children, had some spectacular falls, and was several times rescued by helicopter – the most dramatic when he fell 400m on the notorious 'Tortin' off-piste descent in Verbier, and lay motionless for a few seconds as we raced down towards him, until he sat up and lit a cigarette…

The saddest moment by far was in 2013 when our Les Diablerets next-door neighbour and close family friend, Thomas Schmidt, who had been at Atlantic College with our daughter Sarah, fell while skiing on a local Isenau run. He was found in a coma from which he never regained consciousness. He died in a Lausanne hospital two months later, leaving a devastated widow Bridie and two young children Theo and Katie. We held an emotional memorial celebration in the village, which was attended by the families from Germany and England, friends from everywhere, and many Swiss locals. I and another violinist friend played the slow movement of the Bach Double Violin Concerto, and there were moving tributes in French, German and English. We still stay in close contact with the family, now back in England but still with close ties to Les Diablerets and their loyal Swiss friends there – and the sadness remains.

Since then we all continue to ski, apart from Ruth who has finally hung up her boots, but we do so prudently, as the years go by.

In December 2018 I fell in difficult icy conditions. It was not particularly painful – a slight bang on the helmeted head – but the Swiss guides insisted on my being taken down on a 'skidoo' and being given a concussion and general medical check. All was OK, but I suffered a loss of confidence. At the age of seventy-seven with a repaired knee, I wondered whether it was time to give up? Our children Sarah and Andrew were kind and helped me to recover some confidence. In March 2019 I took a one-hour lesson (cost CHF 70) with Anne Chalus, a charming young instructor from the village. She immediately spotted that one significant fault had crept in – hunching the shoulders forward (a Cecil family 'generic' trait, shared with my brother, father and great-great-grandfather) and thus looking downwards – otherwise she said that all the technique was OK. The next day I was able to correct the fault, and confidence (even cockiness?) returned. It was certainly CHF 70 well spent!

Variation: Chess

After the physical challenges of cricket and skiing, a word about the mental challenges of chess. At school I had played a lot, and, while good by school standards, was not spectacular. In Berne, I played regularly with my *'Herrenabend'* Swiss friend Hans Steiner, who was a sound player and taught me lightning chess – *'Blitzschach'*. Later, like most of the chess world, I was gripped by the Fischer–Spassky epic confrontation in Reykjavik, 1972, and personally analysed all their games in some detail.

My one moment of modestly potential 'glory' was in a simultaneous match at the Athenæum with British Grandmaster Raymond Keene. He must have been playing at least forty of us, speeding from board to board with his cigar and his glass of fine brandy, apparently without a care in the world. However, after about twenty moves I noticed that he slowed down when he reached my board and started to frown, from which I deduced that I had gained a slight positional advantage. With unjustified confidence I then thought that I could capitalise on this positional advantage with a 'stunning' bishop sacrifice – which I did. When Keene came back to my board, he had a quick look, visibly relaxed, re-filled his brandy glass, and duly won the game quickly. Afterwards I consulted Gulnara Sachs, the wife of Ruth's nephew Jonathan, and herself an International Master from Soviet Kazakhstan. She indeed confirmed my positional advantage, which she thought could even have become a winning one – until I had thrown it away with my reckless and over-confident bishop sacrifice.

Since Oxford schooldays I have played correspondence chess with one of my oldest friends, Roland Needham, who once played at county level. We still exchange moves on postcards for old-time's sake, although email about everything else, always adding a bit of gossip. At least we have over sixty years moved on from the descriptive notation P-K4 to the algebraic e4. On balance, he has probably won a few more games than me over the years, although recently it has been mostly even. About twenty years ago, I noticed that he was starting to win every game and suspected that he was using a computer chess programme. I then got a more up-to-date programme, and I started to win every game. We then agreed that, while chess books were permitted, chess programmes were not … and the postcards continue.

As an 'intellectual' adjunct to chess, I have for many years enjoyed doing crosswords, even from time to time winning *The Times* Saturday Prize Cryptic Crossword. The prizes used to be Parker Pens, which have now been superseded by rather more modest £20 WH Smith Vouchers, but the thought counts.

Variation: Poker

For many years from the 1980s a group of us met regularly, foreign postings permitting, for an FCO poker school – including Don Allen, Philip Morrice, Ken Wright and Brian White, with guest appearances from Chris Curwen. Most stunningly, when one of our number was posted to the Paris Embassy, we met once in a mini château near Chartres. A congenial game of poker with good friends, excellent French wine and cheese, and a direct view of Chartres Cathedral – what could be better?

More prosaically, when in London we met regularly at the RAC Club to which Don and Philip belonged, starting in the early evening, interspersed with a quick supper, and continuing to the small hours. Being 'modestly' paid civil servants, we limited the amount of the stakes and bets to one or two pounds, so that one would not expect to win or lose more than £50 over the course of an evening. Nevertheless, we had many 'hard-fought' tussles, as the evening drew on, progressing from normal draw poker to more exotic forms of stud poker with zany variants of wild cards. Don, notwithstanding his 'serious' day job as Head of the FCO Inspectorate, was often the most buccaneering, with the rest of us being more conservative – although the wins and losses usually evened out over the years. Sadly, with the deaths of Ken in 2004 and Don in 2007, this most congenial school came to an inevitable end.

Once I joined the 'professional' poker school of my friend Anthony Holden, well-known journalist and writer of books on royalty and poker, and subsequent President of the International Federation of Poker. Other participants included the literary eminences David Spanier and Al Alvarez. However, the elevated stakes were such that I soon found that, even to get my second card in a hand, I had to buy it with more than my cash limit for the evening. So, with a mixture of regret and relief, I politely made my excuses and left. Afterwards Anthony told me that his friends had much appreciated my 'good manners' – not surprising as they were now sitting on my 'pocket money' for a whole month.

Variation: Sherlock Holmes

When I was a young Bernese violinist, we strayed to the far end of the Canton of Berne to the village of Meiringen with its famous Reichenbach Falls, where the Swiss locals told us that the celebrated 'real-life' British detective had outsmarted the evil Professor Moriarty. We later visited the Château at Lucens near Lausanne in the Canton of Vaud, where Arthur Conan Doyle's son Adrian had moved in 1965. He established a Sherlock Holmes Museum with many authentic Conan Doyle memorabilia, which

I was fascinated to discuss with him. Later, when back in the UK, I joined the 'Sherlock Holmes Society of London', and to this day enjoy the abstruse and the more serious scholarship into the life and activities of the great sleuth.

Notwithstanding his reputation as an 'establishment' pillar of the late-Victorian era, Sherlock Holmes had surprisingly liberal views on social issues such as education, divorce, autocratic monarchy, women and race – no doubt reflecting the personal views and experiences of Conan Doyle himself. Also, although the master nearly always unscrambled the causes of the mysteries which confronted him, he could be surprisingly lenient in letting off a considerable number of culprits for whom he discovered some personal sympathy – naturally, as a good citizen, leaving the clues there for the police to discover, which in their 'hidebound' way they usually failed to do.

Recently I was invited to lead an Athenæum discussion on 'Sherlock Holmes – Man of the nineteenth or the twenty-first century?', and the research threw up some fascinating insights on how some of our latest and cherished liberal values on social issues, as above, were already prevalent with thinkers such as Conan Doyle many years ago. *Plus ça change...*

Holmes also played the violin – another link – a Stradivari, 'narrating with great exultation' (in 'The Adventure of the Cardboard Box') how he had purchased it 'at a Jew broker's in Tottenham Court Road for fifty-five shillings', while proclaiming to a bemused Dr Watson that it was really 'worth at least five hundred guineas'.

Variation: Ireland

I was always fascinated by my Irish as well as by my Cecil background. My maternal grandmother Aileen Phillips – a 'much-admired Irish beauty' according to '*Lady's Pictorial*' of 2 September 1911 – married my maternal grandfather Roland Luker in St Ann's Church, Dublin, in 1911. The

Phillips family were Southern Irish Protestants (Church of Ireland), who had lived at Gaile House in Cashel, County Tipperary.

We first visited Ireland in 1970 for the wedding of Ruth's cousin John Cooke to Tania Crichton in Dublin, and twenty-plus years later for the wedding of their daughter Olga in Sligo, where Tania's parents lived. More recently we visited Wexford on operatic business, to help my photographer friend Clive Barda with his cameras and lenses while he took the official photographs of the performances, also calling on my FCO and skiing friend Ivor Roberts at his spacious Residence outside Dublin where he was Ambassador at the time. On one occasion Ruth and I drove from Wexford to Cashel to explore the Phillips family background. We enquired about the family at the local Post Office. They were not too sure of the history but advised us to ask the 'old lady' in the newsagent's next door – 'she knows everything'. The most helpful 'old lady' initially thought that we were Irish Americans discovering our 'roots'. Fortunately, she did indeed 'know everything', and referred us to Gaile House, which was still there, and to the family graves in the Cashel Church of Ireland graveyard. 'Roots' unearthed.

Back in London, the Irish Ambassador Dáithi O'Ceallaigh, a lively friend, introduced me to Christopher Moran, philanthropist/businessman, who had restored his fifteenth-century Crosby Hall in Chelsea on the northern bank of the Thames. He invited us in 2005 to a Reception, Dinner and Concert in aid of 'Cooperation Ireland', in the presence of HM The Queen and Irish President Mary McAleese. During the Reception, the two eminent ladies emerged together from a private meeting, and Christopher then introduced us guests to them. I thought immediately from the looks on their august faces that 'those two have been plotting something'. HM subsequently visited Ireland for her historic visit in 2011, which we later understood had indeed been discussed at Crosby Hall earlier.

Some years later I considered getting an Irish passport, under pressure especially from my children because of future Brexit travel concerns – if I acquired an Irish passport, so could they. The procedure stated that this would be possible if a grandparent had been born 'in the island of Ireland'. However, when I managed to get hold of grandmother Aileen's birth certificate, it transpired that, although very much 'Irish', she had actually been born in 1889 in Gloucestershire, England – maybe her father, who was an army officer, had been stationed here. We consulted the Irish Embassy in London, but the ruling was quite specific – so no Irish passport. You never win them all.

Variation: Antiquarian Travel Books

While still at Oxford I became fascinated by pre-First World War Baedeker Travel Guides, and I started to buy them from second-hand bookshops for my personal collection. Those were the days when Oxford had at least twenty second-hand bookshops – now there is only one antiquarian room in Blackwell's. As I travelled around Europe and more widely, both for music and later for diplomacy, I steadily added to my collection, often finding real rarities for very reasonable prices in usually quaint second-hand bookshops in obscure backstreets. Unfortunately, in the course of time many of these bookshops have also disappeared.

Recently I did a memory-lane trip round Paris and found that most of my favourite bookish haunts had vanished or become fashion shops. Even the *bouquinistes* on the Rive Gauche of the Seine, some of whom like Michel Le Berre I have known for many years, nowadays have hardly anything of interest to collectors, preferring more sellable touristic items. One reason for this, of course, is that so much of the business today is online, and perhaps with less overall interest in printed books.

Over the years my personal Baedeker collection has grown to over a thousand different editions in French, German and English – including all the famous misprints and censorships, such as the reference in *Palestine and Syria 1894* to a hotel owner as 'Howard an Arab', subsequently deleted when Howard complained to Baedeker that he was not 'an Arab' – and indeed that the Prince of Wales had stayed in his establishment, or the Baedeker censorship advice in *Konstantinopel und das Westliche Kleinasien 1905* to keep the book in one's back pocket when approaching the zealous Turkish frontier. The collection includes some very early pre-1840 'Biedermeier' editions, and rarities such as the complete *Orient Quartet,* and *Russia, St Petersburg, Indien* and *Athens,* and expanding to the editions between the Wars, and during the Second World War such as *Generalgouvernement 1943,* i.e. Poland – still being produced despite the Soviet Red Army then moving rapidly westwards towards Poland – and some selected later post-War ones.

I have related how my copy of Baedeker's *Berlin 20 Auflage 1927* was useful in tracking down Ruth's family's residences in pre-War Berlin.

With the help of 'amateur' Baedeker experts like Professor Reinhard Öhlberger, bassoonist in the Vienna Philharmonic Orchestra, Goulven Guilcher of Bourg La Reine, and the late Dr Laurence Boyle of Kent University, together with 'professionals' like Bernard Shapero and Lucinda Boyle of London, Manfred Nosbüsch of Bonn and Marie-Luise Surek-Becker of Berlin, the English and French collections are now very nearly complete, and the German collection substantial.

Likewise, I have several hundred Baedeker *doublettes* in varying degrees of rarity and condition, which are now being gradually included in the books for sale in our second-hand book business, 'Cecil Books', which Ruth and I set up more than twenty years ago. It is supplemented by other antiquarian travel books such as Murray, Black and other guides, as well as by more general stock. Ruth and I originally ran this as a book-stall in a local antiques arcade, but found the compulsory share of 'minding the shop' unduly time-consuming with our other activities, and some fifteen years ago we went online at Abebooks (www.abebooks.co.uk – Cecil Books).

The upside is that one's books are on offer all over the world, and the downside is that price comparisons are immediately visible – unlike if an enthusiast wanders into a bookshop to browse. So far, I have been advised not to swamp the market with my Baedekers for sale – colleagues tell me that they already represent some 10 per cent of the online market. Recently we hired a stand for the day at the well-established 'Bloomsbury Bookfair', to check out the current sales possibilities. However, we noted, in discussion with some of the other exhibitors, that the specialist collectors did not seem to be physically present and searching for rarities, as I remember that they were in the pre-internet days.

Time moves on.

15

ENVOI: 'WHAT'S PAST IS PROLOGUE' OR 'TOMORROW IS ANOTHER DAY'

Coda

WHEN I NOW LOOK BACK ON THESE MEMOIRS, I ASK MYSELF the inevitable questions about what I might have done differently in my life.

Should I have attempted a career as a scientist, as my father would have wished and as appeared promising at school? No way – I might have been competent and 'safe', but I would have totally missed out on the passions, and of course the frustrations, which music has brought me.

Should I have remained an oboist, developing rapidly at school, as our inspirational music master advised? No. Once I had been smitten by Yehudi Menuhin's Bach and Bartók on the violin in the Oxford Sheldonian, when I was an oboist teenager, there was no way back from the violin.

Should I have remained a music professional, or tried to move into music administration, after my five years with Max Rostal in Switzerland? Possibly, but I had taken the violin professionally about as far as my late start (many soloists begin before the age of ten), and what Rostal described as my 'English' introversion, allowed. Rightly or wrongly I decided to move on, was fortunate to be offered my diplomatic opportunity, and to be privileged to keep music and especially playing the violin as my personal passions. Since then I have done what I can over the years to support other young musicians, including in the UK, Germany, Russia and Switzerland, who need all the help that they can get.

Should I have stayed longer in the FCO, rather than move on after twenty-five satisfying years? No – I was becoming increasingly frustrated by the bureaucracy and had at most one promotion left – so better to move with the flexibility of being in my early fifties, rather than hang on. I am so glad not to have missed the fascinating nuclear clean-up experience with British Nuclear Fuels of working for ten years in the 'window' of the post-Soviet pre-Putin Russia, where I loved the culture, the language and the friendships.

It more than made up for my earlier frustrated Moscow diplomatic posting, as indeed the subsequent ten years plus integrated into the French state energy company AREVA more than made up for my two frustrated Paris diplomatic postings.

I continue to serve on the Board of the UK Nuclear Industry Association, firmly believing – whatever 'political correctness' may imply – that nuclear power remains essential for addressing climate change and our security of supply, especially as the world moves from fossil fuels to clean electricity.

Did I marry and commit myself at too young an age? No – emphatically. Ruth, my dear, independent yet supportive wife after more than fifty-five years of partnership, and our four quite different lovely children and six grandchildren are a source of perpetual joy. We share our pride in the characters and achievements of our now middle-aged children and follow with equal interest the developments of our fast blossoming grandchildren.

What does the future bring? I am lucky so far to enjoy good health, domestic happiness, friends and travel. I play my lovely Stradivari violin all the time, interpreting both familiar and new unfamiliar chamber music with outstanding musician friends, often performing in charity and local concerts. To try to keep myself musically alert, I work regularly, however inadequately, on the formidable Bach solo violin sonatas and partitas and on the slightly less daunting Bach 'cello suites which lie well for my viola with their eternal challenges for musical inspiration and technical discipline.

We see our friends and family as often as we can, and travel sometimes locally and sometimes further afield, both to revisit old haunts and to discover new ones. In parallel, our arts charity work helps to provide vital opportunities for similar aspiring young musicians, who, as I have said, need all the help that we can give them.

Long may it all continue, always with an open mind to be able to explore fresh avenues and ideas. To quote from one of my favourite films – *Que sera, sera.*

Acknowledgements

My grateful thanks are due to: my literary friends at the Athenæum, Mike Shaw and Bruce Hunter, for their wise counsel about venturing into 'public' writing; Naim Attallah, CBE, Quartet Books' Chairman, for his faith in publishing my 'project', together with his staff, David Elliott, Peter Jacobs, and Grace Pilkington; my many friends in the musical and other worlds whose experiences have enriched my life; and, of course, my dear wife Ruth and our four lovely children for all their support over many years.

Index

223